Angels are Black and White

Ulla Berkéwicz

Angels Are Black and White

Translated by Leslie Willson

CAMDEN HOUSE

Library of Congress Cataloging-in-Publication Data

Berkéwicz, Ulla.
   [Engel sind schwarz und weiss. English]
   Angels are black and white / Ulla Berkéwicz; translated by Leslie
Willson.
     p. cm.
   ISBN 1–57113–112–4 (alk. paper)
   I.   Willson, A. Leslie (Amos Leslie), 1923. II. Title.
PT2662.E6826E513   1996
833' . 914—dc20

1

A GERMAN BOY doesn't cry! Even if the firestorm roars through his head, and even if the cavalry breaks through his lines, and even if his chest is burning, he'll be far from crying! Will wipe the wetness from his face with his sleeve, gobble up the horsemen. Will sit upright on the hard chair, even if his behind hurts from the spankings. Will go off, far away, will fight in foreign lands. His father will be sorry yet, but then it will be too late!

"A day without food, a week with no playing, and you'll never see that Rachie ever again," his father had yelled.

Rachie was her name, she had been soft and white, white and sacred. And they had merely played house, whispered and lay down together, as fathers do with mothers, and he had only bent and turned her until he had curved her together with himself, had only felt her heart, the small beat, the whiteness and softness. Until his father had come, had picked up the board. Rachie was her name, and he had thrown himself upon her so that it wouldn't swat her, and his mother had cried, and his father had yelled and had beaten and beaten him with the board that he had planned to build him the knight's castle with. And they had pulled her out from under him. Rachie was her name, and her parents had taken her away from him, and his father had kept beating him, and his mother had come between them, and then his father had struck his mother.

His mother cried. — Women are allowed to cry!

"A German boy doesn't cry," his father had said. "He must sit up straight. Hands on his knees, eyes on his hands."

His mother, Magda, stood at the sink scraping and peeling and was not allowed to look at him. His father had forbidden it.

His father had put on his black suit and white shirt, had taken his hat and overcoat from the hook, thrown open the door, had walked out, had slammed the door shut.

His father, Heinrich! Heinrich Fischer, born in Hesse, bowed down from small-town poverty, parents dead early, the father from gluttony, the mother from an unknown fever. He had been fifteen and had to get along in the world alone and had never stood with legs planted wide, not wide enough for his pride.

Had lived with his parents, who rented from farmers on the edge of the city — his mother helped in the barnyard, his father sat around in his early retirement with a blanket on his knees, staring at the red building opposite, at the brook that flowed along there out into the flat land.

Heinrich had once jumped across the brook, slunk around the red building, gotten in, found himself in another world. Madmen lived in the red building, minotaurs wandered around, butchers with billy clubs out of holsters. Heinrich had to hide, in storerooms, bathtubs, else those with the clubs would have set upon him, too, like upon the poor madmen there. They want to beat the mysterious in them to death, Heinrich had believed. The madmen's mystery bothers them because it is deep seated and true. And because they have none in themselves.

There were long corridors, the great hall and the stench, the cold and the damp. Men and women shaven bald, faces turned away, sunken in morasses of thought, submerged in the pond of memory, the deaf-blind, blind from looking, deaf from listening.

And one time Heinrich had been seen them take a newborn baby from a small woman and throw it away. He had had to ask his father and mother about it. They had said the lunatics were crazy and had forbidden him to go into the red building. But Heinrich had continued to go there and had taken the small woman apples.

Then his father had died, and he had moved to the city with his mother into a house from which the smell of cabbage never left, where women had their heads in slightly opened doors. Men in undershirts, propped on sofa pillows, leaned over the windowsill and stared at the street.

But behind the house there had been a small tract of earth where his mother had planted potatoes. There flowers were still in bloom in November. There a mighty tree had stood. Then he had dreamed of being as mighty as the tree, had climbed up high into the tree, had sat in the top and gazed over the city, had practiced governing, being in charge. And still had suspected that he would never be in charge. Up there he had sung.

Then his time in school had come to an end, and his mother had no money for further schooling. In the cold winter of 1910 there had not been enough wood and charcoal. His mother had fallen ill. Sick people froze to death by cold stoves. The mighty tree had been felled. His mother had died anyway, feverish with the cold.

Heinrich had wanted to become a singer, for his voice had become big and beautiful from his sitting in the tree and looking out over the city. But studying voice would have cost money, and so, because he had seen helpless people and not been able to aid them, he had studied how to help, a profession in social services, welfare work. He had studied how to help as others had studied bricklaying or carpentry.

Then the war had come. At eighteen a war volunteer, at twenty-two back from the war, he had become the district secretary for the welfare office, had gotten acquainted with the daughters of a farm couple from the Vogelsberg — they had five daughters and two sons. Five sons had died in

4

the war. He had courted the eldest daughter, but she didn't want a penniless man. He had courted the youngest, and she was willing.

His mother, Magda, cried. — Girls are weak and cry. Mothers are fat and cry, too!

But he had only played house with the other child, who was a girl. — Girls are different. Girls play mothers, are white and soft, and perhaps get sick from playing and from crying! Maybe his game had made her sick, and maybe his father had hit him for that reason. Her name had been Rachie, and they had often played the game, and sometimes she had cried doing it, but only secretly so nobody would hear.

His mother's sister, who hadn't wanted Heinrich, had married Eberhard, who was rich. He owned a building with a shoe store and a large apartment. His boy cousin and his girl cousin and a big piano were there. Behind the building was an orchard. In the summer Magda was allowed to pick as much fruit once a week as she could carry. The orchard was wild and dark under the trees, marsh marigolds, slugs, enchanted toads, dancing flies, and earthworms. But his boy cousin shot at the flies with a slingshot and stomped on the worms with gleaming shoes. And although the boy was already older and big enough to carry things, he didn't help his aunt when she had picked as much fruit as she could carry. When she dragged buckets and baskets along through the streets, he had hopped along next to her, stealing her berries, thumbing his nose. And his girl cousin was a hussy. Heinrich called her a hussy. She had chocolate cookies, offered them to a person, and then ate them herself. She rubbed hawthorn seeds under your shirt, she never cried.

Magda's parents had sold the farmstead because they needed dowries for five daughters, ten thousand marks for each one, and twenty thousand for each son. Now they were old, now lived in the city on the meager funds they had kept for themselves.

The farmwife had become small. Her legs bent with the weight of years so that she tottered when she tried to walk and creaked when she ran. Her teeth stood solitary like steep towers in her mouth. Her hands were broad and clumsy from digging turnips in the frozen December soil, from threshing, from plowing, from milking, and from spreading manure. But in her face goodness stood firm, even when she slept.

When the farmer had been off to war with his five eldest sons, she had had to take care of everything alone: seven children, house and garden, meadow and field, three cows, a few chickens, pigs, seven goats, and two dray horses. And every time a son had died in battle, she had known it. She had gotten a long, shooting pain in her heart, then she had collapsed. Then she had seen her son, upright in a hail of bullets, to the left a tall bright and to the right a tall dark man, transparent as the wings of flies. Then she had known.

The farmer was the only one to return to her, hadn't wanted to talk very much anymore, and soon had not spoken at all.

Now they sat in their kitchen, waiting for their children and their children's children, and for death. Sat silently beside one another, looked straight ahead, let their thoughts stray, meet, mingle, and separate again, and again looked straight ahead, at the wall opposite the sofa in the kitchen, where an angel was walking in a picture.

The picture of the angel had hung in the farmhouse in the Vogelsberg, and Magda had often looked at it, had heard the angel flapping his wings, had seen him glow, and had put her hands over her eyes and ears.

He was sitting on his chair, his mother was standing at the sink. It was night, the tower clock struck. He could not yet count the strikes. It was winter, the kitchen was heated. His mother put on more wood.

On Friday evenings his father went to the Liedertafel, a choral society. His mother was not allowed to go with him. — Only men could sing! But he was sometimes allowed to go, and then he saw his father in a black suit and white shirt. He stood there tall, taller than all the others, and his voice was the greatest of all.

His father sang with ardor, his mother had said. But he had not known what ardor means. "Ardor," his mother had said, "it makes you glow inside like sunset."

His father was at the Liedertafel, and his mother cried, groaned, writhed. — Something is going to happen, it will be momentous, a fight, a skirmish, a battle! There's no telling how it will end, it seesaws back and forth!

His mother staggered, tried to hold onto the sink, slipped off, fell over, crumpled on the kitchen tiles. "Get Frau Polster!" his mother yelled.

The hallway was cold and dark. It smelled clean, it was Friday, and the stairs were scoured. — The banisters wind downwards, make you dizzy. His mother groans from the kitchen. It echoes in the corridor. The echo twists together with the twisting banisters, slips off and plunges, crashes like his mother, lies below on the gray stones, is shattered!

6

Frau Polster was their neighbor, lived on the same floor, had a sick husband, went into strangers' houses to clean, and smelled like floor polish. She came and called Frau Zopf, who lived on the top floor.

His mother groaned. The door to the hallway stood open a crack. The light fell through the crack onto the boards of the floor. — The gray boards, they groan when you walk across them, why? They groan because they were trees that can no longer stand in the forest, his father said!

The women pushed the door open. His mother lay on the kitchen floor. They rolled up their sleeves, kneeled down, tugged his mother's clothes away until a white, taut sphere was bared. A red trail flowed from his mother, a rivulet across the kitchen tiles, which had a drain in the middle, drained away there.

The women started a fire in the cook stove, put on a kettle of water, began to pray. — They're not about to eat or sleep, why are the women praying?

His mother began to scream, writhed, reared up, started up, collapsed. The women held her firmly, pushed her down, sat on her, rode her naked belly. — The battle has begun, it's a matter of life and death, I have to chase the women away from my mother's belly.

But then there was a rusty, old howl, and it wasn't his mother. The neighbor held high a bloody bundle that itself howled.

"Reinhold!" his mother yelled. "Get your father!"

The women shoved him out the door. He stood on the doormat, which was tangled with the frayed cleaning rag. They had closed the door behind him. The cleaning rag was checkered, green and blue, visible by day. Now it was night, and he was supposed to get his father. But he wasn't allowed on the street, his father had forbidden it. He was supposed to stay in the kitchen, hands on his knees, eyes on his hands. — Father will spank me!

It was still, dark, cold, and wet. The gas streetlights flickered. — The way leads across streets that intersect, over bridges under which water is flowing. The streets are all crisscrossed, at every corner there are corners. But there where the lights are burning and the songs echoing, there his father will be!

There the men stood, singing. And his father was the tallest standing there. The men were standing around tables. On the tables sat mugs that overflowed with foam.

"There rode three fellows over the Rhine," the men sang, "to a tavern mistress to drink some wine." And the chorus swelled mightily and climbed

7

up the walls, seemed to gather under the ceiling, ball itself together, and press against the roof.

"Dear Mistress, you have fine beer and wine," the men sang, "where is your daughter, so fair and fine?" And the room seemed to shake and the ceiling to split.

"My beer and wine is fresh and clear," they all sang with one voice, with one mouth, "my young daughter lies there on her bier," it rose up softly as though from a deep body.

And Reinhold could see how the men ducked down, bent over, how one and the other propped themselves with their fists on the table, how their eyebrows rose, their brows wrinkled. — How frightened his father looks, as though he had dropped something on the kitchen floor and it had smashed on the tiles. His mother is lying on the kitchen tiles, and his father must come and lift her up!

"And when they entered the chamber room," the men went on singing, "in a black casket she lay in gloom." — But his mother is lying in nothing, and nothing is black, only a red trail runs out of her into the drain!

The men went on singing, and Reinhold called his father. "The first one drew aside the veil, and they looked at her with faces pale," they sang and didn't hear him. Then he crawled under the table, where he was between legs, pants legs, table legs, chair legs. — The pants legs are all long and black, and the men spread them wide while singing, standing there on big feet!

"Ah, wert thou alive, maiden so fair," they sang above him. But he couldn't find his father's legs under the tables. — Pants legs are all alike!

"I would love thee for e'er and e'er," the voices trickled softly onto the table and then over the edge and softly upon Reinhold underneath.

"The second covered her with the veil anew and turned away and wept then, too," it sounded as though the men were forcing their throats, and Reinhold could see their knees folding, very slightly, as though they were weakening. And because he could not find his father's legs, he crept out from under the tables, got to his feet, and looked into the faces of the tall men, into their open mouths, their throats.

"Ah, thou dost lie now on the death bier, I have loved you for many a year," the song came out of them, and Reinhold could hear the men's anguish. And was afraid. — They're all afraid here! He could hear it and see it and screamed for his father.

And his father saw him and came to him. He lifted Reinhold up, he held him fast. — As he used to do, but not for a long time, like Sundays on the bridge when a train traveled under it!

"The third one again pulled aside the veil and kissed her on the mouth so pale," the others sang. And Reinhold screamed about his white mother and the kitchen floor and about the red trail.

Then his father ran with him through the rows of men, his father was weeping, his heart was hammering.

"I loved thee always, I love thee sore," they sang when his father was already out on the street and was running with Reinhold tight in his arms. "And will love thee now for evermore," it resounded after them from light into the darkness.

His father races, he gallops, he will win any war! Now there's war, now his father is racing through the night! The war races and gallops, and sturdy hearts beat against one another!

"War!" screamed Reinhold, and his father held his mouth shut.

At the beginning of the war the German Kaiser had spoken to the German people: "It is a matter of the existence or non-existence of our Reich, of the existence or non-existence of German power and the German being. We will defend ourselves to the last breath of man and horse." Then Heinrich became a war volunteer and set off against the French. He carried his songbook in his knapsack.

Freshly trained troops and young recruits marched against Paris. They could already see the Eiffel Tower in the telestereoscope. But suddenly there were hot-air balloons in the sky, Zeppelin attacks. Armies came in waves from the horizon.

"To experience a charge — that must be wonderful! But perhaps we'll live through only one," the comrade next to Heinrich said.

The German troops wheeled to the north. Presence of mind and manly discipline were preached. The front was consolidated. Winter came. Trenches, holes in the earth, dugouts. Heinrich shared his hole with two comrades, volunteers like him. He sang from his book. He could believe in himself when he heard himself singing.

The days were quiet and short, the nights long. On the lookout over breastworks and firing slits, and sometimes from a thousand throats as one, the "Watch on the Rhine" through the darkness, and sometimes a hurrah through the trenches, and then they knew: In the East it is happening, great and true. There the German assault columns are storming across the Russian plains, there hangs the thunder cloud from which the name of Hindenburg rumbles. But in the West it was a matter of watching and waiting, of boring into the earth like worms, and screaming hurrah for the victory of the others.

His muscles taut, nerves tense, eyes straight ahead, one summer morning the General bellowed: "Be confident that light and air will be created for the free unfolding of the German oak. No Frenchy will resist German strength. On the bloody battlefield give your all joyfully to the last man!" And then they stormed, ran, all stormed into the blaze of drums.

Heinrich had been beside his friend, his comrade Deutsch, who with a hurrah for the Fatherland had flown to pieces. His mouth shouted "Hurrah!" and lifted from his face and flew off and landed on a tree.

Later Heinrich had often wondered what became of Deutsch's wife? Had Deutsch not given him a letter if worse came to worst? And had he not looked for Deutsch's wife in vain? And had he not, after years of searching, had the thought of steaming the letter open? Tear it open, he had thought, and he had been seized by a feeling of profanation and then by one of justification that at least one human being on God's earth should know what Israel Deutsch had written to his wife Ruth, if worse came to worst. And then he had opened the letter.

Ruth, Deutsch had written, my wife, my wife! My mother was Jewish, and your mother was Jewish, and from us came a Jewish child. And if worse comes to worst, if I remain lying here, then I will die for what is German, which is the next thing to what is Jewish. And I beg you, if there can be a burial of my mortal remains, to call together the comrades who survive me, that in addition to the Kaddish they sing the national anthem for me. For Germany, after Palestine, is our homeland. God protect you, dear wife, protect my child, and protect our German Fatherland.

The stuff of war, the human raw material, lay steaming on the red field. There a torso crawled, there an ownerless hand twitched. Machine guns hammered, infantry fire seethed, artillery ripped air and earth.

"Many much greater nations have been annihilated," yelled the comrade next to Heinrich. "Or do you want to dawdle your life away like the Wandering Jew who cannot die?"

A grenade landed, flung earth into the air, dug a crater. His comrade gasped. Heinrich lay still. Something was running out of him, running down him. He felt tired. The gasping next to him ceased.

It was a Sunday, summer flowers were blooming. A malevolent streak of gunpowder ran diagonally through the light. A whimpering came from the furrows of the field. The wounded crawled over the dead, a heat fly drank eyes, blow flies followed into the hollows. Maybe from this or that brain something was draining that made the air quiver. The air over the red field was quivering.

"Brightly flaming indignation and sacred fury will double the strength of every man," the Kaiser had said.

Heinrich crawled across the field, saw the edge of a woods, wanted to lie down under a tree and look up at the sky. But ghosts had hidden in the woods, approached him, dragged him across bodies, dragged him under the trees, gave him water, bandaged his leg. And he understood: Frenchmen, deserters!

They crept together. They did not have to understand one another with words. They remained in the woods and let hunger gnaw away their flesh.

Then the war was over, and they did not know it. And if a farmer had not come past with a cow pulling his wagon, they would never have found out.

It had become autumn. They separated, each headed in the direction in which he thought his homeland lay. Scorched woods, destroyed roads, blown-up bridges, Heinrich followed the devastation and in seven days came to his German land.

The war is over, the wetness is not blood but sweat. His father pants, he bounds up four steps at a time!

His mother, Magda, is lying in bed and had become thin. Heinrich dropped Reinhold, he landed, and it hurt. Next to his mother lay a baby. "Your son Helmuth," she said, and held him up to Heinrich.

"Where does a baby come from?" Reinhold asked later, when his father was sitting by his bed.

"Believe it or not," came the reply, "on the other side of the river lies a bright land. There anyone who wants to can fly. Many, because they have wings, are called angels. I've been told..."

"Who told you?"

"I think it was a clever squirrel. I've been told that people would arrive there old and weary and in a short while would become children again."

And as he fell asleep, Reinhold ran across all the bridges over rivers that he knew, but did not reach the bright land, then took the river with one bound, leaped: "Attack!" he yelled, jumped, and flew up to the young and old angels in Heaven.

The next morning his mother was gone with her new son, and his father said that she had gone to the hospital with childbed fever.

Heinrich drove with Reinhold into the countryside.

Wetterau was bounteous, and the farmers were rich. But men were lacking on the farmsteads. The war had taken them, and now a monument for them was standing in every market square.

Heinrich had become district inspector, and a piece of Wetterau belonged to his district. Herr Daumer, who had brought a brain injury home from the war and so received money from the welfare office, lived there.

A humble farmyard, decrepit stables, stones overgrown with weeds. Rusted flails, bent plowshares, battered milking stools, pails, iron bars.

— The pines are menacing, ambush is lurking in the bushes. Fear has quiet feet! Reinhold held tightly to his father.

Herr Daumer's brother has been an invalid since birth and Herr Daumer an invalid from the war. "Before, they still had their parents," Heinrich whispered.

Herr Daumer receives money, but his brother doesn't. His brother didn't even bring into this world the part of Herr Daumer's brain that was shot away. And so he receives nothing, because no one can help that.

Herr Daumer had his feet in a wash basin and his hands in his lap. His brother was sitting on the floor, building a tower with wooden blocks.

"Good day, Herr Daumer," said Heinrich too loudly in the quiet room.

"And who are you?" the man asked. His legs were ulcerated — yellow, red, blue flesh, nothing but meat. His skull was bald, his temple pulsed.

"Is he a woodpecker?" asked Reinhold.

"That was the shot in his brain," Heinrich whispered. "The bone splintered. The skin grew over it. Everything under that is loose."

"What's loose?"

"All the convolutions and thoughts."

"And if the skin weren't there, could I see Herr Daumer thinking?"

Crash! The brother's wooden-block tower fell over. He looked young. He was smiling. And when the tower was standing, he looked into the sky. He did not see Reinhold and Heinrich.

In the corner of the room two iron bedsteads were standing. Over them an angel in a golden frame went through the world blessing things.

"Are there angels everywhere?" Reinhold asked.

"Angels!" Herr Daumer cried out.

Straw was sticking out of the sacks on the bedsteads. The window openings were crusted over and covered with spider webs. There was a strong odor. Reinhold's eyes were burning.

Crash! The tower fell over, and the brother immediately began to build it up again, block on block.

"This is my son," said Heinrich and pushed Reinhold forward.

The man's temples pulsed stronger and stronger. — A woodpecker, a cuckoo woodpecker that, like in a clock, springs out of his temple when it's time!

"Angels are all that matter," the man cried out.

Crash! The brother's tower fell over.

"Angels are magnificent. Angels are lethal," the man cried out, and Reinhold was afraid that the woodpecker would spring at his face.

"I must take off my shoes before their magnificence and bathe my feet," the man cried out.

And Reinhold's fear became intense, for the man's eyeballs were bulging. "Do you know angels?" Reinhold asked.

"They rustle," the man cried out, "they whirr. They set their right foot on the ocean and their left on the land. Angels are black and white!"

Crash! The tower fell over.

"And pray," the man bellowed, and he reached for Reinhold and smacked the boy's head to his chest, like the woodpecker smacked his temple. "Angel child," he bellowed, and his brother threw a block at him.

At that, Heinrich was between them. He picked up Reinhold and carried him to the door.

"And Herr Daumer," asked Reinhold, "is he a brother angel?"

Then there was a great to-do in the house. His mother had come back with her new son. His bundled-up brother lay in a cradle. His father had said that Reinhold, too, had lain in it. But he couldn't remember, didn't want to believe it, didn't believe it.

The Sunday gap between his parents' beds was occupied. There where he had been able to come on cold feet on Sunday mornings, where his dreams had met those of his parents, had run along together for a way, right down the mountain into the vale of day, the dwarf now lay and wailed. And his father who, hardly awake, had told him stories of heroes, had invented stronger and stronger heroes, greater battles, more frightful dragons — now he took the dwarf onto his belly Sundays and sang silly songs.

Evenings Reinhold lay awake in bed. His Kaspar doll lay in a heap on the windowsill. In the daytime he had had to scold it, his pale, weary sleeping companion, had had to threaten and slap it, for it was a patient sufferer. But evenings the blows hurt it, because it was alone in the world, had no father and no mother, looked like souls perhaps do, crestfallen and afraid.

At night he got out of bed, went through the vestibule and into the parlor. On the floor were traces of moonlight, fish, snakes, dragons, wolves. He pulled the curtain away from the cradle, saw his brother — the dwarf, the imp! He wanted to snatch the sofa pillow. Then the moon fell into the room, then everything turned white, then he crumpled. Then he remembered: Angels are white!

His mother carried him back to bed, and although he had pulled the covers over his head, he heard a rustling for a long time. — As though of white wings! Maybe the dwarf was now gone with the angels into Heaven!

And once he was standing at the kitchen window. Below him lay the courtyard with the stone slabs for hopscotch. — Climb onto the window ledge, jump down, lie all dead below! Then Mother will no longer call out the name of my dwarf brother in a voice too high, then she will come to me and warm me all dead in her lap and rock me and cry for me endlessly!

But during the night he saw her come to his small bed, heard her speak his name. She kept speaking his name, and the next morning Reinhold was sure of himself again.

DURING THE SUMMER Heinrich went with Reinhold into the forest, climbed with him into the highest trees, and taught him how to sing. And when together they sang "No lovelier land than in this age," they owned the land that lay below them, green and luxurious, far and near.

But the wage that his father brought home did not suffice, and often Reinhold went to bed hungry, even though his mother had given him her portion. They owned nothing that they could have sold and had no one who could have given them something. And the 10,000 gold mark dowry, which Magda had received from her parents two years after the sale of the farmstead, was later worth merely the purchase of a floor lamp for the parlor.

There was a strike. Electricity was cut off. Candle stumps from the last Christmas festivities were lighted. Those who lived on the upper floors of the block of rental apartments still had gas to boil their potatoes. Those on lower floors had the last water in the pipes. And Heinrich talked about consumption and hungry bellies and said: "Where do they get the strength for a strike!"

Meat, when there was some, stank, the cabbage was withered, Reinhold could mold little men with the bread. Wearing their military uniforms, beggars without arms and legs sat at street corners, and in Germany the word was going around that the poorest son of the people was also its most loyal.

When Magda's brothers came to visit — Uncle Otto, the sewing machine salesman, and Uncle Fritz, the theater lighting director — Reinhold could not fall asleep. The men sat around the kitchen table then, drank beer, and talked louder and louder. Then Heinrich yelled, then he raged: Four years of war, millions of dead, millions of unemployed, inflation, and those who got rich from the war got richer and the poor got poorer and the Reds got redder! Marches, parades through the city, shouting, bellowing on all the squares, speechmakers, setting the world to rights, rabble-rousers on every corner!

Reinhold was standing at the window. On the street a horse collapsed. People came with bread knives out of the buildings and sliced pieces from the horse, twitching pieces of meat. His mother held Reinhold's eyes shut, pulled him away from the window, prayed with him: "Our Father, give us today our daily bread."

Every morning at four minutes to eight Heinrich left the apartment and came back at twelve noon for lunch. When, from the kitchen window, Magda saw him coming across the railroad overpass, she put the soup on, and when he came in the door and hung his coat and hat on the hook, the soup was hot.

15

They ate until half-past twelve. Afterwards Heinrich lay down in his suit on the sofa in the parlor, and everyone had to go on tiptoes until five minutes to two. Then he was awakened, drank a cup of coffee, listened to the two-o'clock news, and left again, five minutes late, for his office. He had been doing that ever since he had become an inspector, ten years after his entrance into public service. He couldn't become more than that. With his completion only of grammar school he couldn't rise higher.

Reinhold had started school, had learned to read and write, and had become independent. Every noontime, after school, he went first to the butcher, who had a shop on the street level of the apartment building, fetched a large tray of liver meat loaf, took it to the baker in the neighboring building, picked it up there again in the afternoon, and took it back to the butcher. For doing that he received a slice off the end, munched on it himself for half the week and, from Thursday on, gave it to his mother, since her weekly allowance was used up then and she had little that she could set on the table.

Often Magda cried on Thursday, then Heinrich yelled, he yelled: "You can't get blood out of a turnip!" And when Magda cried even more, Heinrich had to yell more, and twice they had struck out at one another, yelling and crying, and both times Heinrich had then run out, had slammed the door behind him, and had come back only when it was night. Then Magda had crept into the corner of the kitchen and had kept on crying, so softly and terribly, that Reinhold had not dared to go to her, that he had stood in the entryway until her crying was over.

A lodger was to come into the apartment. A second bed was set up in Reinhold's room. Magda needed money, for she could buy less and less with what Heinrich brought home.

When Herr Butz came to introduce himself, Magda left the room because the men were talking about the war.

"Humanity must work its way out of Sodom and Gomorrah," Reinhold heard Herr Butz say to his father. "Fire and sulfur fell from Heaven and prepared a mighty process of purification that must now come to pass. We must not look around us, we must look ahead and attack."

Herr Butz had spoken more quietly than men usually do when they talk about war. And when he was leaving to get his belongings, Reinhold heard him say: "Only the Jesuits and the Jews are to blame for everything." And when he had left, he heard his mother say: "The Neumanns are Jews, too, after all."

Rachie Neumann had been her name. She had been so white and soft, so white and holy! Before falling asleep Reinhold couldn't help thinking about her and touching himself because he could not touch her. And because he couldn't do anything to keep from breathing faster, when he couldn't help thinking about Rachie Neumann before falling asleep, and because Herr Butz was sleeping in his room, he tried not to think about her anymore.

But one Sunday morning on his way to church, he met her.

Did she recognize him, as he did her? She had black eyes and black braids, and she came to a stop. And she looked at him.

"Rachie," he said.

And she nodded.

Her stockings had fallen down, and she pulled them up. Then she ran away.

She had grown taller than he, she was older. He was six, she perhaps eight.

He looked after her as she ran into a corner building, and because he remained standing there, because he could not walk away, after a while he saw her standing at a bay window. Her face was earnest. She didn't move. Her eyes stared at him.

When Reinhold came home, when he ran into his room so that no one would see his tears, tears of shame, tears of rage, because before Rachie Neumann's bay window he had realized that he was powerless, still as powerless as before, when he had to suffer his father beating him before Rachie Neumann's eyes and forbidding him to have anything to do with her, so powerless that he still had to suffer that Rachie Neumann was forbidden him — on Herr Butz's bed lay magazines with pictures of half-naked women, women with men, and one made an impression upon him: a women with large breasts in a plunging neckline, milking a cow, behind her a gigolo — that was printed under the picture — who bent over the woman with the breasts and gripped the large breasts in the plunging neckline exactly as the woman did the heavy udders of the cow.

Herr Butz was a student. "A studiosus," his father had said, "an eternal student." Because he was almost forty, spent most of his time lying in bed reading books and magazines, and never got up before noon. Evenings he went out.

"To study?" Reinhold had asked.

"No, to duel," his father had said. "Herr Butz belongs to those students who don't study but slash at one another's faces with rapiers. The more dueling scars he has, the more respected he is among his peers." And Reinhold saw with amazement that Herr Butz, the studiosus, had many scars.

"You have be careful that he doesn't get you into a conversation," his mother had said. "He'll entangle and confuse you, he'll involve you in views, lead you astray, and you won't find your way back."

Sometimes when Herr Butz came home late at night, he woke up Reinhold and told him about Nordic men, the knights of Thule, about racially pure Nordic daughters, the young maiden animals and their Nordic young men with their proud, deliberate souls.

"The entire earth," he then said, "once belonged to Nordic men. They are our ancestors, yours and mine," and he shook Reinhold when he was about to fall back to sleep, and he barked at him: "Remember, you, too, were once a Nordic boy."

And Reinhold saw lights flash in Herr Butz's eyes, heard him tell about brave Galand, the one with the rune on his forehead, how he vanquished the killer wolves solely with the power of his indomitable will. And when Reinhold heard that Galand would rather have looked any danger straight in the eye than be the slave and servant of others, that he wanted jauntily to imprint his will on the whole world one day, it seemed to him as though he were remembering himself.

For three years Reinhold shared his room with Herr Butz, who sat with Heinrich in the parlor on Sundays playing chess. Herr Butz gave speeches and Heinrich won. Reinhold had to watch, write down the moves, and repeat them because Heinrich wanted Reinhold to learn to play chess. Then Reinhold heard Herr Butz say: "A new age is approaching. A change in mankind and its measures of judgment is taking place. Strong-willed masculinity, that inner power, that newly risen beauty, is quite simply the specific ideal of beauty for the German race. Out of the horrors of death in battle, out of conflict, peril, and misery, a new race is struggling forth!"

Herr Butz had gotten to his feet. — With the face of a monument and body stiff as a poker, a statue, an empty figure! Reinhold had not been able to look away, until a spasm shot through the figure and freed Herr Butz. He had sunk back onto the kitchen chair, had played on, had carried out the major castling move to ward off the attack of a queen, and had kept on talking, had raised his voice so loudly that Reinhold's brother in the bedroom had begun to shriek, so that his mother had come into the kitchen in her nightgown. But Herr Butz was not to be restrained: "We are the race of change in the world. We must not be in torment if much is demolished. We must understand that much must be demolished so the world can change. A stirring is spreading over German soil as never before in the memory of mankind. The German race is being given a view of the world soul out of which a new order of life is being born!"

After Reinhold had at last gone to bed and listened for a long time to Herr Butz's speeches before he had been able to fall asleep, he heard him at dawn stumbling against table- and chair legs, falling onto his bed, blustering through dreams.

There lay the man, his skin yellow. His large pores seemed to snore with him. The dueling scars twisted into patterns, formed marks. — A marked man! The lodger lay there in Reinhold's room, and it was so full with his lying there that Reinhold had pulled his covers over his head so nothing could get to him.

Reinhold became an altar boy. On his way to church he passed by Rachie Neumann's building each time, looked up at the bay window and thought thoughts. At confession he confessed the thoughts that he had had about Rachie Neumann and her softness. "Sinful thoughts," said the father confessor and punished him with a rosary. After confession he did not pass Rachie Neumann's house, walked back a different way, avoided any thought of her. He even took a different way to Holy Communion, and only after he had received the Body of Christ did he walk past her again, looked up at the bay window and thought sinful thoughts.

At the Feast of Corpus Christi he walked along in the procession, wore his altar boy's robes, and was allowed to swing the incense vessel. Behind him strode a serious young chaplain under a canopy embroidered with stars that four altar boys held over him on poles. He was carrying the monstrance. The sun fell on its mirrors and gemstones. They sparkled blindingly. The trombones resounded. The choristers sang "Praise, O Zion, Thy Shepherd, the Redeemer of the strayed," and a great, holy inner space was in Reinhold. But then the procession turned slowly and solemnly into Rachie Neumann's street. From far away he saw her building decorated with fresh birch branches and saw the German flag waving from the bay window. "The world's Salvation, Jesus Christ, is truly here among us" the choristers sang. And however much he resisted them, the sinful thoughts took possession of him. And then he saw her: Rachie Neumann was standing between her parents at the open bay window. All three gazed down at the procession, and Reinhold saw that Rachie Neumann was looking at him, that she looked earnestly into his eyes. Why wasn't she walking in the procession? Why was she not among the girls who were carrying the large candles, wearing a white dress with ribbons in her hair?

He did not dare ask his father or mother, and he asked Herr Butz, who had marched in the procession also, with the flag pole on his hip bone, with the

German flag in the wind, right in the middle of a group of marchers and flag bearers, with a cap on his head, bright stripes over his shoulders, with dueling scars on his face. Perhaps he, too, had seen Rachie Neumann standing at the bay window, maybe he could explain everything to him. Reinhold didn't want to conceal the reason for his question, wanted to confide in him man-to-man, and said that he was having such thoughts.

Herr Butz sprang to his feet and grabbed Reinhold by the nape of his neck. "That's a Jewish girl," he yelled, "her blood isn't red, it's as black as her eyes and her hair. Do you understand that?" he yelled and shook Reinhold. "Anyone who gets involved with a Jewish girl will be ruined, do you hear me!" he roared. "The Jew is as cowardly as David, who slung the stone at Goliath from a safe distance, cut off the head of his unconscious opponent, and behaved afterwards like a great fighter. A Jew has no heart, has no character, isn't human, just cleverly imitates human beings, do you understand that?" the man roared so loud that Magda came running from the kitchen with flour on her hands, pulled Reinhold away from the man, and faced him herself.

"Be sure you know who you're dealing with," the man came after them with a menacing forefinger. "God created the Jew in anger, the Jewess in fury, do you hear! The Jewish plague rages, seethes, and it would end with the death of the soul of our people, had not the dawning tremors of great days of renewal come upon us. German rebirth is at hand!" And then the man whispered, came close to Reinhold and Magda, whispered: "The pure Aryan race has recognized that it must enter upon a new path of racial purity. Mankind is waiting for its Führer. The battle rages toward a resolution as in the First Year." And the man who before had been Herr Butz collapsed, lay on the floor, shaken with convulsions, with foam on his mouth and rolling eyes.

Magda ran into the kitchen, brought water, made the man compresses for his brow and calves, and took Reinhold along when she left the room, and on the night that followed he was allowed to sleep on the sofa in the parlor.

There he lay awake for a long time, wondered whether his father had hit him that time because Rachie Neumann is a Jewish girl, whether you're allowed to have such thoughts about other girls, just not about Jewish girls, and what is Jewish about Rachie Neumann and whether maybe she needs help so as not to be a Jew anymore. And he vowed he would help her.

But he saw her only seldom standing at the bay window, and whenever he waved at her, she stepped back from the window. — Had her parents forbidden her to look at him? Are the parents of Jewish girls Jewish parents? Are Jewish parents bad?

Reinhold often went to the church. The serious young chaplain gave him pictures of saints on the back of which the lives of the saints were written, and Reinhold dreamed himself into their suffering, wanted to become the holy, mild Francis or the serious chaplain with his intelligent brow and peaceful eyes. He wanted to be like him, was rapturous about him, longed for him.

When he was nine Reinhold wanted to take the vows of priesthood, but the chaplain said he was too young for vows. And when he got up the courage to ask what all the fuss about Jews meant, the chaplain replied that they were the biblical murderers and was not ready to say anything else about the Jews.

Herr Butz, who borrowed books from libraries large and small, who hung a checkered hand towel over his lamp and read through the nights, brought Reinhold books: "You must read, boy," he said. "You have to gain knowledge. Karl May knew a lot and was also against the Jews."

He brought Reinhold one Karl May volume after the other, and soon he no longer had to hang the hand towel over the lamp because Reinhold read through the nights as he did, no longer wanted to be like the serious young chaplain, and less and less went past Rachie Neumann's building. But he could not forget Rachie Neumann's whiteness and softness.

One Sunday morning Reinhold ran out of the house. There was a street fight on the square in front of the railway station.

"They want to make Germany a Russian province," screamed one man and pulled Reinhold into a group of men wearing brown shirts and peaked caps. But Reinhold wanted to go to his girl cousin's, got loose, and kept on running. At the railroad overpass two groups were laying into one another. "Fight the fascists and the Red Front," some were yelling, and "Germany awaken! Down with the Communists," the others were yelling. On the overpass railing a small man was balanced, trying to yell against all of them, and Reinhold saw that it was Herr Butz, and he heard him scream: "We have set out to defend our Fatherland with pure hearts, and with pure hands the German army has wielded the sword. If love for the Fatherland inspires you, if the German soul comes before anything else for you, reach out your hands to one another!"

Rocks were flying. No one was listening to the man. "Brothers," he screamed, "fight for the majestic thought of the German people! Today we are lying humiliated on the ground, but we have now found the root of our power, the consciousness of the forebears of Old Germany, the religion of the

German future!" And the man wobbled on the overpass and cried out: "Blood!" And cried out: "Brothers!" And cried out: "Blood is overflowing!"

Reinhold wanted to get to his girl cousin's. He knew that she would be in her garden. In the summertime she was always in her garden on Sunday.

"Well?" she said when he arrived.

"Well nothing," he said.

"Do you want to go berrying with me?" she asked, took her basket and preceded him.

"You're my cousin," he said when they were among the berries. "I want to see it."

"See what?" she asked and giggled.

And then she let him go ahead and look and find out what was different about her from about him, let him feel everything there that was there to be felt.

"We can do this," she said, "because we're related and can't marry one another anyway."

And when he had felt everything, he looked at it. And when he had looked at it, he went home.

Reinhold was supposed to learn about the serious things in life, so Heinrich took him along during the school holidays to the families that he had to take care of and into the sanitariums and old peoples' homes he looked after.

"People have nothing left," Heinrich often said, "no more honor, no pride in the Fatherland, and nothing left to eat. No wonder they jump out of windows, hang themselves, and slit their throats."

Heinrich went to the Home for Injured and Difficult Children from 3 to 14 once a month. "A House Protected by God" stood over the entrance. To the left and the right verdigris-covered angels knelt with folded wings, bent heads, and closed eyes, as they kneel in cemeteries. In the entrance hall three yellowed paper streamers from a Carnival long past were hanging on the ceiling and wafted in the draft that came in with Reinhold and Heinrich. There was a stench. — The air is thick! Full of disease and privation to wade through with every step! The nurses fly past like owls, mute faces closed off by bonnets, shadows and grit under their eyes, sticks up their backs, proba- bly wheels instead of feet under their five skirts!

They entered the dining room. Reinhold gripped Heinrich's hand: eighty children, no window, light from grilled fixtures, dishes smeared, clothes spotted, quiet, only the sound of the tin spoons in the bowls. "No talking with a full mouth!" was in Gothic letters on the wall.

"What are they eating?" asked Reinhold. "Do they get enough?"

"They die young," said Heinrich.

"Do they have parents?" asked Reinhold.

"They're all dead," said Heinrich and pulled Reinhold along, "died in battle, starved, froze to death, jumped out of windows. Consumptives, drunkards, murderers."

The wash room was next to the dining room: two iron tubs, a wooden bench with holes, on one hole a girl strapped fast.

"You're the son, aren't you?" said a fat man, pinched Reinhold's cheek, and held a hose up high. "Look, boy, anyone who shits in his pants here or pisses in his bed gets squirted off, and anyone who does it twice gets sent to the chamber." The man whipped open a door: "If you were one of those in there and had shit in your pants for the second time, you could spend twenty-four hours squatting in there, 'cause you can't stand up, the ceiling's too low. And you can't lie down 'cause the chamber's too cramped. And so that your eyes stay healthy, there's no light. And so that you won't have to shit again, there's nothing to eat either. And after two or three times we'd have cured this little fellow of shitting in his pants."

In the dormitory the sick and the wasted were already in their beds: iron cots, one next to the other, gray blankets, leather straps, no shelves, chests, toys, two children tied to their beds.

"What's wrong with the little girl?" Heinrich asked a nurse.

"She bit her fingers to the bone."

"And the boy there?"

"Wanted to mutilate himself, too. We don't have enough food for the little sheep," the nurse whispered, "our sheep must go hungry. Erich and Emil," she whispered and pointed to one here and another there, "are twins, were born joined together. Emil has no left arm, and Erich's right one is crippled. They want to be together but aren't allowed to. Touching conceals peril, and tenderness is blasphemy. And that's Klausi," she whispered, "a Jewish boy, but I like him anyway. His parents first abused him and then abandoned him."

"And the one there?" asked Heinrich.

"I don't know what his name is. His father was out of work, killed himself with gas. His mother went crazy. His nine brothers and sisters came to the home, the two littlest ones died. These days," the nurse whispered, "the Good Lord probably doesn't want to put his children down on earth anymore, and so takes them back quickly to Himself in His Heavenly Kingdom."

The next morning Reinhold went with Heinrich to the workers' quarter on the edge of the city. — Brick, hard yellow gravestone, humbled houses, cowering stone huts!

There were no doorbells. Heinrich knocked. A face without teeth, with gray strawlike hair, appeared in the crack of the door: "Do you bring money?"

"I just want to see the little one," said Heinrich.

"He just died of starvation," said the face with the empty mouth that was so empty that it laughed. "Please, sir," and a skeletal woman opened the door. "I can't pay for the funeral. If your office won't pay for it, I'll bury the young one in the ground."

The child lay on the table in a blanket. A candle stub was burning. The woman lifted the blanket. The child looked more dried out than starved. Music came from the street.

"Where is your husband?" asked Heinrich.

"At work," said the woman.

"Did he find work?"

The music stopped, a speech was announced.

"Looking for work is also work." said the woman.

"The aristocratic fundamental thought of Nature," came a voice from the street, "desires the victory of the strong and the destruction of the weak." The loudspeaker droned. Heinrich listened. The bony woman blew out the candle. From the street came: "Therein is found that free play of power that must lead to a lasting, improved breeding ."

In the evening they were invited to his aunt's, his mother's sister who hadn't wanted Heinrich the pauper.

On the street stood a car that belonged to his uncle. The store was crammed to the ceiling with shoes. In the apartment was a dining room with a large table. More food was served up on it than was eaten.

But everything that got onto Magda's table was eaten, and often there wasn't enough for Reinhold's hunger. And though Heinrich and Magda went without, Reinhold had invented "the fair way" for himself and his brother: One divides, the other chooses.

His cousin was there and showed Reinhold his new skis. And his girl cousin crowed: "I'm thinking of something — guess what it is!"

Reinhold turned red. But then he thought of the picture of the woman with the breasts, and the cow, and the gigolo, and he found his cousin ridiculous, for she didn't even have breasts.

A bowl with hard-boiled eggs was standing on the table. Each one took an egg, and his boy cousin took three. But a second one was offered neither to Heinrich and Magda nor to Reinhold and his brother. The bowl of eggs was carried away.

Only once had they offered Reinhold an egg, and he had taken it, and it was hollow, a blown-out egg, a joke. They had all laughed, bent over, slapped their thighs.

Reinhold had run away, had bawled with anger, had felt humiliated, degraded. Had run home and sat down in front of the picture that hung in the parlor over the sofa.

The picture had the title "The Last Man," and the last man was also the strongest man. With flying hair, surrounded by the raging sea, he was standing on the boat's stern, holding the German flag into the wind with one hand and with the other the wheel of his battleship in a solid grip. "The heroic battle of H.M.S. Leipzig, Falkland, December 1914" it said under the picture. And when Reinhold had looked at it for a while, he had come to himself again, had again become sure of himself, and would like best to have torn the flag and the wheel out of the man's hands.

But during the night he had ridden up to his uncle's house on his vengeful steed, had jumped over the garden fence, exploded through the shoe store so that all the boxes fell from the shelves on the walls, all the shoes flew through the air, so that they had lain the whole night through on the floor, broken like empty egg shells.

A few weeks later the uncle had come to Heinrich. He had written checks that he couldn't cover. He needed help. And Heinrich had, for a period of ten days, taken a rather large sum from the coffers of the welfare agency. "I'm responsible for it," he had told Magda, and yet had done it.

The danger that the money would be discovered missing had been great, and the danger that the uncle would not pay him back was, too. Magda had prayed a lot, and Heinrich had sat quietly beside her. But the uncle had paid the money back on time, and a thanks had been the only thanks.

Eberhard Gottschlich soon after joined the Brownshirts, the SA, became a supplier for all SA boots and later also for SS Black Shirt boots in the city and became rich doing so.

"You're paupers," said Reinhold's boy cousin to him. "You don't count," he said. "You don't have a horse or a bike, and you don't study piano."

Then Reinhold's grandparents died, died together, were found clinging together in their bed, with hands clasped, each one in the hand of the other.

Magda knelt with Reinhold and his brother at the foot of the bed. It was early morning. They were alone with the dead. The candles were burning. "Winnetou says the dead walk with the wind," thought Reinhold, and he could not cry.

"It's cold," said his brother. "Why are all the windows open?"

"When there are dead in a room, the windows have to be open."

"Why?" his brother asked.

Magda was lost in prayer. The candles were burning, flickering. Reinhold looked around, could see the picture with the angel through the open door, saw the angel step out of the picture, heard its wings rustle, saw his grandparents at the angel's hand, wanted to get up and go over to them, then the door slammed from the draft that came from the open windows.

"That was the wind," said Magda, startled.

"The dead walk with the wind," said Reinhold.

On December 12, 1932, Heinrich Fischer, too, joined the Brownshirts.

"They don't ask me there: 'Do you have an education, since you want to be a leader?' They say: 'Here you can go beyond of the limits of your origin, if you have the stuff to do it!' " And Heinrich got Herr Butz to go celebrating and drinking with him. They played chess, and after three games he went to Magda in the kitchen and forbade her to go to church.

When he had been drinking he always forbade her to go to church. But she, who had always obeyed him, did not obey him, went to church, confessed, prayed, and asked the Lord God to protect her from evil.

One morning Frau Polster found Herr Butz in the attic room. He had hanged himself. On his bed lay his letter of farewell.

I am a Jew. I was so unconscionable as to believe that my racial soul could be purified, because from my childhood on, my longing was directed solely to what was German. I wanted to walk from darkness into brightness. I imagined myself secretly to be in the Aryan mysticism of light but had to understand bitterly that it can never be the inner sanctum for me. A Jew cannot be purified, for he has no soul, since his origin is in the anti-God. I am what I despise, a parasite. And as Lagarde says, since you can't educate trichinas, you must make them harmless as quickly as possible, so I deal with myself like that, since I must recognize that all of my bells of longing are unable to bring me any help. For the Jew is a danger to the exalted Nordic soul, to all inherently noble creatures. The Jew believes in nothing, neither within himself nor outside of himself, and so he is capable of spoiling even what is most pure. He is the acid that will corrode bright humankind. But if the Jew gains victory with the help of the Marxist deception, he will steer the death ship of mankind through racial chaos and unimaginable destruction into the void that he carries within himself. I must atone for the wrong they perpetrate. And I want to proceed as an example, and all my cursed kind should follow me, for the preservation of the Aryan, the salvation of the world.

Herr Butz was carried away.

Magda aired the room, tore the bed apart in which he had slept just the night before, took down the curtains, scrubbed the floorboards, swept off the walls with the broom, laid a cross on the mattress and a woolen blanket over it, took the clothes out of the wardrobe, bundled them with the things that she found under the bed, found there also the magazine with the picture of the woman with the cow and the gigolo, put it with the other things that had belonged to Herr Butz, put everything in a soap box and put it in the basement until relatives could come to pick it up.

But no one came. No relations showed up. Heinrich took the box to the winter relief office where everything that had belonged to Herr Butz was distributed to the needy.

"You're going to get to see the Führer," Heinrich said. Reinhold had to put on his good pants and accompany his father to the great hall.

Many people were crowded at the entrances, wearing peaked caps, brown shirts, and boots, like those Heinrich was wearing. Policemen were there. A brass band was playing.

Two thousand people raised their hands and began to yell as a slightly built man with a mustache walked to the speaker's platform.

"There comes the Führer," Heinrich called out.

"Where?"

"The first one there, the one with the mustache!"

"Not *him!*" Reinhold exclaimed and looked up his father, who was standing tall and broad beside him.

But when the man began to speak, Reinhold recognized the voice again that had droned up from the street to the woman with the starved child.

The man with the mustache was speaking, and in the great hall a great silence prevailed. — They are as quiet as in church, and they have the eyes of those who pray!

The man talked about his passion for the Fatherland and said that he carried Germany within him.

"Is he a Jew?" Reinhold whispered.

"What makes you think that?"

"He talks like Herr Butz and looks so pale and dark."

A storm of applause whisked Heinrich's reply away, but the motion of the pale man's hand sufficed to quieten the screaming and jubilating people.

"We all have a premonition that in the not-too-distant future problems will confront the people, to overcome which only the most eminent race will be appointed as the master race," said the man. "Germany must necessarily take the place on this earth that is proper to it," he shouted, and the whole hall began to sing.

"But he talks just like Herr Butz," Reinhold insisted on the way home. And Heinrich told him to keep his mouth shut.

Magda's brothers came to visit. Heinrich told about the rally in the great hall. Magda was mending, his brother was asleep, Reinhold was allowed to sit at the table with the men.

"The Führer speaks impressively," Heinrich said, "no smear campaign, no rabble rousing, and he knows how to speak so that everyone understands him. What he says concerns the needs of us all."

But Uncle Otto and Uncle Fritz sat with tight-lipped faces and seemed not to believe Heinrich.

In January, when on the radio "the gospel of an awakening Germany" was proclaimed and the bells of the Königsberg Cathedral were tolling, Heinrich called Reinhold over to him, gave him a fifty-pence piece and said: "Go to the Café Deibl and get two pieces of cake. The Führer has won. Now, boy, everything will get better."

The following Sunday Magda went with Reinhold and his brother to the Church of St. John. Usually they went to St. Elizabeth's Church, which was closer and smaller, in which the light fell like holy light through blue windows and was comforting. But the Church of St. John was gloomy and high. The seeker of God found no ladder there, no step up, so that, crunched and crushed like a beetle on the floor, he sensed vaguely that blessedness reigned in the heights of the tower.

In the city newspaper the appeal had appeared that all the faithful should gather for Sunday services in the Church of St. John. In spite of blizzard and icy cold many had come.

Reinhold saw that men in the brown uniform were in the church, and he told his mother, who held his mouth shut aghast.

When the old priest began to preach, Magda took Reinhold's hand and, as they listened, held it so tight that it hurt him.

"The sign has come to pass. Satan is among us," the old priest said. "In opposition to God he is trying to erect his dreadful kingdom. The might of Heaven shall be shaken, the order of power dragged into chaos. But before I read from the mysterious Revelations of John, be consoled and know: Whoever entrusts himself to God will live in bliss. For whoever opposes God, Heaven will be unendurable, Heaven will be Hell. Hell is where it is, in us, because Hell cannot exist as a place. For what God has created is good, therefore do not be afraid!

"And now hear the Revelation," the priest called out, and solemnly opened the Holy Bible: *Then I saw an angel coming down from heaven, holding in his hand the key of the bottomless pit and a great chain. And he seized the dragon, that ancient serpent, who is the Devil and Satan, and bound him for a thousand years, and threw him into the pit, and shut it and sealed it over him, that he should deceive the nations no more, till the thousand years were ended. After that he must be loosed for a little while. ... And when the thousand years are ended, Satan will be loosed from his prison and will come out to deceive the nations which are at the four corners of the earth.*

"And I say unto you," the old priest interrupted his reading, "I say unto you that the thousand years are just past, and I ask you, will God now, through the highest of the demons, drive the demons from the world? Or does He have in mind to test us through what is evil, as He tested Job? And I ask you further," he shouted, "what is evil? And I say unto you, evil is the absence of God, is not a thing actually, is only a lack of divine light. It is matter itself, populated by fallen angels!"

And the priest continued to read: Now war arose in heaven, Michael and his angels fighting against the dragon; and the dragon and his angels fought, but they were defeated, and there was no longer any place for them in heaven. And the great dragon ... was thrown down to the earth, and his angels were thrown down with him. And I heard a loud voice in heaven, saying: "...But woe to you, O earth and sea, for the devil has come down to you in great wrath, because he knows that his time is short!"

"Because only for a short time, as it says in Revelations," shouted the priest, "only for a short time shall he be loose!" And he started singing the hymn "Blessed Assurance, Jesus Is Mine," and it became mighty song that expanded the dome and made the towers grow.

On the way home his brother asked: "Are angels white?"

"Yes," said Magda, "white and holy." And Reinhold couldn't help thinking of Rachie Neumann.

"And do the white angels sleep sometimes," his brother went on asking.

"Why?" asked Magda.

"Because sometimes black ones are standing there," said his brother.

"When?" asked Magda.

"Right now," said his brother.

"Where?" asked Magda.

"Behind the priest," said his brother.

At home Magda's brothers were sitting with Heinrich in the kitchen, and already in the vestibule Reinhold heard Uncle Otto say: "They pulled out Rabbi Kohn's beard, then they killed him with a shovel and threw him into the pond ditch."

"Who, who?" Heinrich cried out, came out of the kitchen, pushed Magda and his brother aside, pushed Reinhold away, and ran out the door. He returned only at evening and looked like someone who had been lost in the snow, someone who hadn't noticed that he was freezing because his mind was completely disoriented and unable to think.

Magda had still been sitting with her brothers in the kitchen before Heinrich came home. She had sent Reinhold and his brother out and closed the door.

It was a Sunday afternoon in winter. Reinhold was sitting in his room at the window. It was snowing. The flakes pressed on his shoulders, pressed on his heart.

Reinhold had often met Rabbi Kohn. He had the biggest ears, wore long gowns like old women do, wore a hat and a beard, and whenever he spoke he raised his finger and said things that Reinhold didn't understand.

When his mother said goodnight to him late in the evening, he asked: "What is a rabbi?"

"A rabbi is a priest for Jews."

"Is a rabbi a Jew, too? And are you allowed to murder Jews?"

The next morning Reinhold went to school earlier. He wanted to meet his chaplain and ask why a Jewish priest was killed and by whom.

The chaplain was standing outside the teacher's room with a priest. Both were talking with raised voices, as though in an argument, and they didn't see Reinhold.

"But the Jew is not a human being," Reinhold heard the priest say. And the chaplain said: "Jew is a word and a numeral. In Hebrew every letter is a numeral, every word a concentration of knowledge, every sentence a frightful formula that, when uttered with full breath and the right emphasis, causes rivers to cease flowing and mountains to sink."

Then Reinhold didn't want to question the chaplain anymore because he couldn't believe that Rachie Neumann was a word and a numeral.

Reinhold was not yet ten and as tall as others at twelve. He was the first in his age group in the gymnastic society, had an A in the pentathlon, and beat even some who were thirteen. But sometimes he got out of breath. Magda took him to the doctor. "The boy has a heart problem. His heart is enlarged," he said. "He's delicate and must take it easy."

Reinhold ran to the Ziegenberg, which means Goat Hill. It was directly behind the city, was overgrown and deserted: tall trees, thick underbrush, steep meadows, and a shut-down mine. There he imagined the world to himself. He wanted to be a man, a real man like his father, one whom no one can hurt or break. — But can someone with heart problems be a real man? "I will be one," he yelled down to the city and was again sure of himself.

The Reichstag in Berlin had burned down. Heinrich was sitting at the radio. Uncle Eberhard came in his Brownshirt uniform with two men whom Reinhold knew from the Liedertafel, who had also come in uniform. Heinrich went into the bedroom and returned in uniform.

The men were sitting in the parlor, listening to the radio and drinking the beer that Reinhold had fetched from the saloon for twelve pence a bucket. Magda had stayed in the kitchen.

"The radio shapes people in the spirit of the Führer," it droned through the apartment.

And Magda was singing, although Heinrich said that she couldn't sing, although he laughed whenever she sang. That's why she sang so seldom, that's why she hummed mostly when she wanted to sing.

She was standing at the washboard, washing shirts. Reinhold was watching her.

31

In the parlor someone yelled: "It was the Bolsheviks," and someone else yelled: "Now the Führer must take action, now he can't shilly-shally anymore."

Reinhold was watching his mother soaping and scrubbing, heard her humming lullabies, all a bit too deep and fragmentary, heard his uncle from the parlor: "The Führer reacted immediately. Starting today there's an emergency decree. The announcement went out in the late afternoon to all the headquarters."

Reinhold saw his mother's red, cracked hands. — The inside of her throat would look as red and cracked! And he heard his uncle from the parlor: "Every suspicious citizen will be taken into custody immediately for the protection of the people. Volunteers should report to the SA office as auxiliary policemen."

Reinhold heard his mother sing even louder, even deeper, saw her red hands wringing out the shirts and, doing that, turning white, heard his uncle keep on talking in the parlor, heard his voice like the radio voice, as though he were addressing the masses: "The priest of the Church of St. John was the first one they took into custody. He's in jail now and should be glad that the same thing didn't happen to him that happened to the poisoner of the fountain, that little rabbi."

Magda had asked Heinrich to let Reinhold join the Catholic Youth Organization, and as an answer Heinrich had read to her from the newspaper: "A single flag flutters ahead of young people. The son of the millionaire and the son of the worker wear one and the same uniform. For only youth are unprejudiced and capable of a genuine community. Youth is socialism."

"Our Lord God is the only God," Magda had said, "we should serve Him and no one else."

But when the decree came that children of officials were not allowed to be members of religious youth groups, the argument between Heinrich and Magda was decided.

On the Führer's birthday, April 20, 1933, Reinhold entered the middle school and was taken into the Hitler Youth.

More than two thousand boys and girls had gathered in the great hall. The leader of the Hitler Youth had come from the capital and shook hands with every Hitler Youth boy and girl: "Your body belongs to the nation. You have the duty to be healthy and to obey. A great idea can be directed to its goal only when a firmly established, strict organization led with consistent firmness lends shape to its world-view."

Reinhold's group leader was named Hanno von Wolfsberg. He was thirteen years old, tall and thin, with dark hair and gray eyes, one who knew much and to whom Reinhold soon looked up.

And when a year later Hanno von Wolfsberg became cadet lieutenant, the leader of the platoon, it gave Heinrich a small, malicious pleasure that Magda had to hear from Reinhold that he, too, wished to become a leader in the Hitler Youth.

On a summer morning Eberhard Gottschlich stood in civilian clothes at the door: "Last night the Black Shirt SS and the defense force, the Reichswehr, put down a putsch attempt by the Brownshirt SA. Many died in the attempt. Many are sitting in jail!"

Heinrich, who had become a sergeant in the SA, knew nothing about a putsch, told Magda to shut up when she said the godlessness of his belief was beginning to take bloody vengeance, and he shut himself up for a whole day with closed blinds in the bedroom. But he wanted to continue believing in his faith, and at evening he pulled up the blinds again and opened up the doors.

A friend of Heinrich, a unit leader in the SA, was among the dead. His daughter, the small maiden Mechthild, sat with Reinhold and Magda in their kitchen and cried.

"We are the Atlantean German people," said Heinrich. "We must offer sacrifices, whether they be father and mother, brother and sister, daughter and son. Something higher, my girl, than happiness and peace must be wished for by every will that is the German will!"

And Mechthild, three years older than Reinhold and a leader of the Hitler Youth Maidens, was soon ready to make any sacrifice.

WHEN REINHOLD TURNED fourteen, Heinrich traveled with him to Bayreuth.

After a long train trip through forests and more forests, Heinrich said, "Anyone who doesn't know Franconia doesn't know Germany."

They took lodgings at an inn on the edge of the city: white walls, fresh-made beds, window overlooking the courtyard, in which chickens were running around.

Reinhold had never slept in a strange bed and didn't want to think about the strange dreams that might have infused the pillows. Strange dreams, he couldn't help thinking, are like a contagion to me, like danger. And he resolved to place his rucksack under his head for sleeping.

They were sitting in the tavern bar eating sandwiches that Magda had made for them. Reinhold got a fruit juice and Heinrich a beer with a head.

At the next table were sitting two old men. They watched Reinhold and Heinrich and then asked where the newcomers were from and what had brought them to Franconia. And when Heinrich answered them that he had wanted to show his son the house, city, and land that had been Richard Wagner's place in this world, the old men invited them to their table and told how they had been singers in the choir at Dresden at the time and came every year to Bayreuth, for Richard Wagner, with his powerful music, had gotten the change in the world going. Mankind had for centuries been cut off from its mystic past and limited by space and time, and left to its own devices had looked for fabricated comforts. But the age of the new God-men had begun with Wagnerian fanfares.

"The future will reach out its hand to the most distant past," said one of them. "Look at your son," he said, "a sturdy German boy, look at the aggressiveness and pugnacity in the eyes of your son, and on the rudiments of your memory the sense of the whole thing stirs. And Richard Wagner, does not he not lead us back to that sense, to the heroic poem of this world?"

From the radio that was standing on the bar there came a report that the Führer was devoting special attention to equipping his troops. A man sprang to his feet and with raised hand shouted: "Whatever is called German soil should recruit hordes of fighters, then no one ever again will revile the German Reich!"

And another one said: "I am convinced that the Führer has been called to be the executor of German destiny. He has the strength of soul to exterminate the lower races and to prepare eternal Germany for the arrival of the God-man."

Reinhold heard the men begin to sing a curious song, tones that expanded, that went forth into the room. He still heard Heinrich's voice, strong and clear, heard the tones expand into the eternity of a great bell that struck and rang and sucked him into its throat.

In the gray of dawn he woke up disoriented, kicked the wall when he started to get up, bumped his head when he got out of bed. His father was snoring, hoarse from beer and the singing that ended only late at night, long after he had put Reinhold to bed. The sun was creeping into his father's open mouth, into his nostrils.

"Father," Reinhold cried out, "wake up!"

Then he was awake, sprang out of bed, and cried: "Boy, we're in Franconian lands. Today we'll get to roam everywhere!"

It was seven o'clock when they left the inn with their rucksacks. — The forest heights and the vales roll, surge on and on, the sea of forest is whipped up by the wind, the church spires ring above the crests of the waves! To be air itself, to be wind itself and woods, to be myself to the limits of wind, woods, and air, filled with myself, imbued by the depths of forest and meadow land!

They made a rest stop in a mill taproom, and his father told about the mill ghosts, about the white miller in his smock, with his embittered face and his long-pointed cap, who came all night long into every German mill to disturb the sleep of the living, to steal the breath of babes in cradles, to give young brides consumption, old women warts, and old men the gout. Those who met him would say that his long-pointed cap hung down as deeply as the corners of his mouth, and stick-thin legs with flour-white stockings stuck out from under his smock. Cockroaches and meal worms crept away when he appeared, and owls flew shrieking from the old linden trees that stand around every mill.

They walked along a wild brook, went past water mills, past oil mills and hammer mills, past powder mills, flour mills, and sawmills, wandered through the valley of fear and the valley of horror, reached steep rock ridges, found the Devil's Cave, and Heinrich pulled Reinhold down into the underworld, told his son about the Nibelungen, and the echo of his voice resounded back mightily:

> I know an ash, called the Tree of Earth,
> A whitened fog moistens its crown,
> From which dew falls down to quicken the depths,
> Ever green the tree stands at the well of Urd.

35

Night birds flew up, flying bats screeched, fluttered around their heads. Reinhold's fear was immense, but Heinrich recited verse after verse until something rose up in Reinhold, pulled him out of his fright, up onto the top of a peak.

"Edda means 'there of old.'" He heard his father's voice as an echo, heard about the misty home and the flame home, saw himself with the sword in one hand and the maple staff in the other, and heard out of the primeval roar, out of night and abyss the call of Urda. Or was it Heinrich's voice?

In the afternoon they arrived at the druid's stone. The heat was steady, the crickets were shrill. And seemed to get louder and faster until everything was a turning, racing, screeching. — A shrieking chorus from the dim and distant past breaks through the barrier of time and invades our ears as a horde of crickets. Had the shepherd said that, who suddenly stood before them in a flickering light between the gigantic stones?

The shepherd knew the names: baptismal stone, altar stone, star stone, and pointed to one in the middle of all the stones, one with a circular hole through which the rising sun on the day of the summer solstice and the setting sun on the day of the winter solstice sent its rays. And the knowledge of that, said the shepherd, came from his father, who had gotten it from his father, who had gotten it from his father. He pointed at the sky, where the birds flew in a great V from which the initiated who once observed the flight of birds had known in advance of things that had not yet happened. And suddenly he had vanished again in the darkness of spruce and fir, into another story.

It was already growing dark when Reinhold and Heinrich inquired about a place to sleep in the castle inn of a small village. A raven tower menaced the sky. From the church came the stroke of ten.

In the inn farmers were sitting at cards, eating fat sausages and drinking dark beer.

From the church came the stroke of eleven. A party was taking place in the castle hall. Light gleamed from the windows, the music came down to the inn.

The farmers told how a ghost visited the castle. The White Woman haunted it. Her sighs could be heard even in the village. Almost two hundred years ago the young princess had committed incest with her brother. From that a horrible changeling had crept into the world, whom the princess had killed and buried in the castle garden. Thereupon she had become ill and wasted away before the eyes of everyone. On a black All Souls' Day at the twelfth stroke of high noon she had closed her eyes. And her brother could find no priest who would consecrate the earth where she was buried. Ever since, the castle walls would crack open and collapse, and on nights of a full moon the night walker returned to compete with the cats with her yowling.

Laughter came down from the castle, and when it struck twelve the farmers drank up their beer and went home.

Reinhold and Heinrich lay down on wooden benches, shoved their rucksacks under their heads, and went to sleep into dream castles.

The next morning they left the inn, went past the castle with its raven tower, out of the village. Birds were still plunging through the air, trying out their voices and clearing their throats with squawks.

They stopped to rest at a castle ruin. There was rainwater in the well, the first leaves of autumn were floating on it.

But when Reinhold continued to look into the well, saw flower blossoms, lily leaves, garlands, he began to get dizzy, he began to feel a pull, down into the well saga of the young novice nun who had fallen in love with a farmer boy. On the day of taking her vows, wearing her white bridal gown with a lily wreath in her hair, she had jumped into the well and since then sings up from the bottom where a great, colorful garden grows, sings and sings, and entices men. Reinhold grew afraid, and he stepped back quickly from the edge of the well, for from deep below had come something like choruses, like the laughter of women adorned with flowers, wreathed with lilies.

"Boy!" his father called, "we've got to get back to Bayreuth today."

A farmer's wagon took them along to the next village, which was called Tüchersfeld, where they stopped off. The innkeeper told them that a long time ago Jews had fled to the village and for a large amount of money had received permission to reside there. At that long-ago time sixty of them lived there, and some were still there today. The Jews were possessed by death, the innkeeper said. Recently he had seen a Jewish girl sewing, and when asked what she was sewing on, she had answered: "On my fiancé's shroud." And the innkeeper slapped his fist on the table and then made the sign of the Cross.

"They're just strange customs," said Heinrich.

"Too strange," said the innkeeper, "too strange for us to put up with them. When they sing their songs of lament in the Jewish quarter, where they still live, then you'd actually like to forbid the Jew from even being in this world."

And Reinhold couldn't help thinking of Rachie Neumann and the shroud she would have had to sew for him for their wedding, if his father had not forbidden him to associate with her.

37

When they arrived in Bayreuth, they walked through the bare, stone city to a house before which his father removed his cap and said it was the house in which Richard Wagner had lived, and when Reinhold read the text that stood over the windows to the left and right of the door: "Here where my dreaming freedom found, let me name this house Freedomdream," he had the feeling of again being entangled in a story, of being drawn into a saga.

And then, when they stopped at the foot of a hill and looked up at a mighty gabled building, when music came forth from it — chords that grab hold of you here and deposit you there, where darkness hides in darkness, where nothing continues to think, where everything broods — Reinhold would gladly have taken flight.

"They're playing the saga of Siegfried, the *Ring of the Nibelungen*, the conclusion, the end, the twilight of the gods," Heinrich shouted. "Listen," he shouted, "the call of the horn! That's the Rhine journey."

Small, friendly clouds that didn't fit the music had gathered, and a few impudent evening birds were making noises in the air. Reinhold and Heinrich took a seat on a bench. The music broke off. They saw people coming out of the building, saw the great squares fill up, saw colorful clothing, heard distant talk. The sky grew darker, fanfares, the people went back into the building, the music came again.

"Does he belong to you?" a man called and pointed at Reinhold. "Would the boy like to go backstage?" The man was wearing a suit of armor made of iron. Black streaks were painted onto his face. His black hair stood straight up, but he laughed.

Reinhold and Heinrich followed him into the gabled building, went up steps. The dark tones overflowed. Reinhold held tightly to Heinrich's hand. A horn called as before when they were sitting on the bench. And then there rose up before them like broad daylight, like really being in the countryside: a woods, a rocky gorge, and in its middle a river. Women were swimming there, fish, fishsong, and up on the wooded heights stood the one who had called to them, and next to him stood a singing hero. And the one who had called to them, whom Reinhold had seen laughing, shoved a lance into the back of the singing hero. Then came the funeral procession.

Music is a sphere. We're all in the music, are shut up in the music. There are no windows, soon our air will be all used up!

"Let the embers blaze high and bright that will consume the noble body of the sublime hero," sang a woman holding a torch. She thrust the torch into the pile of wood on which the dead hero lay and rode on her horse into the fire to him. The river flowed over its banks, the man who had called out to Reinhold and Heinrich sprang into the river, the fire ignited the sky, then the heavens burned, then the music burned.

38

2

A FTER FEVERISH DAYS — in which Reinhold had walked through great halls and had died away with his footsteps, in which his mother had held him and he had let himself be held, had hidden with her from the great hall and the dying away, when he had hidden from the men who had come through the great halls, men with long, menacing fingers — lords of warning, warning of what? — days on which he had heard his mother say: "The boy is delicate, you expected too much of him!" and had heard his father say: "His heart is just enlarged, he must take it easy!" — he had run out of the house, had run to the Ziegenberg, sat up there and looked down on the city, broke branches, burrowed, dug holes in the earth, sat there until it got dark.

On the way home he met Utz and Gummi, who were in his class, and found out that the social evening of the Hitler Youth was to take place the next day in the gymnasium of the Wagner School.

Reinhold picked up Schade, who was his friend, was in his class, and stood under his protection. He was frail, played no sports, and read a lot. Reinhold could always talk to him about the inner conflict that he sometimes felt, about melancholia and anguish.

"You're reaching middle age early," Schade had said, and was not joking. He had no gift for making jokes. "It's the first stage of the great gradual malady called death that you're confronting. Don't read novels from the small library, read the poets," he had said and had given Reinhold some books. "Reading helps — the gloom of others cheers you up. Read Hölderlin, Novalis! Read Kleist and Büchner! Then you'll read what such feelings mean, and you'll learn to enjoy your most anguished thoughts."

Schade was small and delicate, didn't eat everything, didn't drink everything, didn't grasp everything. His father was dead. It was said that soon after the seizure of power he was caught embezzling. He had fled, went underground, and a week later was found — he had hanged himself. Schade had then been absent from school for two weeks.

Reinhold wanted to take him along to the social evening, wanted to strengthen the weak, thought that belief in strength could certainly strengthen him, infused him with the seven sword words of the Hitler Youth boys: toughness, bravery, composure, loyalty, truth, comradeship, honor.

"You must believe in Germany, so sure and clear and fine, as you believe in sunlight, evening's glow and in starshine," he yelled during the long-distance run to the Wagner School, which he had demanded of Schade. "You must believe in Germany as though Germany were you. Just as you believe that your soul strives for the eternal, too. You must believe in Germany, else you're in a living death, and you must fight for Germany until your final breath."

Fifty-two boys had gathered in the gymnasium: Platoon 7 with its platoon leader Hanno. He was standing on a chair and spoke as though from a mountain, as though to an army: "We youth stand today firmly resolute under one flag. In service to what is exalted we will grow beyond ourselves. Through our work we will assist in the erection of the future national community. And one day we will be the people ourselves who must bear and master history. Then when our fathers are no more, we will carry the flag on, in order to hand it over to our descendants one day."

Schade never returned to the Hitler Youth evenings, stayed at home, built castles in the air and sometimes, when the doorbell rang and Reinhold was standing outside, he opened up an air castle door and let him come inside and showed him its splendors.

But Reinhold plunged into service to the Hitler Youth, into comradeship and community. He became a private first class, then a corporal, and, when Hanno became a cadet captain, he became a sergeant. Reinhold's platoon belonged to Hanno's company: "Whether rich or poor, we are all the same" was the motto. The uniforms, the brisk marching, the rousing slogans, the flag ceremonies, camping and campfires, the celebrations of winter and summer solstices fulfilled him and filled out his days.

Every morning he went to the early morning exercises in the platoon quarters, to gymnastics and wrestling, to squad boxing matches and friendly brawls. Sometimes he still went to church first, and he liked it when no one saw him there. He put his acolyte's robe over his uniform and performed his service to God as he did his service to his Fatherland.

Eight platoons, two companies, two hundred and eighty boys assembled for the flag ceremony on the Ziegenberg, gathered up wood, made a fire, sat down in a circle. Darkness fell. Hanno hoisted the flag up high. He stood next to the flagpole and spoke in a clear voice: "We step up to the flag. It is the symbol of our commonality. We follow it. Our loyalty belongs to it. We can make mistakes, act contrary to honor, be cowardly and disloyal — the flag remains pure. To serve it, to follow it is battle, is the battle which we agreed upon here untold thousands of years ago. Be aware of the fact that we are all Atlanteans and wish to erect our Reich here anew. Therefore I demand of you that you honor the flag through your composure and staunch salute."

The boys had gotten to their feet, the fire flamed high.

"Anyone who cannot get a grip on himself before the flag," shouted Hanno, "has no business among the living."

A wind came up, the flag flapped, the boys stood with intense eyes and sang:

> Our flag flutters before us,
> Our flag is the new age,
> And the flag leads us into eternity,
> Yes, the flag is more than death!

Reinhold and Hanno stamped out the embers. Then, quiet with lofty thoughts, without looking at one another, they walked back to the city. The intimacy with his older companion was so close that Reinhold's throat became dry, that his pulse throbbed in his temples, that he could have walked next to him on and on.

But Hanno stopped. It was cold, it was winter. From their mouths and noses came white clouds that touched and flowed together. In the cold and quiet they stomped one leg and then the other. Then their gazes crossed, they shook hands. Then they parted and did not look back.

One Sunday morning, when Magda had gone to church with his brother, and Reinhold — with the certainty of not being allowed to waste a thought on a religion other than the one that he had in common with Hanno, not to have any more time for being an acolyte and going to church — had gone jogging through the morning streets, and his enlarged heart had beat in his throat, when he had become furious about his enlarged heart, had run on, when with his heart in his head, soaked with sweat, he had gotten home, had heard a slam and had run into the kitchen, there lay his naked father. He had slipped and hit his head on the edge of the bath tub that he had started to get out of, in which he bathed every Sunday morning and read novels from the small library — he was unconscious. — Or dead? He was lying on his stomach, face down, air bubbles in the bloody water.

Reinhold pulled at the heavy body, still more air bubbles. He pulled but did not have enough strength, called his father's name, bawled, yelled, braced himself under his father, his head and his shoulders under the head and the shoulders, swallowed the bloody water, was able to open the drain, could let the water run out.

Was able to turn him over, turn him onto his back: there lay the big, naked man. Reinhold pushed on his chest as he had learned to do in life saving. Water spurted out of the man's mouth. The face became his father again.

43

That evening Reinhold went to Hanno, who lived in the most exclusive area in the city. The house was a fortress surrounded by a high wall, with a golden bell over a golden nameplate, with an intercom: "What do you want?"

"My name is Reinhold Fischer. I would like to see Hanno."

The gate opened. He walked along a graveled path. In the great doorway stood a servant: "The young master is in his room."

A large vestibule, a marble staircase, many steps, a long hallway. Hanno jumped to his feet: "Welcome, friend, to my holy four walls!"

The walls were bare and white. Only the rune of victory and the black sun were hanging over the bed. Hanno had been sitting at his desk in front of the window. The window was open. It was already getting dark. Wind blew into the room.

"Do you hear the voice of the wind? The Valkyries are riding, the horse maidens," Hanno laughed.

Reinhold could not speak. Then Hanno spoke: "Here I can be quietly by myself. This is my kingdom, my chamber of quiet, my homeland solitude. I'm peculiar, I know, but it's good to sit here and stare or climb around in the stars up there, produce thoughts, to branch out in my thoughts, get lost in my gaze, you know?"

And when Reinhold then talked about his father, Hanno said: "Fathers are mortal. You and I, we're mortal, mere mortals, mere weaklings when we don't look inside ourselves. Believe me, the ways there are freer and the points of view higher. And when things are lying too heavily on your soul, you must send your soul into the dream.

"You ought to keep a diary," he said. "Writing means waging war. It means looking into blackness, where shapes are standing. As long as you write, you won't die. And you win the war against gloomy thoughts when, with the word of the shapes in your ear, you write against it."

A gong sounded through the house. "The might of men intrudes," said Hanno and laughed. "I have to go to our evening meal."

He showed Reinhold down the stairs to the door. "I'm sorry that I can't invite you to dinner. We have visitors. Something or other important from the capital. They're sitting inside in the light of new promises."

Hanno's father came through the vestibule. Hanno introduced Reinhold. Herr von Wolfsberg took Hanno's chin in his left hand — his right hand was of leather. "He's one from among the people, isn't he? One who, seized by the simplest idea, can move mountains!"

Reinhold and Hanno stood for a while at the door, and Hanno said: "You really should keep a diary. Keeping a diary helps you to think thoughts to their end and evaluate them. Keeping a diary is self-control and accountability."

"How do you keep a diary?"

"You take a regular book the size of a tablet, bound in oilcloth."

"And what do I write down in it?"

"Everything that's important to you. But don't just write what happens, write what you think and feel. Watch out that you don't write down everything that's unimportant and pay no attention to the big things that happen inside of you."

"But why?"

"You should be able to review the segments, the events, and the feelings of your life. When you read it later, what is past should rise up in you so that you can test yourself, take your measure, and overcome with it. If you talk to yourself about yourself, then you can write your innermost things out of yourself, understand, organize, and change them without confiding in someone else. Unless," said Hanno and looked Reinhold in the eyes, "you want nothing more than just that."

That night Reinhold woke up. His bed was wet. Until morning, until Magda came, he lay in stiff terror that seemed to him inexplicable. Magda saw that, saw everything, said nothing, and Reinhold said nothing, and they never talked about it.

On the way to school he bought a notebook bound in black oilcloth, the size of a tablet. And when it became quiet that evening, when his parents and his brother were asleep, he turned on the lamp on his night table and, like Herr Butz once did, hung a checkered hand towel over it, held the notebook on his knees, his pencil in hand, on the right-hand white page next to the left one drew black — lines, so that I can hold on to something. It's the beginning. I can't spoil the beginning. "Beginnings are holy or already contain lies," Hanno said. And so I look into my soul and am ready not to pretend anything! And he wrote: It is November 5, 1938. I am fifteen years old. I am in trouble. I wet my bed. I don't get that. I am a miserable bed wetter! I'm ashamed. And Father? Can I still love him? Must I despise him, as I do myself? Helpless flesh in a bathtub, that was my father!

And since then I see a lot of things differently.

My bed is dry now. My father is strong again, and still, I know now that I'm on my own. Schade advised me to read poets when I am in need of a comrade in suffering. I've been doing that for some time now, inform myself from Schade and Hanno and read great things that get into my sights. But for me it's not merely the inner man, it's also Hanno! He reads and writes, and a second head to my own would not be able to think up and capture what this single Hanno head thinks. And I admit, I would gladly read and write like him, even breathlessly.

Heinrich was promoted, became a unit leader of the SA and received three stars. That took him beyond the limits of his origins, lifted him above his origins, up into his great tree that they had chopped down thirty years before. He forgot the limitations of his conditions and from then on walked upright, went twice a week to the meeting in uniform and was somebody. At every opportunity and on holidays he wore the uniform with its three stars and the squeaking boots, held his head high, and pushed his strong chin out. But once a week he still went to the Liedertafel and then said every time, song was the most beautiful thing on God's earth.

One morning in November — Reinhold had gotten up at six o'clock to go off to early sports — his neighbor Herz met him on the stairs, being led away by two men. He had his hands behind his back, looked down as though he were remorseful, as though he were ashamed of a disgrace, turned around on the last step, and said: "Please, Herr Reinhold, take care of Freund."

Herz had said "Herr Reinhold" and addressed him formally for the first time, and his voice was like it had been when it was changing, high and at the same time low like Reinhold's voice.

His neighbor, Herz, was a friendly, shy man, proofreader at the daily newspaper, unmarried, not young, not old, lived for as long as Reinhold could remember in the two-room apartment next to Frau Zopf, and had a wire-haired dachshund that he called Freund, friend.

When Reinhold came home at noon, Magda had heard from Frau Zopf that the neighbor, Herz, had been arrested because he was a Jew.

"I didn't know that," said Heinrich.

"What did he do?" asked Reinhold. "I can't imagine that he broke any law."

"Me either," said Heinrich, "I liked him."

"Will he be coming back?"

"If he didn't break any laws, he'll surely come back."

That afternoon Reinhold went up with the caretaker to Herr Herz's apartment to get Freund. He lay dead in a corner of the kitchen.

"Poisoned. The Gestapo," said the caretaker. The dog's eyes stared at Reinhold. "I'll go get a sack," said the caretaker.

But Reinhold didn't want to stay in the apartment by himself and ran back down to his parents. There was Uncle Eberhard in his new SS uniform, shouting: "I saw that haggling Jew in the movie house. That Jew Herz was in the movie house. Instead of reading his Old Testament pimp and livestock-dealer stories, he had his lecherous eyes on our actresses. All the Negroes and Syrians have lecherous eyes when they look at our women. Their foreign blood starts heating up." And he yelled: "Since the start of the month a Jew is not allowed in movie houses, it's over, through! A Jew is not allowed to do anything at all, otherwise he'll always find a way, a sneaky way. Since '35 no Jew has been allowed to marry a German, and now the bastards come into the world illegitimately. Since '38 the Jew has had to surrender his wealth, but he still craps surreptitiously in a golden chamber pot. A Jew has no right to vote and has no passport, and if he goes into movie houses anyway, it just shows that a Jew can't be allowed to be allowed to do anything. That's that!"

That evening Heinrich left the house wearing his uniform. When Reinhold couldn't sleep and got out of bed to go to his mother to ask her about Herr Herz and the Jews, when he opened the door to the kitchen, his mother was standing there naked. He slammed the door, ran back to his bed, pulled the covers up over his head, and lay stiff and still.

The next morning, sitting at the kitchen table and drinking his coffee, he couldn't look her in the eye. She was making sandwiches for school. Reinhold drank the hot coffee much too fast. He heard his father getting up. His mother took his hand. Her hands were rough. Reinhold hugged her around the neck. He was shaking. She talked to him as to a child. He wrote nothing in his diary about it.

In the first class at school he had instruction in world-view with the chemistry teacher. There was no priest. Religion had been replaced by the new course in world-view.

"Here you will learn the genuine faith appropriate for bloodlines and the species," the chemistry teacher had explained. "Humility, renunciation, subservience — or honor, dignity, self-assertion? Tell me: Church or the religion of light?" he had said. "The papacy is carrion, and the European churches have developed into protectors of the inferior, the sick, the crippled, and the criminal. At the extremity of degeneration," the teacher had said, "nuns drink foreign spittle and vow never to wash. That's the odor of holiness!" he had yelled and flung open wide the windows in the classroom.

Reinhold had then dreamed of nuns. He had lingered all night long in convents with frail, scab-covered lady nuns, had heard the nuns singing, and had seen a nun's hand reach through a curtain into the air like into water.

On the seventh of the month the Jew Herschel Grynszpan had attempted the assassination of the German ambassador in Paris, during which the secretary of the legation, von Rath, had been struck fatally. The chemistry teacher was standing in the doorway, his black uniform very tight, the skin of his face taut, his hair short, his lips thin: "The Syrian fiend has struck, and we will strike back. We struck back last night, and we'll keep striking back until the constant lies of the Jewish enemy race are obliterated from our cultural sphere."

Pupils who were able to report about smashed windows of Jewish shops in the neighborhood, raised their hands, reported about beaten Jewish men and their weeping wives and children. And Reinhold thought of his neighbor Herz and the dog Freund. "Is it right," he asked the chemistry teacher, "to punish all the Jews just because a Jew somewhere in Europe killed a German?"

"Right is what Aryan men decide is right," the chemistry teacher barked at him. "You're a Hitler Youth sergeant. How did a question like that get into your head?"

Since Reinhold didn't know how to answer, he would have to stay after school.

At four in the afternoon he knocked on the door of the chemistry room. The teacher opened it, laughed, invited him in, led him from one table to another, showed him this and that experiment, laughed, slapped him on the shoulder: "We teachers want to be comrades to you students!"

Dusk was coming through the high windows. "Shall I turn on the light?" Reinhold asked.

"No, no light," said the teacher. "Today we began to dream again, my boy. Nightfall is good for that." And he sat down, had Reinhold stand in front of him, and looked at him. "You boys," he said, and laughed, "you live in a tent while the parlor waits at home. You wrestle and box mornings before school, you march, you fight, and when it must be, you go without eating, too. You swim through cold waters when others are lying in warm beds. You're true, you're loyal, you hate base sentiments. Someday a steamroller will be about to run over you, but it will groan, will have to lift up, because you are granite that cannot be rolled flat."

It had gotten dark. It was quiet. Not a sound reverberated through the school corridors. Reinhold was still standing.

The teacher laughed, laughed for a long time. "You're not interested in chemistry but in a world-view," he said and laughed. He got up, put two stools together. Reinhold had to lie down on them. The teacher laughed as though the punishment were a joke. Reinhold had to lie down on his stomach. The teacher pulled the stools apart, pinched Reinhold's cheek, sat down on Reinhold's back, rode him, rode up and down on him, a silent ride, a dogged one. Then he got out of breath, got off, went to the wall, stood there out of breath.

Reinhold ran to the door.

The teacher turned around, an assertive man, a clap on the shoulder.

There is something that runs counter to what is healthy and to daylight, Reinhold wrote in his diary. I don't know what it is, but I'll ask no one, for I'm ashamed and don't know what for.

In January Reinhold found Schade whimpering and bleeding on his doorstep.

"They were waiting for me and beat me up when I was going to my piano lesson."

"Who's *they*?"

"Four guys."

"Do you know them?"

But Schade didn't answer, was a bundle on the floor, neither wanted to nor could talk, whimpered with pain, whimpered with humiliation, held fast to Reinhold's feet, gripped them tightly until Reinhold pulled him up. "Man, Schade, pull yourself together!" And then he saw that a piece of Schade's ear had been cut off.

Schade had been taken to the hospital. Reinhold had visited him. Schade hadn't said anything.

When he was at home again and Reinhold was sitting on his bed, Schade burst out: "I'm not fit to live!"

"Who says that? Who? Who?"

"And as a sign of that they wanted to notch me like cattle!"

"But the guys, you have to remember!"

Schade was lying so small in his bed that Reinhold didn't press him further, stayed sitting quietly with him and stroked his hand. Schade fell silent, possessed by secrets that he wanted to keep to himself. Then he fell asleep, and Reinhold sneaked out of the room. His small mother was standing in the hall, and Reinhold saw that she, too, was defenseless.

They cut off a piece of Schade's ear, and they threw the piece of Schade's ear away, into the gutter. That seems to me to be the worst! Reinhold wrote in his diary. Schade is mutilated, and I think he won't live very long. Today he looked like a baby and an old man at the same time. And that frightened me, because the angel of death, they say, is also the angel of procreation. That came to my mind when Schade was sleeping like that. And if he dies, I thought to myself suddenly, he will probably die into himself. But most people probably die out of themselves, like somebody leaving himself.

Schade knows who the guys were. Why won't he say?

"A box with cut-off children's hands has been found," said Uncle Otto.

"Where, when, by whom?" Heinrich cried out. "What are you trying to pin on us?"

"The box was found," said Uncle Otto quietly, and Magda spilled the malt coffee.

"There wasn't anything about it in the newspaper," said Uncle Fritz. "If they haven't got anything to do with it, why do they suppress it then?"

It was quiet in the kitchen until the tea kettle whistled and Magda sprang up and took it off the stove.

"They sent the artistic director of our theater packing," said Uncle Fritz. "If you're a Jew today, you may as well hang yourself."

"Now what does that mean?" Heinrich yelled. "Is your artistic director a Jew?"

"Yes, but not a practicing one," Uncle Fritz said. "He converted to Christianity, with an Aryan wife and two pretty daughters."

"And what did he do wrong?"

Uncle Fritz didn't answer, he just looked at Heinrich steadily, right in the eye. But Heinrich looked steadily and right in his eye back.

"The Neumanns are said to have disappeared," said Magda. "They say that the rest of their evening meal was still on the table. The girl's bed — wasn't she called Rachie? — they say had been thrown out in the yard."

Reinhold ran to the building with the bay window. — Rachie Neumann — who could have done something to her? He stood in the front of the building as he had often stood in front of the building. There was no light in the apartment. — Aren't there dark eyes in the bay window blackness? Aren't eyes looking over at me?

He went to Hanno's. He wasn't at home, they said. He was at the Hitler Youth main headquarters next to St. John's Church.

Reinhold ran. — Fog in the lanes, fog around the merlons and pinnacles of the church, thick clouds of fog through the arches, out of the mouths of the stone gargoyles, light from within to the outside. Songs of comfort through the walls!

He ran into the sanctuary, where he had been the last time, when the old priest had talked about the Devil. A young priest was standing where the old one had stood, singing mass for two sleepers.

In the headquarters he found Hanno: "I've been looking for you!"

Hanno packed his books and his pennants and left with Reinhold. And because he didn't know with which of his questions he should begin, he asked: "What do you want to be when you grow up?"

"Writer," said Hanno, poet. "*That I be banned from all truth, a fool! Only a poet!*" and he laughed and said: "Master Nietzsche!" And looked around and said: "Just look. People run around like pairs of ducks, searching for one another, mating, making babies. Bestial and boring! Apathetic souls, paltry breasts, blind eyes, but delicate fingers. — These very ones here! All have death breathing down their necks and don't know it. Don't even know it!" he yelled. "When you're writing you know death, and then you forget him, forget yourself, sit night after night bent over a word, and when you've found the word, you hold death off by writing it. You sit at night and write and are the beloved of the night, and that love is fervent because it's secret. And since a great number of sighs and cries are buried in your breast, you have the sources that you need, and you can write with blood! So, die in battle, pour out your soul for a great cause. The best thing is to waste your existence, but the second best thing is to write about it."

They kept walking quietly for a while through the darkness, and since Reinhold still didn't know how he should ask Hanno, Hanno said softly and with an unhappy laugh: "I'm ashamed of my torrents. Other people are not ashamed of their rivulets."

Then it gushed out of Reinhold: "What's happening to the Jews? Did you hear about the chopped-off hands of children? And Schade's ear? What do you say about that?"

They walked along next to one another. They had their hands, their fists, shoved into their pockets. They didn't look at one another.

"It's the same old vile situation," said Hanno. "It comes along particularly when the world purges itself. The history of the National Socialist movement will one day be handed down to posterity as the heroic epic of the German nation risen from rubble and ashes. The heroic world-view of the German people has experienced a rebirth through the heroic battle of the National Socialists, such as no saga can convey more quickly and more cleverly. The Reds rise up for the last time to plunge Germany into chaos. I'm convinced that they are attributing things to us, atrocities, that we would never dream of! And don't worry about the Jews. They've been surviving for five thousand years."

"And Schade?" asked Reinhold.

Hanno said nothing.

"But Schade," said Reinhold.

"He'll survive, too." And then Hanno said: "I'll walk you home. Nothing will come anyway of my intention to write ten or twelve poems today, and besides I have to watch out for your ear."

Reinhold visited Schade every afternoon. Sometimes Hanno or Utz or Gummi came along. Schade wore a cap that he now never took off.

"He's dying on me," said his small mother. And Reinhold could not comfort her, for he saw, too, what she was saying.

What is life? Reinhold wrote in his diary. Where is Schade's life heading? Where will it drain away? Through which hole? And Rachie Neumann? What has happened to her?

A pain is within my body. I must do something about it. I don't want to lie here and dream of lost things or of great things that may arise in the future. I want to release all the strengths and possibilities within me. I am fifteen years old, I want to fight, want to devote myself to the light with body and soul.

Reinhold became a master in the pentathlon. His heart beat too fast, but he didn't want to admit it, forgot it, and he even won the hurdles. After the honors given to the victors there was a festival on the river meadow. His parents came and were proud, and his comrades in the Hitler Youth celebrated Reinhold. He became a first sergeant, and since his company commander Hanno became a cadet colonel, he took over Hanno's company and now wore the green-and-white leader's braid on his uniform.

In the evening, fires were burning. Hanno stood under the flag and spoke: "Those who know history only from textbooks have never observed the splendor of our people and never felt the obligation toward our ancestors who demand an accounting from us at the fire of the solstice." And he spoke about the time of the Peasant Wars, of suppression, serfdom, burning villages, about Florian Geyer, Thomas Müntzer, and Götz von Berlichingen.

The wind fanned the flames. "Storms of springtime," Hanno whispered to Reinhold.

The boys looked at the blaze. — Fire, symbol of never-diminishing loyalty to the people and to the Führer! The purity of flames, comradeship!

The Hitler Maiden Mechthild had baked cakes with her girls and made sandwiches. Soft drinks and beer were poured, and Mechthild nudged Reinhold and said, "Someday you're gonna amount to something!"

At the end of the evening Reinhold was sitting next to Hanno.

"Shall we become blood brothers?" asked Hanno.

"Yes," said Reinhold. And heard his own reply as though out of a tube that reached down inside the earth.

"Fine," said Hanno. "Tomorrow night at midnight on the Ziegenberg."

At school Reinhold worried about how he could get out of the apartment at night unnoticed. At recess he looked for Hanno and didn't find him. He managed to get through the day, and when his brother was sleeping, when the light in his parents' bedroom had gone out, he ran in his socks out of the house, his boots in his hand, didn't look back, and ran up to the Ziegenberg. — Night, the moon! Glowworms and the rustle of leaves! In rustling springtime I walk through woods and meadow at midnight!

On the Ziegenberg, high over the city, far from the city, from sleepers, his parents, his brother, his bed, the night was cool. But Hanno wasn't there. — Out of the woods around him, though, the glowing eyes of wild animals, or only rotting wood? Cones fall from the pines, night birds fly up, the moon has its corona, the stars are close enough to touch. Suddenly his heart stops, then a comet flares, and then Hanno appears! Breathless, completely breathless, Hanno with fiery eyes!

They didn't talk. They stood facing one another. They sat down and looked into the sky and at the ground, at the ground and into the sky.

Hanno took out his knife. They got up. Hanno shoved his left sleeve up high, Reinhold did the same with his. Their arms were smooth and firm, the veins stood out like strings, blood in the veins, each could see it in the other.

Hanno grabbed Reinhold by the nape of his neck with one hand and held their faces together: "If I could be you, how could I stand not being you!" turned Reinhold loose, put the knife against his skin, and cut himself across the palm of his hand. He had tensed all his muscles, not a quiver went through his face. Then he gave the knife to Reinhold, who did the same thing.

With raised, bleeding hands they stood facing one another. The knife had fallen between them. One gripped the hand of the other, felt the blood of the other, rubbed it, pressed it into his open hand.

"Blood brothers," said Hanno. He picked up the knife, wiped it off on the wet grass, and put it away again.

And then they left, not looking at one another, ran fast, their boots pounding on the ground.

"Will we see one another tomorrow?"

Reinhold nodded.

"Five o'clock in the afternoon, at the same place," said Hanno.

Reinhold found his way to bed without anyone noticing him. — Everyone was sleeping deeply and purely. Am I now impure? He was horrified that the thought came to him, and wanted to think it out and didn't want to. He was hot and he was shivering. His hand hurt. He fell asleep.

After his first sleep, fires assailed him. What was within him tried to get out, broke through, tried to break down the wall. A torrent of tears, a surge, an onslaught, a force. And then Rachie Neumann's shape came into his head and her softness into his feelings, and a small-emitted cry was liberation from the force, and he lay trembling in the morning freedom. And then his bed had gotten wet again.

All day long he argued with himself, tormented himself — the flagellations of the saints came to mind. — Doing penance for bad dreams! But they weren't dreams, they had happened to him awake. Doing penance, he discovered, meant not going to the Ziegenberg at 5 o'clock.

He went to Schade, who looked lost. Gone, completely gone, Reinhold couldn't help thinking.

Sitting on the edge of the bed, he told Schade everything that came to his mind, the roughest acts of men of combat and musclemen. Schade had to laugh and then spoke: "I want to tell you that I'm odd. I'm afraid something could grab me and hold me tight, constrict me, rob me of my breath. Or that a spot from the touch would remain on me, a dark, smoldering spot that would grow in size, that would grow into me, grow through me, and extinguish me in the end."

"You're just sensitive," said Reinhold.

"And," said Schade, trying to get closer to Reinhold, wanting to whisper, "unlike you in the last year, I've read as little as possible so that strange thoughts wouldn't nest in me that I couldn't get out of my head, that would make me strange in my own mind and make me wander around there and not know myself anymore."

Reinhold didn't know what to say to that. He looked at his friend as he fell back onto his pillow exhausted, looked at the hand on the clock on the night table, how it kept moving.

"I'm so wonderfully weary," said Schade. "I could drown in my weariness, and as a drowning boy drift on the weariness water like on hope. Weariness, you know, promises me a lot."

And then he was asleep again. Completely exhausted by his short life, he slept the exhausted sleep of the old with heavy hands and empty eyes, the sleep of those who have it all behind them.

When Reinhold got home, his mother gave him a letter that Hanno had brought.

Reinhold went to his room. He closed the door. His head was hot. He tore open the envelope.

Spring evening, terrible bliss that seduces me out of myself so that I lose myself in the whole world. Sunset. I stood under invisible stars and waited for someone who did not come. I had become mindful of the unthinkable. Hanno.

Reinhold did not speak, did not eat, sat with his mother in the kitchen, watching her wash and rinse.

Magda knew it well and had said to Heinrich: "Our boy became a man last night. Be good to him and ask him whether he needs advice from you."

And Heinrich had gone into the parlor and had called Reinhold to him. "So, boy," he had said, "you're fifteen now." Then he had not known what to say further and had finally said only: "Any questions?"

Reinhold had sensed what his father meant, but not for anything in the world had he been able to ask or say anything. With his Hitler Youth voice he had said: "How come? Everything's fine." And that's how he left it.

I don't know how I should describe what burned in me all day long. I'm going disconsolately to bed, he wrote in his diary that evening.

The next morning he met Hanno at early exercises. They said hello curtly. When Hanno quit doing his pushups, he ran past Reinhold without looking up. Reinhold could hear him roaring outside, and he saw Hanno start a big brawl. He ran out to the schoolyard. Several boys were punching one another, throwing one another onto the ground, hurling themselves upon one another. There was fist-fighting going on everywhere, nobody looked to see whom he struck, to whom the fists, the noses belonged, nobody knew what the fight was about. Kicks by nail-studded boots, elbows in stomachs, knees under chins, gasping, yells, and suddenly Reinhold found himself pulling hair with Hanno. They thrashed one another. They were laughing. A whistle, the chemistry teacher was on duty and separated the boys from one another.

In the third hour of classes Reinhold was called out of the classroom: Schade was dying and was asking for him. It was quiet in the class. He took his belongings from the desk, threw them into his school bag, ran off, driven by the fear that he might arrive too late.

Too late for what, he wondered as he ran along. For the last look, he answered himself. But what will he get from my last look, and what will I get from his? And when he got to Schade's building, he would have preferred to keep on running, away from the building, from the delicate old man who had been dying there for fifteen years and had called for him.

People were on the stairs, in the vestibule, and in the apartment. Building residents, the doctor, and the priest were standing around, standing too close to the small mother, robbing her of air so that she had to struggle for it, pushing Reinhold into the dying boy's room. The priest asked whether he could be of assistance. Reinhold wanted to ask Schade.

He was asleep. Then the priest came over, sat at the window, looked down at the street with the blooming linden trees, with birds and their song and their cries in the trees. Reinhold sat down next to Schade, whose cap had slipped and whose mutilated ear protruded. His hands lay long and pointed on the bedcover. Reinhold took one in his own.

A shadow fell, and he looked up and there was nothing that makes a shadow, nothing had changed, everything was like it had just been and was before. And Reinhold felt how something withdrew from Schade's hand that he was holding tightly in his own, like something inside the hand was less and less in his hand, kept withdrawing, and finally he was holding only a hand. It turned white and cold. Schade had stopped breathing. The priest had fallen asleep at the window. The afternoon sun was shining into the room. The shadow remained over the bed. Reinhold held the cold hand. But all of a sudden the air above the hand trembled, and as he looked up, the air over the whole body of the dead boy trembled — like waves it swam upwards, flowed off through the ceiling and took the shadow along so that the afternoon sun shone golden yellow in the room.

Then Reinhold was able to stand up and wake the priest, so he could do his work.

It is June 11, 1939. Schade is dead, Reinhold wrote in his diary. All things, the solid ones, the buildings and the trees and the mountains — they remain. But we? And still I can't cry and I find no sadness, no despair inside me. I feel he is near to me, very close by, but somewhere else entirely, like the two sides of a coin that can't see one another and can't feel one another yet are on one coin. I looked at him, I touched him, held his hand. I can't persuade myself that death is the end. He will dwell in my soul. He will think himself into me, and I will receive his thoughts. — Maybe everything that seems strange, everything instantaneous, unthought, are thoughts of the dead. But the angel of death is black and soundless, if I've seen one, if there is one. Good night, Schade.

Magda came and checked on Reinhold.

"What do you know about angels, Mother?"

"Angels," said Magda, and looked out of the window and stayed sitting beside Reinhold until he had fallen asleep.

The next night a secret vigil was to be held. Schade was lying in state in the cemetery chapel. His class comrades, Hanno and one from the upper class, whose name was Beilharz and who wanted to become a priest, had agreed to meet.

They met at the gate, wearing their uniforms. They climbed over the wall. They walked along the wide gravel path to the chapel. Hanno was next to Reinhold. "All human beings walk into sunset, and then comes the naked night!"

"No," whispered Reinhold, "I believe that only the thread of outward intelligence has snapped."

"Is the moon making you crazy?" whispered Hanno, for it stood round and red right over the graves.

Lights were burning in the chapel. Shadows were spinning around on the walls like night birds. Between small box trees stood the black coffin. — Much too black for the little pale fellow, much to heavy. It will crush him!

The coffin lid was closed, but the locks not yet locked. — If I open the lid, Schade will be there, but our gazes could offend him. But probably only absolute flesh is lying there, and that it can be so absolute is what is horrifying!

It was shortly before midnight and had just become totally dark. "But vigils for the dead must be held in darkness," Hanno had said. Not everyone from the class had come, of forty-seven only thirty-two. They took positions around the coffin. And for many it seemed more to be a test of courage than a vigil for their friend, whom they had called a weakling when he was still in the world.

Reinhold was seized by rage, and out of that rage he began to give a speech: "You're standing there trembling and ashen but with shameless eyes on the misfortune that has come here to one of our comrades. Misfortune, as you believe! But I assure you, our comrade wanted to die, to get away from the circle of your cold souls, away, just get away! The archfiend, the arch enemy, death, was for him no misfortune.

"'You ought to kick whatever falls.' Didn't one of you, who deliberately chose not to appear here tonight, recently quote that? And maybe that was one of those who really did kick our comrade by cutting him like cattle, who notched him and marked him."

Reinhold looked around among the boys and saw that hardly a single one could look up. But Hanno looked at him, so that he could say: "Schade had grown weary of the world. Now he is dead. His death hurts me."

After a long silence the one named Beilharz, who wanted to become a priest, took a position at the foot end of the coffin and spoke: "I have been requested by some of you to give a speech for the dead. Even without that request, which honors me, I wouldn't have managed to keep my mouth shut here. It won't be a pretty speech and will be a short one, for the life of our comrade was short and his end anything but pretty. Sneaky, cowardly cutthroats sliced off his ear. That's what killed him. The angel of death kissed him for a long time, for too long, kissed him too tenderly, for he was well pleased by that gentle mortal. Now peace to his soul. He has his rest now. The sneaky pigs will pass sentence on themselves. That's the lot of Nature. And now let us pray, each to his God. Take your nocturnally dazed souls in hand, bundle your thoughts and send them in the direction of Schade, wherever that is in all the immensity."

No one said anything else. They stood by the coffin until the morning dawned, then they slunk home shivering.

"Opening oneself to love means being open to death," said Hanno in farewell before Reinhold's building.

"Of everything that has to do with death, nothing repels me except the pomp that they surround it with. Burials spoil memories for me," Hanno said at Schade's open grave. "Let's go," he said, "why are we standing around here?"

They walked to the Ziegenberg and sat down in the grass.

"You don't think of death, when you're alive like this," said Hanno.

They lay down in the grass and looked into the sky. Evening was approaching.

"The shadows are getting long. They'll touch you," said Hanno and jumped up and ran around Reinhold, throwing his shadow on him.

"And death, and life?" asked Reinhold.

Hanno remained standing over him.

"Have you done it with girls?" Reinhold asked.

"That has nothing to do with love," said Hanno.

"But have you?" asked Reinhold.

"Did the blood brotherhood hurt you, brother?" asked Hanno.

Reinhold nodded. Hanno kneeled next to him. "It hurt him," he said and took Reinhold's hands.

Then Reinhold ran away from him.

Hanno was taking his high school exams. Reinhold neither saw nor heard from him and was almost glad.

Often I am so befogged in my mind about new emotional states that I can't figure out, he wrote in his diary. And the question of where the place is in my life where I must stand, where only I can stand and no other, only I alone — that bothers me. And often at night the ground moves under me, and it shakes and rocks and asks me: Where is the deed that will not be done if you don't do it? A longing is in me, but its aim is vague. Dreaming of greatness is my indolent main occupation.

Hanno had passed his examinations with "very good" and was permitted to deliver his essay about George's *Maxims* in the auditorium of the Wagner School.

Reinhold received a letter in which Hanno invited him to a party at his parents' house, and he received a second letter.

Reinhold, I climbed around among the stars, but they went out, one after the other. I fell when I was dreaming on the most distant one. I stood in the fire of thoughts. I had succumbed to ideas that, born out of the face of night, are in such desperate opposition to what constitutes day.

And now I beg you, my friend, let our dreams of consecration drain away as mild brooks of tears. Germany needs its men. I am ready! Eternally, Hanno.

"You must wear your Sunday suit," said his mother. She parted Reinhold's hair, combed it down flat with water, stuck a fresh handkerchief in his pants pocket, pressed a bouquet of daisies for Hanno's mother into his hand, plucked for a long time at his tie, again and again brushed a grain of dust from his suit jacket.

Although it was just becoming twilight, the von Wolfsberg house was brightly illuminated. Torches were burning to the left and right of the gravel path. Young gentlemen streamed in with their ladies, men in black tails and white gloves showed the way. But when the sound of the fanfare came, which Reinhold had heard in Bayreuth, he would have preferred to stray into the high bushes, under the old trees to the left and right of the path.

He saw comrades from his school who ignored him because they came from the upper classes. He saw men in black uniforms, saw Hitler Youth cadet colonels and cadet captains in uniform and was ashamed because of his Sunday suit, which he had long since grown out of and which had a sheen on the seat of the pants.

Hanno's parents were standing in the great door opening. Hanno stood next to them. "This is my friend Reinhold," said Hanno.

59

"Oh yes, the boy from the people," said the father, slapped Reinhold's chest with his leather right hand and with his left, the real one, turned to the next guests.

"Enjoy yourself," said Hanno's mother with pale lips in a stern face, flaxen knots on her neck, a stick in her back, and handed on the bouquet from Magda.

Reinhold was crowded through the door, shoved past Hanno, who laughed — that infuriated him. — I don't go to parties like this every day, and I don't want to go to such parties every day. I'll never again go to such a party. It'll have been the first and the last party!

He was crowded into the great hall, which was as high as a church. A chandelier hung in it, and it had a marble staircase. The fanfares sounded for the second time.

Hanno's father was the chief justice of the state court of appeal and a high SS officer, and Reinhold knew from Heinrich that his mother was the heiress of a cologne manufacturer and had brought wealth into the house. Wealth and influence were great, Heinrich had said, and he was proud that his son was invited to that house to such a party. Reinhold had not been able to endure that pride, had run to his room, had beat his bed, and then written in his diary: For my pride I need my father, it can't be the reverse! My father is a unit leader of the SA, and I'm proud. I will go forth proudly and take hold of life.

But when he looked around in the great hall, he found no one who was wearing the brown uniform. Only black uniforms were there.

They knew one another, greeted one another, talked, laughed, cascades of words, cascades of laughter. A boy from Hanno's company came up to Reinhold and knew just as little what to do with his hands and feet as he did. They both set one leg in front of the other, let their arms hang, grinning at one another.

When the fanfares sounded for the third time, a lane opened up, Herr von Wolfsberg strode through the great hall, ran up the staircase, two steps at a time, turned at the first landing, on the balustrades of which there were two onyx sphinxes bigger than a human, surveyed the hall, assumed a stance, and spoke: "Heil Hitler, and a welcome to the youth of this city. Friends of my children, German boys and maidens, welcome to my house. Creative blond race, the key to world history lies in your hands!"

The man stood stiffly. His leather fist lay on the back of a sphinx. The sphinx was lying in wait in the hall. "The German dream — many still do not have the courage for that dream, visions alien to our species impede us still," the man continued. "But the Nordic soul is beginning to be effective again from its center, from the consciousness of honor. And it works mysteriously, similar to the time when it created Odin, when the hand of Otto the Great was palpable, when it gave birth to Meister Eckehart, when Bach wrote poetry in musical notes, and the peerless Friedrich strode upon this earth. The task of our century is to create a new kind of mankind out of a new myth of life. One of those epochs is beginning in which world history must be rewritten."

The man raised his leather fist: "Since '33 we know with the help of what powers the non-state of November 18 has been replaced by a German Reich! Since then law has been under the command of the Führer. Since then a judge has been bound not only to the law but also to the uniformly complete world-view of the lawgiver, he is, as my friend Rothenburger, the director of the state court of appeal in Hamburg, says, the most noble enforcer of the will of the Führer. And since it is his most noble will to bring to life a new German order, I want to support him with my own blood in the form of my son Hanno. What the Führer has in mind are monasticism and knighthood, the two primary forms of male society. Through superior breeding and improvement of the primeval bloodline a new high nobility will arise. The future belongs to them!"

The man, who Reinhold could not believe was Hanno's father, looked around the hall. — He looks at each one, right in the eye! And his wife was standing two steps lower and following his gazes. — If you get close to her, you'll get hurt, sliced!

The man continued to speak: "Friedrich Nietzsche's tempestuous sermon about the Superman, his wistful premonition in the midst of a world gone mad, and his mystic memory of the Nordic-Atlantean form of life of our ancestors shall be a model for the new core race to be bred. In Atlantis, too, those who were chosen to be warriors and leaders were raised in camps in the high mountains. There the best characteristics of choice exemplars were developed and the elite of that master race prepared for their initiation by the oracle of the sun, the symbol of the sun wheel, the four-armed swastika. Thereupon the initiated took over the leadership and became mediators between the people and the invisible higher powers."

The man went from one sphinx to the other and looked around in the hall and spoke: "In our Ordensburgen, our training castles, our castles of order, the beautiful God-man in command of himself will arise. Heroes shall be trained there who will realize the plan of Providence. Mankind is not yet perfected. He stands before an incredible transformation that will lend him the powers that the ancients ascribed to the gods!

"In our Ordensburgen merciless discipline is demanded, the necessary rough indoctrination for the special education that follows when the first consecration is completed. The rules of the order are hard, the cadets will through their vow be intended for a superhuman destiny."

The man ordered Hanno to his side with a toss of his head and slapped his shoulder with the leather fist. "I am proud today that I can celebrate with you the graduation of my son, but incomparably greater is my pride that Hanno has fulfilled the prerequisites for acceptance into an Ordensburg. Faith, obedience, and struggle is all that he will now learn, and I'd like to toast that with you, that and the religion of the German future. Heil Hitler!"

Glasses were raised, all assumed a position, their glasses suspended in the air, a long gulp was taken. The lady of the house invited everyone to the cold buffet and wished them, in plain everyday German, a hearty appetite.

In the dining room long tables laden with food had been set up. Reinhold was shoved and pushed. Next to him two young men in black officer's uniforms squeezed their ladies through.

"Well, found our way home to the ancient eternal values," said one and looked at Reinhold's plate and laughed, and the other laughed, too, and the ladies laughed after them.

"This is the Nordic-Atlantean lifestyle," said the one and delicately took a Russian egg from Reinhold's plate. The ladies laughed.

"And what brings this young hero to us?" said the other and grabbed Reinhold by the nape of his neck.

"I'm Hanno's friend," Reinhold heard himself say, and he was livid with anger.

Then Hanno was standing beside him: "Reinhold, may I present my brother Edzard to you. Sometimes he misbehaves out of a mystic failing." He put his arm around Reinhold and turned away with him. His arm lay tight around Reinhold's shoulders.

He led him through the library and the smoking room into the gentlemen's drawing room. There stood judges, officers, there the talk was muffled, as though secret things lay in the air.

The master of the house called his son: "He's a quiet boy, with the withdrawn soul of a poet. He'll have to take control of himself."

"He who will one day have much to proclaim keeps much to himself inside. He who one day the sky will inflame must long as a thundercloud glide," said an officer and laughed as though it were a backstairs joke. They turned away again, and the conversation was renewed without transition, soft and tense.

Reinhold followed Hanno through the great hall. A band had set up around the grand piano. The first couples were dancing, smiling in embarrassment, had uneasy eyes.

In the ladies' drawing room Reinhold took the glass of champagne that was offered him and emptied it with one gulp. — Chatter! The air buzzes here with chatter. Whispering in corners, coloratura laughter! Rumor, character assassination, slander! Feeblemindedness or paucity of ideas? Women are phantoms. When you open them up, there's nothing inside. Put-on, hollow, a sheer ghost!

He drank a second glass. He had never drunk champagne. His father sometimes drank wine, first tested it, pursed his lips, sipped, chewed the wine, shuddered, and then said: "Sour!" And his mother said then: "Why do you always buy such sour wine?" And then his father drank his wine alone. Sometimes Reinhold was allowed to try it, and when he didn't find the wine sour at all, his father winked at him, put his finger to his lips, and they had their men's secret.

"Have you met my sister?" asked Hanno and introduced Reinhold. His sister was hard like her father and severe like her mother, and Reinhold couldn't believe that she was Hanno's sister. — She has fish eyes and a terrible mouth! Her whole mouth is twisted. As though she had once drawn it down and it got stuck at the strike of the clock, pulled down tightly for all eternity!

"Your friend has such dark eyes, little brother," said his sister, and her mouth was drawn down even more, for she was laughing. "Is there a danger of tainted blood?" She laughed out loud and said: "Ladies' choice," did a hackneyed curtsy before Reinhold.

He turned hot. "I don't dance," he said.

The sister got too near him, rubbed her hip on his, said: "You probably don't trust yourself!" and turned to the next boy.

The music was loud. You had to scream against it. Hanno had joined a girl. Reinhold drank another glass.

"Music must strike fire from the mind of a man, but it goes to the legs of us women," he heard the girl yell. And then both laughed. And then they looked at one another. And then Hanno kissed the girl's hand. And then he whispered to her.

Reinhold had drunk another glass and yet another, and when Hanno returned to him, he looked at him through milk glass, heard him through cotton, heard himself say: "Tears are rising, and I, all alone, drink them and look for brother- and sisterlands."

"A poet whose time has not yet come," he heard Hanno's sister's voice. The floor started to race, raced away from him.

Then he didn't feel good. He looked for himself and found himself in his bed with his bedtime Kaspar doll in his arms. Images that had been there before and up close rose up in him, whirled and flowed into one another. He had to throw up, and his mother held him.

When he had choked up all the food and the images, he asked: "How did I get home?"

"Hanno brought you," said his mother.

At noon, in the light of day and the noise of day, Reinhold didn't want to believe what had happened the evening before. But his mother gave him a letter, which Hanno had put in their letterbox that morning.

Dear Reinhold, shut yourself up in your cottage. Drunken gods are also gods, and sometimes they overflow. I have to go now, the direction is called Rheingau. Farewell, farewell, think of me! Hanno.

Then Reinhold heard nothing more from his friend. June passed and July, and August passed.

"T HERE'S WAR," MAGDA exclaimed. "There's war, boy, there's war!" She waked Reinhold up. She was trembling. "Since five o'clock this morning they're shooting back!"

School had started again. The music teacher composed a military symphony. The chemistry teacher reported about atrocities that the Poles had committed against German men, women, and children. He had newspaper accounts read and photographs passed around.

No one can ever forget them, Reinhold wrote in his diary. They appear in your dreams and make you scream from deep in your throat. Pictures that mark life as an illusion in the face of the great empty horror, death. Pictures that illustrate the counter proof of any hope of existence beyond death. Murdered and emasculated, the face knocked off, where to? Graves after graves, a man with a gunshot in the chest, heartrending! With a grenade in the face, and there's only a hole left of the man with his chin and lower teeth. They talk about bloody Sunday on which the worst things are said to have occurred: our women and children tortured, slain, destroyed by agony! And, what never leaves me: the photograph of a young woman, all her ten fingers carefully cut off — a baby protrudes out of her body.

The war expanded. Heinrich was certain of victory: "The Polish crime is black on white before us. Right is on our side," he said with a tinny voice, so that Magda shuddered.

They were sitting in the kitchen, listening on the radio to the tinny voice that had infected Heinrich so that Magda shuddered again, so that she sat down with her brothers, who had come to the evening meal. She drew up close to her brothers.

"Those who fight with poison will be battled with poison gas. Those who distance themselves from a humane conduct of war can expect nothing different from us," came from the radio.

Reinhold's district as company commander was the Ziegenberg. He often marched with his company over the forest clearing that had been his and Hanno's place. There the autumn fires were burning. There he wrote in his diary: My soul, it seems, has taken root in his, and he went away, and his soul pulls and stretches mine after him so that every day I brood, and even the greatest ideas, even the most successful strings of words are completely senseless to me. He had grown up to be the grandeur of earth to me, and now the ground is pulled out from under me. I set my foot on no-man's-land.

I miss Schade, too, of course, but differently, only in everyday things. Usually I am in contact with him all the time, let thoughts occur to me that don't seem to have grown out of my manure and that I then try to reply to with my own thoughts. Beyond that, this is also an amusing game in which it's a matter of looking beyond my own boundaries.

But what will warm me against the winter without Hanno? Utz maybe, he's a solid sort. And Gummi, the jokester, those are my snowmen in the ice.

The end of October 1939 was harvest help time, grape picking in the vineyards of Baden. Eleventh and twelfth graders from the Wagner School had to work for two weeks on model farms and vineyards. Reinhold came with nine other pupils to a Newwei farm. All belonged to the Hitler Youth. Utz and Gummi were among them.

Until the freeze they didn't mind sleeping in sleeping bags in the shed, working among the vines, and not receiving anything but salt bread and soup. In the evening there were reconnoiters and tests of courage, potato fires and flag watches.

When they were sitting in a circle around the campfire, when all their limbs were aching from bending, picking, and carrying baskets, when the storm swept past over them and the birches and the alders were swaying, they sang their songs, saluted the earth, saluted the air, saluted the water, saluted the fire with the proud feeling of having accomplished their part, having done their duty.

Autumn storms and the light so slanted and the fields so empty and the longing so great, Reinhold wrote in his diary. Just as man is made of earth and returns to earth, all of love is made of longing and returns to longing. Like the rotten wood in the forest glows! Like we pursue it, pursue love! Like it lights up and dies out! Like we pursue it until it becomes longing again.

But when they had to go out at the crack of dawn in the fog and cold, when they stumbled up to the vineyards drunk with sleep, and freezing, no rousing song occurred to them.

Weakling, wretch, mama's boy, Reinhold grumbled and was homesick.

In the second week, when after five hours of harvesting they had returned to the village from the vineyards to eat their lunch in the village inn, there were girls — Erika, Renate, and Trudel. They brought the boys milk and salt bread, sat down with them, ate with them. The boys stared straight ahead and grinned.

"Seventy-two Hitler Maidens from the Droste-Hülshoff School have been distributed to farms in grape country," said Erika. "Here we help with dairying and sleep in threes in a room for farmhands."

The boys grinned, poked one another, and agreed to meet the girls for the evening at the campfire. When they then walked through the village back to the vineyards, their nail-studded shoes sounding in marching step on the cobblestones, they sang rousing songs, imagined the girls at the windows, at open windows, leaning far out of the windows, with ears that listened even as far as the vineyards.

That evening the maiden Mechthild came.

Strange, something like a piece of home, motherland has come to me. Mechthild isn't a woman, she's something better, Reinhold wrote in his diary.

A boxing match was arranged. The horns of bulls sprouted on the boys. They thrashed, snorted, pushed, pranced, couldn't separate from one another until Gummi, who was the referee, blew the whistle to end the fight. With a rolling gait the boys left the fight, gathered up wood, made a fire. The girls brought potatoes. They ate, talked, they sang: *Wild geese are swooping through the night with shrilling cries all northward, unstable flight, beware, beware, the world is full of murder.*

Reinhold and Mechthild were sitting next to one another. "What are you reading?" asked Mechthild.

"Poets. And you?"

"I'm reading our magazine, *The German Maiden*, and I like to read about the women in sagas, our mythic models, the proud generations of women in our heroic epics." And the girl told Reinhold about women in Iceland who built farmsteads and founded generations, about Unn and Thorbjörg who met male attacks victoriously in battle, and about shepherdesses from the Northland, curious solemn forms in black gowns, who carried men off from the valleys, dragged their prey to mountain huts for the purpose of reproduction, and after begetting had exposed them in the wilderness.

"Utz wants to trot out a speech," Gummi yelled, "but I think it's the girls' turn today."

They hemmed and hawed for a while until Mechthild got up and with a clear voice said: "The eternity of the German people and its mission applies to girls just as much as to you boys. One of my favorite books is Walter Flex' *The Wanderer between Two Worlds*, and from it I want to read you two pages about the heroic death of the friend, for we girls, too, are filled with burning longing to belong to those for whom it's a matter of life and death."

And when she read, it seemed to me that her soul entered her eyes, Reinhold wrote in his diary. My comrades stopped carving on their pieces of wood, the stars were standing high above. Everything was simple and grand.

On the last Sunday of the two weeks, Reinhold, Mechthild, Utz, and Gummi set off for Dusterlingen. There, deep in the Black Forest, lived an uncle of Mechthild, one of the last organ builders. They were going to visit him.

They got up earlier than usual, packed their rucksacks, marched to the nearest bus station, and rode for an hour through darkness and early fog. No bus went to Dusterlingen, there was no road, there were only footpaths, very steep through the Black Forest. It was damp and cool. The pines were standing so quietly that no one spoke.

Reinhold got out of breath. He thought about his heart. He became furious at his heart and climbed all the faster. — Toughness regarding oneself is the beginning of all soldiering because only someone who has the will to win and the toughness to endure will achieve victory! And he climbed on and on and let his heart hammer. — Hammer along, hammer my chest cavity through and through for the battles that lie ahead for me!

"There's Dusterlingen," exclaimed Mechthild.

In the blazing sunlight were seven buildings, two of which were burned down. No church, no cemetery. Mechthild knocked on a door. A man opened it, pulled the four right into his room, set bread, bacon, and wine on the table, laughed, asked nothing and watched them while they ate. He might have been sixty years old, wore his hair long and had a pointed beard. And his laughter wouldn't stop.

The room was so low they had to bend over. Doll-house windows, a bench along a tile stove, old books and strange pictures, dried summer flowers in bowls and glasses.

After the meal Mechthild told about the harvest project. Then the man interrupted her. His laughter came to an end: "In the service of something you believe to be great, you think you're growing out of yourselves, into a kind of infallibility. The thought that God could be against you doesn't occur to you! Germany is your religion. In the place of belief in Heaven and its angels you have set Bismarck towers and Valhalla. You pray to Germany. You are nuns and monks for Germany and are following its godless call with the eternal: Here I am! Germany, which like something fallen from on high lay under the soil of your childhood. Germany, that like a strange little song was sung over you by the last Rambler's Association members. Germany! Into your emptiness and desolation crept God's darkness! And claimed to be the form of your beginnings and your future simultaneously, and the charade is believed! But God is upright, and the things of His Creation will follow the Commandments on the way to the abyss."

The man sprang up, ran through the door of the room, went up the stairs. Organ music swept through the house, fair music and church music together.

The four, who had sat quietly in fright, ran after the sounds. In the attic stood three barrel organs, and the man was standing behind the largest, turning the organ with gigantic swoops. And at the same time yelling: "Many a night, when I look up at the sky here or out to the open fields to feel the stars over me, to sense the spirit of the Creator, the demon that walks through the night, there comes an angel. And then, freed from the boredom of my inferior understanding, I can see. And I say to you: There are angels of light and angels of darkness. The angels of light stand for the powers of construction, those of darkness for those of destruction. They work hand in hand, for light and darkness are mirror images, are one and the same thing. The angels of light pour forth from the center of their sun into our bloody Reich, and if you see them and hear them, the evil of your soul sinks into all of eternity. For angels, music and dance are one, so that dance brings its music along with it. I'll play you the music now, and you go back into the woods and find your way home, for the darkness will soon break through the light, and then the woods gets claws."

The barrel organ tones increased. The man was turning all three at once, running from one to the other. The tones were jubilant, and the four of them ran out of the house.

"Why did two farms burn down up there in the village?" asked Reinhold on the way back to the bus station.

"Hotzen lightning," said Mechthild. "Once my uncle told me that when the spirit in the walls become too much for the farmers, lightning shoots out of the Hotzen Woods, starts fires, and frees the farmers."

Overnight the first freeze came.

The cold fell upon me, made me stiff, made me old, lay on me like a gravestone. Because of weariness I couldn't wake up, because of forest, organs, and angels. The wake-up call came to me from out of the world, out of which I felt I had long since died. But Utz and Gummi shook me back into the hay, Reinhold wrote in his diary.

The boys wanted to go home, but the girls wanted to stay because their room was heated. The departure was to be solemn. They put up a flagpole, invited all the farmers, the farmhands and farm girls, raised up the flag, stood in a circle, held hands with one another, and expressed their gratitude for the community, for the harvest, for the beauty of the summer, of the fall.

In December Reinhold got worried about Hanno. He asked the teachers who had him in class, asked comrades who had known him — no one had any news of him, no one knew anything.

At first Hanno's silence was a hurt, and I defended myself against that hurt, Reinhold wrote in his diary. Thoughts that came to me of my friend I covered up with others, with some about Schade, for example, whom I vowed to think about every evening, for whom I set up an inner space for thought in which I could meet with that sensitive boy to make him strong. And I feel strong doing that and avoid coming to terms with whether Schade — if there is existence after death, if he plunged into that existence or vanished into it or appeared in it — is in need of my strengthening. But until recently I drafted defiant, arrogant letters to Hanno, since occasionally I cannot help feeling betrayed. But even if I had known where my letters would find him, I would not have sent them. But now I am worried about my friend.

Reinhold went to the von Wolfsberg house, to which he had never wanted to go again, in the neighborhood of which he had not gone since that time.

"I am Hanno's friend," he said into the intercom. "I would like to speak to Herr von Wolfsberg."

"Herr von Wolfsberg is away on a trip."

"Then I would like to speak to Frau von Wolfsberg."

Reinhold waited, freezing, his forehead and hands hot. The gate opened. He walked along the gravel path. The main entrance was opened up.

He stood alone in the great hall. The superhuman-size onyx sphinxes that lurked to the left and to the right of the stairway seemed about ready to leap upon him. He turned his back to them and followed a voice that seemed to be reading aloud.

In the ladies' drawing room was Hanno's mother. Women were sitting around her in a semicircle. Two candles were burning on an advent wreath. The women were embroidering, knitting, crocheting. Tea was standing next to them, liqueurs, pastries. Hanno's mother was reading from a book:

Our most recent decline repeats the myth of the Edda. When honor and right and the will to power collapsed, a divine race sank, an epoch in world history disintegrated in a frightful, blood-red bath in 1914.

The woman interrupted her reading, let the book sink, looked at those who were sitting around her: "German hands cannot erect enough heroic monuments, not dedicate enough memorial groves to your sorrowful destiny, your life in fulfillment of duty, reverence, and renunciation, women and mothers, to your fallen men and sons."

The woman's voice trembled, broke off. The woman picked up the book and continued to read:

Dark, satanic forces were at work everywhere behind the victorious armies of 1914. Diabolical powers raged more uncontrollably than ever through the world. At the same time, however, in the humbled souls of those who survived the dead warriors — and here the woman looked up again, looked into the eyes of each of those sitting around her — , *in the humbled souls of those of us here who survived, that myth of bloodlines for which heroes died is renewed, deepened, and experienced. That inner voice requires today that the two million dead heroes did not fall in vain, it demands a world revolution.*

"So, dear ladies," the woman interrupted her reading again and held up the book and again looked into the eyes of those who were sitting around her, "that was written by the master Rosenberg in 1920, and who will contradict me when I maintain that he is more than a philosopher, he is a prophet." The woman poured herself a liqueur. Those sitting around her clapped their hands in applause. The woman saw Reinhold standing in the doorway: "Well, little friend, what are you doing here?"

Reinhold was wearing his uniform, not the too-small Sunday suit as at Hanno's party. The uniform made him strong. "My name is Reinhold Fischer. I am Hanno's friend," he heard himself saying. "I have heard nothing from Hanno for too long. Now I'm concerned and want to ask you how Hanno is and also ask for his address."

"Thank you, he's fine," the woman answered. "I can't give you his address, but I can tell you that he will be at home for the Christmas festivities." And the woman turned again to those who were sitting around her in a semicircle, looked them in the eye, and said: "The age of Christianity is past. Before us lie the millennia of the Hitler era!"

Reinhold ran away, ran through the great hall, dashed out of the house. Hanno's sister was coming toward him on the gravel path: "Oops, oops, little friend!"

Reinhold kept on running, would like to have run around her. — Run over and run down her oops, the first and the second oops! "Goat!" he said to himself and ran. "Stupid cow!"

Magda was baking cookies, his brother helping her cut them out of the dough. Reinhold came running into the kitchen and embraced her wildly, so that she was startled. At the evening meal Reinhold could not hear enough about Heinrich's experiences in the war, and when he said to his father: "You are a true hero, a real one, there haven't been many like you!" Heinrich, too, was startled.

Who is it who smashes a social order that thinks very little of a young man who came into the world not the son of a manufacturer, an officer, or a senior judge? And who creates those who judge a person in accordance with his real worth? Reinhold wrote in his diary.

Must the former consider himself cheapened and lost? Must a desperate person be destroyed? Or must he take things in hand himself and pound on the table of society until it breaks to pieces?

But first Christmas will come and will make everyone mellow again. Christmas is coming, will lead us back into our childhood and at the same time make us aware that it is long past, that an earnest life is awaiting, as is an earnest death, that both are already calling, that one is already demanding.

The apartment is full of familiar steps. Father and Mother are keeping secrets. I climb to the attic with my brother and steal Christmas cookies out of the cabinet. Evenings two candles are burning. But when I think of Hanno, the sky falls down on me.

On Christmas Eve Hanno was standing at his door.

"Come in, man!" said Reinhold.

"No, I want to go to the Ziegenberg. I came to take you along."

Reinhold looked for his jacket on the hook, put it on inside out, had rubbery knees.

Hanno walked half a stride ahead of him, had turned up his collar, didn't look at Reinhold. Stopped, turned halfway around as though he were listening to the echo of their footsteps, said: "Evil follows its urges," laughed bitterly and walked on.

When they had reached the top of the hill, had found their place, were sitting there out of breath, looking into the sky, Reinhold said, "The stars are battling in their way for the just cause of mankind."

"No," said Hanno, "everything's just cruel and lonely." He stood up, walked away from Reinhold, turning his back to him. But then he hurried back, then he reached for Reinhold, grabbed him, held him fast. "Anyone who blabs will be rubbed out on the authority of the hard, ruthless laws of the order."

"What order?"

"The black one." Hanno turned Reinhold loose, again turned his back and said with a voice that was more a croak and a squawk: "It all involves magic socialism!"

Reinhold came up behind Hanno, laid his arm around him. Hanno was hard pressed to keep himself too much in control and was trembling. Then it burst out of him: "It's a matter of gaining a clear conscience for cruelty. You learn to do that by, among other things, gouging out the eyes of little mice. You have to free yourself from all humane and scientific prejudices, free yourself from the self-torment of a chimæra called conscience and morality. Conscience is a Jewish invention. Like circumcision it is a mutilation of the human creature. Only what is hard and masculine will endure," Hanno barked out. "To be magically clear-sighted is the goal of human progress. And, friend, you understand, the SS is a religious order for which it is not a matter of removing inequality among men, quite the contrary, for which it's a matter of enlarging inequality and of making it a protected right by means of insurmountable barriers." Hanno clawed at Reinhold, pulled at him, clung to him: "The fighting monks of the Death's-Head SS have vanquished God and put Him to flight, do you understand me?"

They fell down. Hanno clutched Reinhold tightly.

After they had lain on the ground for a while, Hanno turned him loose, got up, went back to their place. They sat down, and Hanno started to talk: "First you arrive at a national political school, a Napola — that's just preliminary training, not half bad. Just drill, total isolation, brisk, hard, and not much more. Then you are admitted to an Ordensburg. I went to Bavaria. An old castle has been renovated into a monastery there. My cell is nine by nine feet, four white walls, plank bed, writing desk, locker. You run your head off. In the first weeks you're just with boys your own age to beat them up or get beaten up by them. And if you throw up because you can't stand the sight of blood, you have to eat your own throw up. And if you refuse to brand a rune onto the flesh of your defenseless comrade, someone else brands him and you get branded twice."

Hanno scratched up the ground all around him, dug, didn't look at Reinhold: "And if you're real cold, and real thin, if you even shiver and call for your Mama, then they come.

"Ordensburgen, man," he exclaimed, "are schools in which you learn to give death and to accept death, in which you learn to kill off your Self. They're temples, sacramental schools in which a generation of youths is trained — arrogant, imperious, and violent — before whom the world must be terrified. That generation will learn to conquer the fear of death, to endure pain, and it will learn what can be clothed in no words born of reason.

"But first comes the vow to superhuman, irrevocable destiny," Hanno exclaimed, "and then comes the consecration! The consecration!" He grabbed Reinhold by his neck, by his arm: "We find ourselves outside of the world. The castle has a cellar. I'm undergoing the first degree of initiation. The grand master lights a light. It is the cold light of Lucifer that rises above this realm. The secret priesthood of the Death's-Head SS sits masked in the circle. The most sacred ones hold the maple staff turned downward. 'The eye of the Cyclops will be opened to you,' says the grand master, and pulls down my pants. I lie naked on a stone slab. A book by Aleister Crowley is placed on my chest: 'And now you will say the Lord's Prayer backwards without bothering to understand it!' And I did that, and I kept doing it. And then I remained lying there and stood up, and stood up and remained lying there, and ran right into my no-man's-land. And then I saw it," Hanno cried out, he roared, "then I saw it!"

"What?"

"The racial spirit. I saw it! It crouched there and looked at me, and I knew I will never escape it. It has placed me on record. Now I must ride and destroy for it. It does exist, you know," Hanno shook Reinhold, "and it doesn't exist, just as everything does and doesn't exist. And that's the horror of it all!"

"And?" asked Reinhold, when Hanno did not go on speaking, and he didn't dare look at the boy sitting next to him, whimpering, "and then?"

"The Black Corps, they brought me back. I came like a sleepwalker. They told me I had passed the test. I received the first rune of consecration. And since then they've been preparing me for the second consecration. There are degrees of initiation of which I know nothing. But my comrades talk about human sacrifices."

Reinhold and Hanno sat silently next to one another. "What is it, what was it that you experienced?" asked Reinhold then.

"They call it the new heathen magic. We're supposed to be possessed so that the powers can serve us. They actually say that! We're supposed to transform our souls into containers empty of Self, so that spirits of high rank can descend into us. They say that, too!"

"And now? Since then? After that?"

"I didn't believe they would let me come home for Christmas."

"How long can you stay?"

"Until day after tomorrow."

They sat next to one another and were silent. Then Hanno said: "I've thought of you often again and again, Reinhold. At night I often held tightly to your name, for I have none other. You don't know what nights are like in which images and voices come between waking and sleeping and don't let you stay awake or be asleep. Dirty ghosts attack you in that gap in which you can't defend yourself, squeezed between here and there. So you awaken from your fear into your solitude, into which no ones takes you, out of which no one can take you once you're in there. Solitude is not my home, my friend, it's the end of me," said Hanno. He stood up and whisked the dust off of his coat. "Come," he said, "I can't be helped anymore."

They walked back silently.

In front of Reinhold's house they stopped.

"So," said Hanno, and didn't look at Reinhold again and walked away.

"Where are you going?" Reinhold called.

"I want to be alone," Hanno called.

That night Reinhold crawled into bed with his brother. He was sleeping the sleep of a child and noticed nothing.

The next morning he wrote in his diary: Sometimes what's incredible seems familiar to me, as though invented by me, thought up. And sometimes everyday stuff seems like madness, and I can't put cause, sense, and connection together. Today, for example, it's Christmas.

IN JANUARY EMMA Zocher from Schlüchtern came into the house. The Reich's women's organization had made Magda responsible for teaching the housemaid cooking, washing, and cleaning for a year and granting her contact with a family. Emma Zocher moved into the attic room.

A chest stood there, in the lower drawer of which his mother had kept Christmas cookies locked up for as long as he could remember. But because he and his brother kept climbing up to the room, the cookies, which were handed around every day after Christmas and were supposed to last until Easter, lasted generally only until the end of January. They both had discovered that they could pull out the top drawer and reach into the locked lower one in which the cookies lay. They had learned to control themselves and never take out more than two hands could hold and at most to climb up the creaking steps to the room once a day, past Frau Zopf's door and Herr Herz's, in which strange ladies now lived, very brusque, maybe sisters, about whom no one in the house knew anything. They had gotten used to sitting looking mournful when it was a riddle to their mother that, although she baked more every year, only crumbs lay in the locked drawer at the end of January.

Emma Zocher was seventeen, still wore pigtails and thick, knitted hose, and regarding her Reinhold always thought of the word *handy* — why, he didn't know.

One time when he once climbed up to the room again, knowing that Emma had gone shopping, when he did not find the door locked and then, as usual, pulled out the top drawer, there lay Emma Zocher's underwear.

Reinhold had started trembling, had touched the soft fabric, had to sniff it, had to touch more, had to stare at it. — As though under the pile of underwear something else would be revealed, something of flesh and blood maybe! He had gained control of himself, shut the drawer, forgotten the cookies, had run down the stairs, out of the house, to school, had done physical exercises, had done gymnastics on the high bar and the parallel bars until he was senseless.

At supper he had not been able to look at Emma Zocher. Had then gone to his room, had then sat in his room. It was too much for him and not enough, and he had written in his diary: My head is heavy, my heavy head is indecent. That's what I am! Even though my heart is heavy, for it clings to Hanno, still something happened to me in a new way. Something expanded in me for a moment and extended past my boundaries. It was pure chance. So a person follows chance and wanders around in this world and lets thoughts sneak around in himself that in the final analysis are nothing but sinful. I had a woman's underwear in my hands!

But the nature of her soul, what is it like? And does she have one? Whenever she's not walking at my mother's side, she sits around the live-long day reading paperback novels and staring out the window, as though she had to fill herself from outside because inside she is so empty. I don't like her at all.

Fine, I'm my world, but she's one, too, but is she hers? My idea of it is critical. And still deep down I am attracted throughout my being. The feeling about her, of what is taboo about that feeling, and feeling the feeling makes everything new. But if a man must really be attached to a woman, I want to keep myself for the One, the pure one.

Just be good and sensible, I tell myself, while my fantasies roam wildly and violently.

This evening, when I was sitting opposite her in the kitchen, there was a rushing in my skull and a glowing in my face. I ran to my room and kept quiet so that my inner thought would awaken. It took a whole, quiet hour, and then, as I was about to think about Schade, a moth came, and I had to laugh and took it as an emanation of my friend that alighted on the shade of my night-light and seemed to be all ears, if moths have ears.

"Schade, your grave is already old," I would like to have said to him. "The earth is already used to lying on you. It has already sunk down into your contemplation. Schade, my secret thought is, of course, that life is natural and death against nature, so in the final analysis I don't believe in you anymore at all, and yet still do. Our worlds are probably drifting apart, because your Now is gone, and my Now now wants to be and glows. But women, Schade, what am I going to do about women?

"Hanno is almost as far away from me as you are, only I know I don't have to worry about you. But Hanno makes my fear deadly. So much for tonight, my friend, for now I'll bury myself in my bed to find a refuge from myself."

"For women learning is a game and knowledge a performance. Knowing is for them like a fluttering little feeling, and wisdom, a toy, a humming top. It penetrates their brain as a humming and puts them instantly in the worst mood," said the chemistry professor the next morning in world-view instruction. And Reinhold agreed with him, although he would make exceptions — Magda, and maybe also the maiden Mechthild.

On Sunday at noon Emma Zocher was sitting at the table as always at noon. Reinhold was forced look at her, and he saw that she stuck out her tongue when she opened her mouth to insert a spoon or a fork. Her tongue was long and pink. It bothered him. It angered him, angered him more with every one of her bites.

She looks as stupid as an animal, he wrote in his diary. How can a human being be so contemptible!

That afternoon it rained. Emma Zocher sat in the kitchen reading paperback novels. She was wearing a dirndl, had her breasts, which were white in the middle of her open neck-line and in plain sight, propped against the table so that Reinhold was forced to think about Herr Butz's photograph.

The maiden Mechthild came and invited Reinhold to go to the movies.

The film was called *La Habañera*. Zarah Leander played the main role and was so beautiful that Reinhold didn't notice how Mechthild's shoulder pressed against his.

It was already dark when they came out of the movie house, and Reinhold intended to see Mechthild home. It was still raining. They walked along next to one another. Mechthild said nothing and Reinhold couldn't help thinking about Zarah Leander. "If there is a woman, then one like her. You can just forget all the others," he said, after they had walked for a while. Then Mechthild ran away from him.

Reinhold could easily have caught up with her, but he had seen her face before she ran off. She's insulted, I guess, he told himself. God knows why girls are always constantly insulted! And he crossed out another entry in his account of feminine exceptions, so that, undamaged and distinct, only Magda remained.

When he got home, he saw his father in the stairwell wearing his hat and coat, coming down from above, and opening up the apartment door. Heinrich had not seen him. Reinhold had hidden and stood there in hiding and didn't know why. And when he entered the apartment, Heinrich was sitting in the kitchen behind a newspaper. Magda was standing at the stove. His brother was playing nine-men morris against himself.

"Where's Emma?" asked Reinhold.

"This is her evening off. It's Sunday, after all," said Magda. Heinrich said nothing.

"I was with Mechthild at the movie," said Reinhold.

"Are you hungry?" asked Magda

"What film?" asked his brother.

"Didn't all of you eat supper yet?" asked Reinhold.

"Your father was out with his friends," said Magda.

"It's raining," said Reinhold and through the open kitchen door saw Heinrich's dry coat on its hook.

He ran out of the house. His mother called after him. He didn't turn around.

He ran to the Ziegenberg. It was still raining. The last snow clung gray and crusty to the edges of the path. Up there in the quiet, in the emptiness, he began to bawl.

When he came home, the lights were out. He sneaked to his room. His brother was asleep. Reinhold wrote in his diary: I'd like to set fire to her skirt! I'd like to cut her hair off!

He could not fall asleep. He thought that glowing wisps of flame, rising from his head, his chest, traveling through the air, would set the attic on fire. He got up and wrote in his diary: I've never wondered whether my father is happy.

Then Emma Zocher was no longer there. And Magda said nothing and went about her work as before. And Heinrich brought her a blue neckerchief. She wore it then every day until spring.

No news came from Hanno. But Mechthild had written to Reinhold.

Dear Reinhold, my thoughts were often with you in recent days. Our comradeship is worth as much to me as mother and father. Everything that life brings should be seized courageously, and the higher powers that stand above us will prepare what is right for every one of us. Who knows where we'll end up! But at the bottom of our souls, deep within us, we think and dream together anyway.

But you, Reino, always seem to me as though you were born for greater things. So, now I've said it!

Just think! My cousin is getting married. She's not much older than I am and is regional Hitler Maiden leader in Westphalia. The last time we saw one another, last April — we laughed a lot together.

I reach out my hand to you, Reino, and wish you the best, Mechthild.

In February a decree went to all the schools from the Municipal Youth Guidance office that all boys and girls were to sift through their parents' and grandparents' libraries and bookcases. Material was still to be found there that could besmirch the German spirit and the German language. Books that were on the list were to be removed and brought at nine o'clock in the evening of the first Sunday in March to the square in front of the university building.

"Why shouldn't a person have all the books in his bookcase that he wants to have in his bookcase?" Reinhold had asked his father.

"There are books that lie and corrupt. There are books that endorse evil. You're young and still believe what's in print," Heinrich had answered.

Some came without a book, but many dragged sacks and boxes. Most were in uniform. Those wearing civilian clothes were conspicuous.

The books were piled into a heap and set on fire. "Here the anti-spirit burns!" someone yelled. Firelight and shadows fell upon the faces. — As though leaves of a book were being turned at night before a lamp!

"Anyone who burns books will burn human beings, too," someone said next to Reinhold. "I know you," he said, "you're Hanno's friend."

"What do you know about Hanno?" Reinhold retorted.

"Why do you act like that to me?" the other smiled as though he were tired. "You're intoxicated by the fire."

They took one another's measure, circling one another.

"I'm Gabriel," said the other one. He had long, curly hair, wore long pants.

"And where could we know one another from?"

"At Hanno's party. You didn't see me. You'd been drinking, were talking in verses, had retreated into your own being to turn off the bothersome effect of a society whose soul is rooted in the spiritual underworld. You were talking and talking, and your talk was like writing in the air, with the certainty that having the right word guaranteed protection from the attack of matter."

"And Hanno? What do you know about Hanno?"

"I suggest that we meet tomorrow at five o'clock in the Café Deibl," said Gabriel. And then a little bleating laugh came out of him, one that Reinhold set against everything that seemed to be appropriate in regard to firelight and darkness, to worry and doubt. Gabriel pointed with his long finger at the earnest faces in the circle: "Look, the ancient images of the soul flicker and rule. The prevailing poets in service have dyed their fog blue. Time is ripe for the Messiah." And he laughed his laugh and walked away.

Gabriel was already sitting in the Café Deibl when Reinhold arrived. He had had a wild night of dreams. Hanno had blown his trombone, and the Valkyries had made a haul, had snatched people and let them fall at the door of Reinhold's house. And then Gabriel had appeared and, with the laughter that was so characteristic of him, had raised his long finger and said: "The task of the divine poet is to describe what is godless."

Gabriel's curly hair seemed to Reinhold to have gotten longer, and he saw the checkered bow tie and crepe soles and didn't know what he should think about him.

"You must know," Gabriel began, "I'm twenty-one, student of literature. I'm the anti-spirit that they conjured up last night." And then the laughter came again.

"What do you know about Hanno?" Reinhold asked curtly.

Gabriel gave him a slip of paper. Reinhold recognized Hanno's writing and read: *Gabriel, I'd like to send you something in writing from me. I'd like you to publicize it among your circles. I want my story to be terribly simple, simple just like the mysteries that I have to describe. For it is a mystery that I have to describe: pure, eternal horror. I'll send it to you, as quickly as I have it and can, and will depend on its being made available to as many as possible. Hanno, December 26, 1939, on the way to destruction.*

"*Destruction, go your way,* Schiller writes," said Gabriel, laughed his laugh, took the paper back from Reinhold, put it in his shirt pocket, kept his hand on its outside.

"But that's months old," Reinhold cried out, couldn't help springing to his feet, grabbing at the hand on the shirt pocket. "Have you gotten any other mail since?"

"No," said Gabriel, "nothing since. And so I assume that Hanno was sacrificed, that he bled to death on secret sacrificial slabs, that the murderous ghosts of the Troisième Reich there have gnawed at him and long since buried his sucked-out body."

The waitress came, bringing Gabriel cream cake, and when Reinhold said nothing and ordered nothing, Gabriel ordered another piece of cream cake.

"I am not one of the faithful," said Gabriel, "but I believe that the horseman of the Apocalypse has already come to a gallop. When I met Hanno at Christmas, he talked about fear, had gotten entangled, lost in fear. Not a thought of running away! He wanted to investigate and find out, write down with his blood, what enchantment is being praised in the innermost calyx of the brown flower."

Gabriel was whispering, bending over the table toward Reinhold, who sat leaning back, who wanted to feel the wooden chair against his back: "We're doing a secret newspaper, *Song of Defiance.* We fasten banned flags on poles that are accessible only to free birds. Kierkegaard says an individual cannot rescue a declining age, he can only show how it declines. Hanno knows what we're doing. Indeed, he's known it all the time, even though his mind was somewhere else, even though until this very day he's been in the middle of the Fatherland stuff."

The waitress brought the cream cake for Reinhold.

"Understand," said Gabriel, falling back into his chair, leaning his head backward. "I'm not a believer, and I don't believe in predestination, but I do believe that fine threads have run through time and that one can get caught in them."

Reinhold became aware that the café was filling with people. He heard their talk and saw that Gabriel was eating the cream cake ordered for him.

"Did you hear?" he said, when he had scraped the last cream from the plate. "The German Association of the Blind has expelled its Jewish members. And did you hear, too? Reparations of a billion Reichsmarks was imposed on the German Jewish community for the damages of the pogroms that were mounted against them. And have you perhaps still heard nothing" — the young man laughed his laugh — "have you really and truly heard nothing about Jews taken into protective custody who are the victims of suicide?"

"Go to the von Wolfsbergs," said Gabriel all of a sudden, as though agitated, "and try to find out something. Try to find out whether Hanno's dread has come true. And if you do find out something, then come on a Wednesday evening after eleven o'clock to the Church of St. Mary on the Graben. Knock three times on the left double door and say: song of defiance. And if you don't find out anything but want to know in what way traitors of the Fatherland in protective custody again learn to enjoy Fatherland songs or how, to get out of custody, they stick needles into their hearts, pencils into their eyes before they play the execution game, then come anyway."

Gabriel got up, paid, left. From his place at the table Reinhold could see him walking across the street. He bobbed up and down while walking, his hair bobbed up and down as though he were dancing an American dance, a forbidden one.

It still got dark early, although the smell of spring was already in the air.

Reinhold was on his way home. — Although it is spring, the darkness lies like a shadow, a harsh shadow, a foreshadowing of death or an aftershadowing! He started to run, heard himself calling Hanno's name in the noise of the afternoon rush hour, realized that he was running on the way to Hanno's house — the way of devotion! Came to Hanno's house, saw the house lit up. — A house full of light. No dead person can lie in the background there! And stood and looked and listened to the voices and laughter of people through the windows half opened to springtime. There Gabriel's words seemed unbelievable to him, and he again took the way back home.

But he had gone hardly two blocks when doubt assailed him. What had just seemed sure to him seemed unsure. He looked at the sky in search of a star that he knew, in search of an oracle that he had vowed not to believe in. He exhorted himself: "I am a believer, I believe in the faith, I believe in the German national community, in its heart and in its being!"

He saw Cassiopeia standing above him. Followed the streets in whose courses it was visible, looked into the sky, paid no attention to the streets, ran, pursued the constellation, and found himself at the foot of the Ziegenberg again.

At night Reinhold wrote in his diary: My diary has become a night book, it has no light. I sit on my chair at my table — all around it is cozy as usual at my hour — and wrestle with the standstill of my thoughts and afterthoughts. The sound of my heart ought to wake everybody, but they sleep, and I'm glad about that and wish no one, not my brother, and not my Father, Mother, to stand at this abyss where a human being has an inkling of the last great plunge.

Hanno! What am I going to do? Where shall I look for you, whom ask about you, and whose answer believe? I called for you through the streets and was led on strange paths to the foot of the Hill that we share with one another. I stood there alone with racing heart.

Now, cold with dread and feverish from the disorder of my feelings, I sit in the quietest midnight, where dogs and cats themselves believe in ghosts, in my cell and let one shiver after the other course through me. Of course, the night view of all fancies and truths is particularly darkened. Still, I don't know what to do about you.

The next morning, after a bad night in which Gabriel's words had fallen upon Reinhold as living images, in which his mother had come to his bed because she had heard him screaming, from the Wagner School a wild rumor came to him: "The chemistry teacher, they've arrested him"

"Queer as Winnetou," grinned Gummi

"Did he ever get into your pants?" Utz almost fell off his chair with mirth.

The one grabbed the other, whirled him through the classroom: "For ceremonious dances you form pairs. Elderly bachelors meet one another through ladies' choice!"

Great laughter.

"The law provides expressly for the possibility of the castration of homosexuals," someone yelled.

"Then they'll just chop off his prick now," someone else yelled.

An assistant teacher had been standing for a long time in the doorway and had to shout three times until he was heard: "Sergeants in the class are to go to the director!"

Reinhold, Utz, and Gummi, Gottfried and Rich, both of whom had just become sergeants in Reinhold's company, stood at attention before four SS men and the director.

"You are old enough, boys, for me to inform you about a regrettable instance of unnatural behavior here in the school, right on our staff." The director sat fat and wilted, taking cover behind his desk: "Does any one of you not know what homosexuality means?"

The boys shook blushing heads.

"You know that such unnatural behavior is heavily punished?"

The boys nodded.

"Are you prepared to be interrogated for the welfare of the German people?"

The boys nodded.

"You know that there is justifiably nothing as reprehensible as a man turned into a woman. Such a man is respected less than the Jew himself or the most common criminal. The pure man is the image of God — let the man be competent in war, the woman competent in giving birth! But when a man becomes feminine and does it with a man, that is the greatest crime against the nobility of nature, against our heritage and our ancestors. I want to mince no words with you: Did this man ever approach you at any time in any way?"

Both the SS men had sat by without speaking and motionless until now, when one then stood up, came to Reinhold, and grabbed him by the chin: "Talk, boy, go ahead. It's not your neck."

"We teachers want to be the comrades of you pupils," the chemistry teacher had said! Last night's images came before Reinhold's eyes and merged with the fate of the chemistry teacher, so that he couldn't help saying: "I don't know anything to say." So that he had to yell: "Really, nothing happened that I could ever have considered as unnatural or indecent."

Days later it was said in the Wagner School that the chemistry teacher had been tried without his having been permitted to have a lawyer. He had arrogantly and aggressively defended himself, admitted his homosexuality, and at the end of the trial put a bullet through his head.

Reinhold received the news that he was to be a cadet colonel. All the companies in the city were put under him. He would wear the commander's white braid, the *aiguillette*, would know the ways and name the goals. As a chosen one he would serve the Fatherland, fight for the Fatherland, for the new faith, new hope, the future of mankind!

He ran, he raced, out into his world, up to his hill. His feet were standing on the earth, his world roared up, his head reached into the sky, the blood in his temples thundered over his eyes, ears.

Heinrich grabbed him hard by the nape of his neck: "Boy," he said roughly and shook him, "now you're the one who's in charge!" And Heinrich's large tree they had once cut down, which was rooted deeply in him, blossomed and swelled.

The maiden Mechthild came with cookies. They sat in the kitchen, together read the letter that the Reich's Youth Leader had written to Reinhold,
and Mechthild admired the white leader's braid that Reinhold would wear
on his uniform from now on.

"Do you know a guy named Gabriel?" asked Reinhold. "He's twenty-one
and goes to the university."

"What does he look like?"

"Tall, narrow-shouldered, dark-haired, white-skinned, long hair, long
pants, bow tie, crepe soles, et cetera — you know."

"Oh, one of the shady sort," Mechthild said and laughed.

"It's about Hanno," said Reinhold. "You know, this whole thing with
Hanno," he continued, interrupted himself, didn't know how to proceed.

"What's going on with Hanno?" asked the girl.

"My worry casts black shadows. If my fear turns out to be true, I'll
crumble with the world."

"Anyone who wants greatness must get control of himself," said Mechthild and laughed. "Doubt belongs to greatness like loyalty to honor. I wrote
you," she said, and her laughter trembled, "what I believe about you."

I can't talk to anyone about Hanno, Reinhold wrote in his diary. It's the third
of May, 1940. I've become a cadet colonel. Wings thrust out of me when I
was standing on our Ziegenberg. But the thought of Hanno shatters my
wings, crackling and painful. The roar of happiness, the storm of longing for
battle and victory falls silent, when I think of my friend.

"Song of defiance," whispered Reinhold, knocked three times. "Song of defiance," he called in a low voice. The church door opened. — Creaking, of
course, like in flicks!

It was Wednesday night at ten thirty. He could not recognize who
opened the door for him. Darkness came from the church, darkness from the
street.

"There's our cadet colonel. Attention!" And then Reinhold heard Gabriel's laughter. "I'll vouch for him," he heard him say, "he's Hanno's friend."

Reinhold was pulled away from the door and into the sanctuary. Several
figures were standing around him. On the altar, the sanctuary lamp.

"You weren't at the von Wolfsbergs?" asked Gabriel.

"No," said Reinhold, "not yet."

Gabriel led him through the door behind the altar down some stairs into
the church basement, into a room in which others were already sitting
around a long table, older than he, students, to judge by their clothing. A

priest was also sitting there. In the corner of the room stood a large box hung with cloths.

"Friend Reinhold," said Gabriel, "up to now we've escaped the *Völkischer Beobachter*, which nothing escapes, as you know. I'm counting on it that the Brown plague hasn't infected all the two hundred thousand billion cells in your skull and that therefore you'll keep your mouth shut about what you hear and see here tonight. Otherwise, my son, you will deliver us to those whose blond hearts tremble with the ecstasy of the emotion of cutting into strange bodies with a knife. In a word, you're Hanno's friend, and that's why you're here. You know his letter, you share our concern and expectation. We stand with hands that are tied. For that reason we are letting you in on things. The deluded crowd at the department on Friedrichstraße imagine and fancy themselves to have been operating against us for some time. But you, let it be said to your credit, are yourself a still very youthful follower of our current national drama and the popular, simple ideas of its directors. With a mere wave of your aiguillette are raised beyond any suspicion by them. Now, before we reveal the plan we have for you, we'd like to request you to join our weekly meeting and, after you have heard things that are bound to keep you from sleeping, to take our solemn vow of silence. After that, all the rest, my son.

"And now, friends, let us together say a few verses by the most famous German emigrant at the moment, who a long time ago was denied the right of lending his name to a little street in our home town because he was a Jew hostile to Germany, to whom the respect of everything high and holy remained unknown, and who pulled Germanness into the dirt."

Everyone, the priest, too, spoke the words like a vow.

> When at night I think of Germany,
> Then sleep is stole' away from me,
> I can no longer close my eyes,
> And in me stinging tears arise.
>
> Since the time I left that land,
> So many sank there into sand,
> Whom I did love — and when I try
> To count them, then my soul bleeds dry.
>
> And count them must I — With that sum
> Swelling higher, torments come,
> To me it seems that corpses roll
> Upon my breast —

"I hope it's clear to you, my son, that we've just recited forbidden verses," said Gabriel, "just as forbidden as those that recently burned through you. And now, open up your ears, now you will get to hear something that will cause your eyes to overflow!"

Reinhold was shown to a chair at the long table. Gabriel sat at one end, the priest at the other. Everyone had paper and pencils in front of them. A girl with long, curling hair and a red-painted mouth said: "He'll think he's stumbled into a seminar on ethnology. We've got to explain to him what's going on here."

"Take it easy, take it easy. I suggest that we let everything proceed as usual, and he can ask questions when it's Greek to him. Our meeting has as always three parts: first a report on the newest incidents, second a short paper, third a discussion. Gisèle has the floor," said Gabriel.

A delicate blond girl stood up: "In my parents' home town in the Vogelsberg, not far from Laubach, lived a Jewish family, peddlers just as before, as they had always been, in the markets of the small towns. The man and his wife had seven children, four girls and three boys. What I tell you now, I know, as confirmed by plenty of people from that same village: The SS came to their house, demanded five thousand marks from the man. But he had never had such a sum in his hands his whole life. Then they beat him, drove him with his wife and children into the damp basement. All had to undress completely. The woman was having her period, which among Jews is the equivalent of being impure. They bound the children and tied them to one another. But they made the husband and wife drink gallons of castor oil, bound them, too, stuck them in a sack together and tied it tight around the necks of the two unfortunates. Not one of us can imagine what that humiliation means for a pious Jew.

"No one heard their cries. Together they had to endure the effect of the castor oil. When after several days and nights they were found — the woman unconscious, the man half out of his mind, two of the children dead — the parents' bodies were eaten away by their own excrement, urine, and blood as though by worms. The wife could no longer face her husband and sons and hanged herself. Thereupon the man went completely insane, and they carried him off. The five children have been taken to a Jewish orphanage, which was closed this past November. There is no further trace of them."

"So," said Gabriel, "and now Charly has the floor."

"I live in the workers' quarter on Klingel Brook," someone said, whom Reinhold knew by sight, a red-headed youth who walked through the streets always whistling, books under his arm, his head thrown back. To himself, Reinhold had called him the bird watcher. "I still live with my parents," he said. "Over us lives a man about whom it was always said that he was an old Party member. Last week they hauled him away — six men from the SS. They beat him out of the apartment and in front of the house, in the small garden — on the small piece of lawn made him rip out grass with his teeth, and then took him away. Two days ago the Party member returned, with a bald head. They tore out his hair. Parts of his scalp went along."

"Does anyone else have anything to say?" asked Gabriel around the table. And when the others remained silent, he said: "Then we come to the second part of the evening. Father, sir, I ask you for your short paper."

"As you all know," the priest began, "Jews steal the consecrated Host, which they slash with knives in back rooms, reciting from the sixth book of Moses at the same time, until blood wells from the Host. And as you know further, there are many who have seen how the Jews caught the Christ Child, stuck Him in a sack, and dragged Him away to slaughter Him. Kosher meat from the Christ Child!

"So much as an introduction. And now, my friends," the priest continued, "I'll explain how the Antichrist has taken residence among us. The Book of Revelations has opened up, and he has stepped into the light of day and has settled into the soul of a man of flesh and blood. His voice has a magic sound, and like the Pied Piper of Hamlin he is seducing people to follow him. He is convincing the old and the young, great and small spirits, to give up their moral responsibility. His exterior is plain. Maybe he even wears a funny mustache."

The priest interrupted the laughter that followed: "So far, so good. But what untruths lie at the base of his inexorable rise? One, my friends, I will endeavor to reveal this evening.

"One or another of you here will be familiar with a work that is entitled *The Protocols of the Elders of Zion*, a work that cleverly attempts to assert that the Zionist movement was not founded to gain a homeland for Jewish refugees in Palestine, rather its secret goal is absolute dominance over the world. In Basle, it is asserted, leading rabbis and cabalistic occultists from Europe, North and South America met in 1897 at an international Jewish congress to draft plans for the enslavement of all of mankind. *We want to stir up unrest, dispute, and hostility everywhere,* it can be read in the ostensible protocols of that gathering. *We will unleash a terrible war on earth, will cause such difficulties among peoples that they will voluntarily offer us the leadership through which we will be able to dominate the whole world. We* — the beast always says we, for his numbers are legion — *we are the chosen, the only true human beings. We want to stretch our arms like tongs in all directions and erect such a tyranny that all peoples will submit to our domination.*

"The Reich's philosopher Alfred Rosenberg," the priest continued, "put this shoddy effort into circulation, knowing very well that it concerned a fake by a Russian named Nilus, a pupil of the distinguished philosopher Solovyev, who, inspired by the Book of Revelations, once wrote a work with the title *Tale of the Antichrist*, which was made fraudulent use of in the supposed *Protocols of the Elders of Zion*. Solovyev's Leviathan, however, does not take possession of the soul and the body of a Jew, as does the Antichrist in the *Protocols*. Quite the contrary, the wise Solovyev understood that precisely the Jews — who have preserved their ancient wisdom and piety, who in the Kol Nidre prayer implore their God once a year for forgiveness for promises not kept that they made also to themselves — will necessarily be among the few who recognize the dragon and call it by name. And Solovyev predicted that for that reason the Jewish race also would fall victim to the frightful persecution of the Antichrist.

"The so-called *Protocols of the Elders of Zion*, however, did not fail in the desired effect. Finally, certain circles in Germany believed they had found the right explanation for the defeat of the Fatherland in the World War: the common Jewish conspiracy! This thesis appeared in almost every country in the twenties. Thereupon hate against Jews coursed like a tidal wave over the Western and Eastern worlds, one of those waves that bore the Hitlerites to power. And the terrible irony of the story: The dæmon, friends, don't misunderstand me, the spirit, the thought, the impulse that speaks from the *Protocols* furnished the Hitlerites in fact with a plan to achieve absolute power.

"Today Jews are held responsible not only for their Jewishness, for their murder of Christ who, as Houston Stewart Chamberlain asserts so convincingly, was in no way a Jew but a handsome Galilean Aryan of the blondest race — so-called international Jewry is also held responsible for the radical-materialistic ideas that lie as a basis for Bolshevism. *The wirepuller of Socialism and Marxism, the Wandering Jew in battle for domination of the world.*"

Herr Herz! Reinhold couldn't help thinking of Herr Herz. — An international conspirator, hunchbacked from conspiracy, his body bent and twisted, a conspirator's body! Herr Herz, the beast with the Red staff of power in his claws! — "Maybe many, but never everyone!" Reinhold heard himself say.

"How do you mean that?" Reinhold heard Gabriel ask.

"It can't be real," Reinhold heard himself saying, "that you're sitting here and in one world uphold still another! What do you want from me? What do you want anyway?"

"From the inside out we want to cure the darkened, wounded German spirit that has been led into error, driven into a corner, and gone mad!" Gabriel snapped at Reinhold.

"We want to save what can be saved," said the priest.

"If there's anything left to be saved," said Charly.

"Assume," said the priest to Reinhold, "that a people learns to believe in itself through idle enchantment, through parades, oaths to flags and loyalty — a people that no longer believes in itself. And afterwards it then believes those who restored that faith, and it begins to get entangled in the dark error advanced by them. Then they raise that people to the idol of itself, and an idol needs sacrifices, else it isn't one."

"Hanno!" Gabriel exclaimed. "Think of Hanno!"

"And those powermongers are the slaughtering priests of the idol called the People," exclaimed the girl with the red lips and the curly hair. "Horror turns into glory, the bestial part of man starts to march. Jews, gypsies, communists, homosexuals, and Bible scholars are arrested. Forced labor, torture, pogroms."

"They are taken to KZs," exclaimed Gisèle. "Have you heard of Dachau? Do you know that a KZ is?"

"A simple definition of a KZ," said Gabriel: "A temporary limitation of freedom with an educational goal, or: The enduring of every kind of pain. Pain and blood heat up the lust of that caste of priests."

"Did you ever hear of concentration camps? Of Dachau, Flossenbürg, Sachsenhausen, Buchenwald, Mauthausen, Ravensbrück?" someone screamed at Reinhold.

"Did you ever listen to Radio London or Beromünster?" another screamed.

"Enough!" yelled the priest. "It looks like you're out to get our friend."

"Cadet Colonel," cried the girl named Gisèle, "do you know that last week four Hitler Youths kept pummeling the old iron monger Salzmann in his shop in Kathrinen Lane until he died!" And the girl went for Reinhold so that he had to defend himself.

"No," he shouted, "never!"

"And Hanno!" yelled Gabriel. "Where is Hanno? What's going on with Hanno?"

Hanno! Lonely, cold, with fever in his eyes, crying, clinging, shaken! — "What is going on with Hanno?" cried Reinhold.

"No one knows," said Gabriel quietly. Everyone fell silent. Then he said: "You must go to the von Wolfsbergs, in your uniform with the aiguillette. You must try to find out what has happened, it doesn't matter how. Something has certainly happened."

"So, friend Reinhold," said the priest and put his arm around him, so that he felt on his own arm the other's trembling. "You now take a vow of silence about everything that you've heard and seen here among us." And the priest held out the Cross to him.

The others went to the large box draped with cloths in the corner, took the cloths off, took positions around the box.

"What is that?" asked Reinhold.

"A printer," said the priest. "Here we print the *Song of Defiance* and the fliers. We still have to work all night."

Gabriel led Reinhold out through the dark church. "Take care of yourself, Cadet Colonel," he said at the door. "Until next Wednesday."

I am forced to write, I am driven and I am written. Me? Am I him, Reinhold Fischer? Others think into me, want to rethink me.

"Are you him, Reinhold?" you could probably ask me now, Schade, and I would hardly know how to answer. My inner chorus has gotten off key. I was my world, and now? That reality is only one view and its description, so I must be present to see other views and to be confronted with other descriptions. But truth, the result of the sum of all realities, views, and descriptions, the essence, so to speak, truth is unique. Isn't it, Schade? And, my friend, what am I going to do? Should I have to determine that there is another truth? Or even worse, that the truth in which I was safe and righteous is experiencing an eclipse, so that I stumble and fall into a little ditch?

Schade, Schade, what could be wrong with our Hanno?

And what's this about prohibited radio stations, and why are they prohibited? If the cause is right, it doesn't need prohibitions.

War is being waged against my thoughts, Schade. They have struck me with missiles of mistrust. What is being done to Jews, and where can Herr Herz be?

The familiar bell is striking outside, but how am I, Schade? Today I received a wound that won't heal until I know how to make sense of things. And what's going on with Hanno. And what does his letter to the *Song of Defiance* mean to me?

And if I had to say right to my face: You have erred, Cadet Colonel. A most bitter error. Your holy hills are heaps of garbage. Not generals sit atop them to direct coming battles, rather rag-and-bone men rule and mask your people with their wares, knead them, enchain them, blind them. But what then?

The next morning, in the light of May, in bed, in his room with its chair and its table, with the view of the gray wall of the house next door, with the aroma of coffee and with his mother's face, her wake-up face, Reinhold wondered why, since nothing had changed, everything should have changed.

91

The room under the church seems to me, considered in the light of day, so separated from reality that I can believe that yesterday evening a kind of delusion of the senses happened to me, he wrote in his diary.

The celestial creatures with a body, mind, and soul living on the earth have a predisposition, perhaps unique in all of creation, to confuse fantasy with reality. So the more creative you are, the more it could happen to you. And people like us, less interested anyway in stories of reality, slip on the decidedly slanted slide behind the veils and run, like yesterday evening, the risk of getting entangled in them completely.

You must know that about yourself, Reinhold Fischer! And look more objectively into your future as a man! But as far as your future as a poet is concerned, if such a thing can be intended for you, you can ride on the broad back of the fabled creature to the isles of the forbidden.

"Have you read the *Protocols of the Elders of Zion*?" he asked his father at breakfast. But he didn't know what Reinhold was talking about.

"What do you know about the Jews who are disappearing?"

"They're getting their own land in the East. In the open countryside there, a new homeland is being created for the Jews. They can settle there. They can live there undisturbed according to their customs and not bother us here in ours."

Reinhold got a new chemistry teacher, a friendly old gentleman in a black frock coat dissolved in his world of formulas. A young woman, just arrived from Africa, where she had taught German to German children, took over the instruction in literature and world-view.

For weeks Reinhold would not admit the respect that he felt for Fräulein Dr. Freitag. He read his poets, read as much as he could, made outlines, plans in a notebook bought special, about how in the course of two years he could have read all of world literature: three to four days for a large novel, two days for a small one, a play a day, and as much poetry as possible on days that were filled with Hitler Youth work! He took heart, went to the young woman, asked her for advice regarding his plans, told her about what he had already read, read a long time ago, showed her his notebook, in which he had noted pedantically the contents and assessment about what he had read.

"How did you happen on Hölderlin and Rilke?" the young woman asked.

"I had a friend," said Reinhold, and was appalled at the use of the past tense.

The young woman saw it and questioned him.

"He has disappeared," said Reinhold.

The young woman looked at him.

Curtly Reinhold said: "He hasn't showed up again," and was about to turn and leave. But the young woman insisted on more. She was dark-blond and medium sized, wore glasses and wore her hair in a bun. — *Has a sweet mouth*, Reinhold had written in his diary, and now looked at her mouth.

And saw the young woman's mouth say: "No one disappears in our Reich. No one is allowed to disappear. The people have gathered each one rigorously in their service. Solitariness has no right anymore. No one can get lost here."

"But disappear," said Reinhold, "like the Jews." It burst out of him.

"Oh, the Jews, the Jews!" laughed the young woman. "You can forget them! Think about the Germans, think about your Hölderlin. Do you know 'Patmos'?" she asked and didn't wait for an answer and spoke, no, sang:

> But the father, who presides
> Over all things, loves most of all
> that the firm letter is nurtured,
> and that what exists is well
> interpreted. German song follows that.

Reinhold ran through the city, ran home the long way around, did not run to the Ziegenberg, got home late, ran to his room, and wrote in his diary: I went walking through the springtime, I wanted to walk under the trees. I was sitting under the trees at the river, plummeted to the bottom of my soul, strode out, and arrived in the old heartland, entered by so many already. The land of my childhood lies behind me. The limits that were set on emotion up to this point have opened. I laughed, spoke, told it to the river: I put an arm around her shoulder, put my arm around her hips, she trembles, her sweet mouth stands open! Then I struggled home through the bliss of springtime into my realm of shadows. And here I am terrified, for amidst certain thoughts, it seems to me as though I were harboring a predator within me that wants to rend flesh.

On the day of the great games competition, Reinhold, Utz, and Gummi walked together to the playing field. One of the Hitler Youth wanted to join them, but full of contempt they gave him the brush-off. "We're from the Jungvolk branch of the Hitler Youth," yelled Utz. "We're not just good on our feet."

"And anyway," Gummi yelled, "that Friedeberg Miller, I know him. We used to squeeze one another's paws often, but then I came to my senses and really got to know him: His father is a native of Negroid, degenerate France.

He's a chip off the old block. He's like a beefsteak — brown on the outside and red on the inside."

"The square is packed full," exclaimed Beilharz, who wanted to be a priest and had been held back in his last class. "Man, boy," he said to Reinhold, "your first appearance as cadet colonel— congratulations! The high and mighty Parents' Association is already filling the seats. Work up a good sweat! Yow!"

They gathered on the street and moved into the arena: meticulously lined up, brisk marching. A whistle from Reinhold, and the battle began. In the intermission the Hitler Maidens formed circles and did field gymnastics. Mechthild was in charge. As a finale "Our Flag Waves before Us" was sung.

"I'm proud of you, Reino," said the maiden Mechthild at the contest fest. "You're a classic example of a cadet colonel. If you ever get to be a solder, I hope that you get into battle and that you take part in assaults. You have the stuff to become a hero, Reino."

"A hero has power," said someone from the rear. Gabriel was standing there, laughed his laugh, and looked at the circle. "Thunderation, a whole forest of youngmen and youngwomen!"

"Who's that guy?" asked Beilharz.

"Eyes are gleaming," said Gabriel, "hearts trembling, souls are overflowing!"

Reinhold went to Gabriel, pulled him away from the others: "What do you want here?"

"What do you know about Hanno? What have you found out? Nothing! And what have you undertaken to do?" Gabriel asked, taking him to account.

"Nothing yet," said Reinhold. "I wanted to wait first."

"Wait! Go on!" exclaimed Gabriel. "Until your Hanno is done for? But oh, what am I saying! Miserable human fear, better to say get rid of that, otherwise it'll get you in the end, won't it! I'm sorry, Rookie Reinhold. You disappoint me," he said and left.

"Who was that?" asked Mechthild.

"I don't know," said Reinhold.

That evening Reinhold, Utz, Gummi, Beilharz, Rich, and Gottfried agreed to take a long bicycle trip during vacation.

It's not cowardice, it's just pure fear, Reinhold wrote in his diary. That house, and that father, that mother, that sister! When I walk into the house, I'll lose my head, run around like a headless chicken and not have a mouth to scream with. Shame and contempt will run over me in one and the same car, and I'll lie deathly silent under the wheels, and that sister will say hooray.

During the night he dreamed that Hanno was sitting on a stone, was himself stone, hewn ancestral stone, gravestone. *No mortal has ever raised my veil* was written on his stone chest. Dust came, towered up, buried the Hanno-stone. Reinhold woke up, got up, tried to write a letter to Hanno, wrote one and tore it up, wrote one again, and tore it up again. When morning came he had written what he wanted to write: *It is June 13, 1940. Hanno! for almost half a year now I have heard nothing from you. I'm at my wit's end. And I don't believe that you've forgotten me. When I think of you, I get a heaviness in my head that won't stop until I get my mind off of you. But it's just that I miss you in each and every thing. Since then I've had no one with whom I can discuss human questions. Where are you, Hanno, and how are you? I need to know! Reinhold.*

When he was on his way to the von Wolfsbergs' house with the letter, he met his cousin. She was wearing a red skirt. He hadn't seen her for a long time. In his thoughts she was only his cousin. But there, wearing the red skirt that was flapping, he thought of the female thing that she had once let him see. She laughed so much, his cousin did. She had filled out.

"Can we meet some time?"

His cousin laughed.

"In the ice-cream store?"

His cousin laughed. "You've become cadet colonel," she laughed. "All right, then, tomorrow at five."

He had become warm. His shirt collar had gotten tight. He started to run and at the von Wolfsbergs' gate met Hanno's sister.

"Well hey!" she said. "Who do I see there?"

"It's about Hanno," Reinhold burst out and blushed, for the thought of the femininity of Hanno's sister came to him, and that the sister also had to have that female thing, so this very sister, too, infuriated him and swept him off his feet. "I haven't heard anything from him for half a year," he exclaimed beside himself.

"Oh well," she said, "just calm down," she said. "It's probably just that my little brother has figured out how to replace his little friend in the meantime. I can assure you, he's getting along splendidly." Her lips rose up before Reinhold, pulled down.

"Please, I have a letter for Hanno," he heard himself say. "It's urgent! I beg you to give me his address or to forward the letter as quickly as possible."

"May I?" said the sister and took the letter out of Reinhold's hand. "We'll see what can be done. Heil Hitler!" And she walked over the crunching path to the house.

On the last day of school before the long vacation, Hanno thought that Fräulein Dr. Freitag had gazed at him for a long time.

And that gaze burned through me, he wrote in his diary, and he would like to have been by himself and would like to have looked at pictures that portrayed his wishes, and colored them in.

But he had agreed to meet his cousin, and she was wearing a different skirt.

She eats ice cream like a cow gives milk, he found himself thinking and nevertheless had to watch her and couldn't look away from the ice cream on the little, flat, square tin spoon that she pushed into her mouth. She sticks out her tongue like Emma Zocher, he couldn't help thinking. She has a red tongue like Emma Zocher, but she has smaller teeth with gaps.

"You're a have-not," she said. "Where do you get the money for ice cream?"

Have-not, she had said. She had said it in English. He wanted to leap on her and beat her, wanted to make a mess of her.

"My parents have forbidden it," she said.

"Forbidden what?" he berated her.

"That I make a date," she said. "But you're my cousin," she said and put her hand on his bare knee and scratched him a little with her fingernails. "They won't mind this," she said.

Then they talked about the future, and Reinhold told her about the planned bicycle trip, and his cousin talked about getting married and having babies: "Marry someone who can ride, play tennis, and play the piano — only someone like that comes into consideration!"

And Reinhold, certain that he could never learn all those things, since money for them was lacking, and certain, too, that his cousin knew it, and certain that she had said it for that reason, lashed out at her: "I'm going to be a poet. I'll never get married. I'll go into solitude. Only in seclusion can I understand my existence and carry it out. Novalis says — do you know Novalis? Have you ever even heard of Novalis? Novalis says: 'Inward goes the mysterious path. Within us or nowhere,' do you hear, cousin, 'is eternity with its worlds!'"

"Check!" he called into the ice-cream store and didn't intend to waste himself on this cousin of his anymore. But she hung onto his arm and pressed against him and led him on the way to the house with the garden in which it had happened, in which she had let him see that time.

"My parents aren't home. Want to go into the garden?" she asked.

He nodded. They went through the gate, past the house. It was already the cool of the evening. — She doesn't have the red skirt on. If she just had that one on!

He reached for her, she laughed and ran, ran up the steps to the veranda. The glass door was standing open. She ran behind the glass, shut the door, turned the key twice, her sides about to split from laughing, turned on her heel, sat down at the piano that stood half in the veranda and half in the room, bent back her upper body, reached for the keys, and bawled out: "Yes, you'd have to be able to play the piano. Anyone who plays the piano has luck with women."

Reinhold ran through the city. — She left me standing there. She laughed at me. She died laughing. Now she's dead. I'll not bury her!

Magda had gotten up two hours earlier than usual, had buttered bread, made coffee, and watched Reinhold eat breakfast. Then she had hugged him. Reinhold had hardened himself for that, regretted it when he was out the door, but then did not turn around on the long, smooth street to wave to his mother, and on his way imagined how she might have stood behind the window, face and hands on the glass.

He had not been able to go to sleep the evening before, had gotten out of bed very late and written in his diary: It's probably nervousness, excitement about traveling that drives me onto hills and through valleys. Just before falling asleep I'm already on trips, and some cities emerge in me in which I would probably do better to submerge than to dive into the foreign cities of this world. Maybe someone to whom writing is important should kind of see the bridges and palaces of Florence built within him instead of their standing solidly built before him and he can build nothing onto them. Also, the closed doors of palaces are open in me, and like Orbasan I can step on secret paths over backstairs, always following splendid Hauff's hero, into the shaded rooms of the pale Bianca. But I'm really standing on the Ponte Vecchio, I'm the one standing there, and Orbasan is far away from me in a book.

But nothing helps. If you start something, you have to finish it. My bike is saddled. I'm meeting my comrades early tomorrow morning at five thirty at the town hall square. Utz, Gummi, Beilharz, Rich, and Gottfried are part of the party, and Siegmund Eis, though he's not a Hitler Youth. But we're a liberal organization, and Sigi is one of the fairest and most sportsmanlike in our class.

But I, who write in my diary day and night, will put my fine pen away and take up a pencil, for outer things will leave little room for inner ones over the next few days.

When Reinhold arrived at the town hall square his friends were already gathered, talked without stopping, laughed louder than usual, said one strong adage after another.

They rode over the river bridge out of their city, rode through the city gate, bore down on their pedals as though it were a matter of riding away from something, pumped against the empty feeling in their full stomachs.

They took a rest at midday, and Reinhold sat apart from the others and took his diary out of his rucksack, opened it to a new page, and wrote:

Report of the Great Summer Trip 1940.

July 15: Move out into your German homeland and be astonished and admire the mighty creative power of long-ago times in the proud works of German architecture and German industriousness. Learn from the historical places about German history, German culture, and in the midst of nature grasp your German homeland in your inmost heart as a part of your own Self!

July 17: After two days of steadfast travel, with little sleep in louse-filled hostels, we reached Germany's south. At twelve noon we rode into Augsburg, past the open-air theater to the Messerschmitt Factory in Haunstetten. In the magnificent factory canteen we were factory guests at lunch. We rode then past Königsbrunn and Klosterlechfeld through flat terrain toward Landsberg and put up for the night in the youth hostel there, a bare, severe building. With 120 kilometers behind us we were soon fast asleep. It probably will be the last time for a long time that we have a solid roof over our heads.

July 18: The Alps took us gradually in their arms. On a good highway we pedaled through Unter- and Oberammergau. Beilharz, who wants to become a priest, told us he had heard that the people of Oberammergau who play the apostles in the festival pageants have to endure pangs of conscience because they have to play Jewish types. Therefore, according to Beilharz, recently there is an Oberammergau pageant rule according to which the portrayers of Jesus, along with his twelve apostles, have to be blond and blue eyed, since to an especially great extent they are supposed to embody the Aryan man.

The mountains didn't leave us until Garmisch. There we admired the Olympic Stadium with its ski jump and the artificial ice-skating rink, located a tent ground on a meadow behind the town, unburdened ourselves of our rucksacks, took off our hot uniforms, tightened tent ropes, and pounded in the tent pegs. The tents were organized — Rich, Sigi, and Gottfried slept in one, Gummi, Utz, Beilharz, and I in the other. The sleeping bag roll was at the foot end of the rubber mat, at the head end the rucksacks. There must be order, and let there be no impediments for those who are capable. Gummi and Rich set up the place to cook, Gottfried and Beilharz gathered wood, Utz, Sigi, and little me put up the flag pole, raised our flag, and hung the Hitler Youth banner on it. A well was there, too, so we could cook our favorite nigger rice. But Gummi let the rice burn and to disguise it shook so much cocoa on it that the walls of our stomachs stuck together.

We sat for a long time in front of the tents by the fire. There was a gleam coming to us from the slopes. Twilight haunted the paths, the forest seemed to thicken, the mountains seemed to grow together.

I am standing flag watch. Flag watch is a watch of honor. You have to be permeated by it. And after days filled with air, landscape, and just body, I now finally have time to look around again for stars and dreams. Old favorite ideas become awake and wild for me, storm and stress, longing flies, where to, for what? — But why is it necessary that you know that! Just enjoy your thoughts: before you, the nameless immensity, or perhaps merely the quiet stroll under trees, thinking, rhyming, sunk in observation of the divine composure of drifting clouds.

But first a path of thought while we often traveled along in silence during the day: We are the representatives of the almighty German youth of the age, who will seize their heritage and will conquer new realms. But the greatest deeds are not the loudest, they are the quietest. They are born in quiet and grow there, and only there, to become hushed greatness.

But much in our days seems to me fairly drummed up. And I now often wonder whether all the noise is necessary, the processions and the boisterousness. Hanno, it seems to me, would have been on my side with this thought. What side might he now be on?

But I don't want to go astray in this and want to find my way back to the thread that's important to me.

There's a leafing in the trees of the night. What pages may be opened up here? Dew falls onto the grass. The life of dreams begins. I'm still, I'm profoundness — what else is necessary? Here what is truly German lies well founded, and not in the clamor, not in the foreground. You can't talk about that with anyone. Only Hanno would understand the doubt that now and then comes over me. Gabriel, too, he'd have the head for it, but he's on the left side of the Rhine, and therefore he sees with a distorted perspective.

July 22: The camping ground remained our location for three more days. The Wetterstein mountain range, with the Zugspitze, the Alpspitze and the Höllentalspitze, lay at our door. On an excursion to Lake Riesser it was decided that one of us would have to undergo a test of courage every night. It was my turn for the coming night. The others withdrew at once to come up with "something horrid." In the evening the streets were full of people.

The town is full of women. — Oh, women walk so buoyantly in the summer! "Breasts give you an itch," Beilharz remarked once. That's probably the July madness that's bitten us. There's no serum against that rabies.

We were loafing around. Secret urges still drove us into the darkness and around this or that corner. No one admitted that to anyone else. Just that we suddenly had something going with biology. Gottfried, for example, knew that the individual who copulates has taken the first step toward making himself superfluous. It's been that way since the Ice Age. It was most threatening for the males. There were actually female spiders that began to eat copulating males while they were still copulating.

Then, when toward eleven that night we were in our tents, my task was given me: I was to go to the nearby cemetery, climb over its wall, there, armed with only three matches, find the third grave in the seventh row and read the inscription on the gravestone. To pass the second part of the trial, I had to find my way in the dark to a chapel that stood in the middle of the graveyard, get into it somehow so that inside I could draw a sketch of its layout. For that purpose a flashlight could be found on the way on the edge of a fountain.

They were sitting together, babbling and grinning. I wanted to tell them that I found their world ridiculous. I'd like to have said that I was way past that. Before, it was all about women, and now you've regressed to the Stone Age, I didn't say, and I put my tail between my legs and headed out into the night.

The little cemetery and a howling dog, dark light from the watery moon, a screech owl, a crinkling and crackling. Really, I told myself, you don't believe in things that swirl through the night in their grave shrouds and cry out hoo, hoo! and I climbed over the wall in the darkness of the grave shrubbery and half fell down and hit my left knee on a gravestone, looked around with the light of one of my three matches, saw the tall angels standing around formidably, found the small path between the dead stones. With the help of the second match I counted off the seven rows. The air was still over the place. There really do seem to be nightmares that settle in feathery dress with owl eyes onto the white backs of angels: That way white angels become black, and many an angel drags a tail around. But then something scampered across my path and was, after all, just a hedgehog or a mouse, but my heart was about to fly out of me, out of my throat, out of my mouth. It wanted to do like the night birds, take off, never to be seen again, and abandon the heartless being among the lightless angels. I lighted the third match, found the second grave, and was just reading the name inscribed when the stone angel that I had recognized as the guardian of the grave in the sulfurous light lowered its paws on me, and I fell to my knees with a shrill shriek. Horrible laughter followed, which liberated me, since I knew it well, and at the same time it overcame me.

After the sound of running steps of two or three pairs of feet over stone and gravel had reverberated and the laughter died away, I swore sweet revenge, ran away from the graves, came to the fountain, found there the little flashlight standing dependably on the edge, and lighted my way to the chapel. It was standing so stoutly in the middle of this acreage that I broke one of its windows with a certain tenderness, a genuine regret. I squeezed myself inside and found it freshly whitewashed. At its centerpiece I saw a lovely Mother of God. I felt a milder mood again toward the world and its coarse jest and walked around and measured and drew the ground plan as well as I was able to.

I then got four or five hours of sleep amongst my comrades, who lay outstretched with open mouths, completely out of it. I generously refrained from filling their empty mouths with sand, refrained, forgave, forgot, and slept away.

July 25: Early in the morning we left Garmisch and traveled past Mittenwald and Giesenbach toward Innsbruck. We pushed our bicycles up the eternally long Zirler Pass, just to push them down the other side (in part a 24% decline). From Zirl on, there was an asphalt bicycle path to the city of Maximilian: proud German Renaissance at the gate to Italy. In a broad valley it lies at the foot of a wall of cliffs and looks toward the south, greeting the land of Etsch, greeting the Germans around Bozen and Meran. It was uphill to Innsbruck. Twelve kilometers before the Brenner Pass, we turned westward. The people who live in the mountains are solemn and poor, the soil steep and rocky. The side valleys have their entrances high above the main valley, and the rivers plunge down into pathless gorges and ravines.

At an inn at Gschnitz we put away our bicycles and climbed up to the Tribulaun cabin. The Tribulaun is 3,103 meters high. We panted our way up for two and a half hours. The cabin lies at about 2,300 meters. After we cooked in the open air, we sang with great feeling on a height above the cabin as darkness fell.

A great clarity is in me, as though my emotions found expression in the mountains that stand with clean lines against the sky. The fog begins to drip, magic pearls appear on every blade, the green slope stands faintly gray. The grayness assails me. Memories spill through my heart. Hanno comes forth from the gray zones. Hopes tower up — it is only the mountains of clouds.

After a sixty-kilometer ride and a two-and-a-half hour climb up the mountain we slept through the night as though content in the cold mountain air, and a whispering rain with icy toes secretly pushed together over the hard bed of blanket and stone.

July 26: We wanted to conquer the mountain! Over the rubble of cliffs and past gigantic slopes of gravel we went upward past our singing camp, upward in serpentines through snow and glacial debris.

To be alone with myself for once and to look for my truth and then tell it to myself in the stillness in quiet bliss in this tranquillity and clearness, in the face of that grandeur! To invent new, wild words of jubilation for that!

July 27: We put our tents up by the waters of the Inn. In the mountain forest it is damp and cool. Mist lies over the pines. From time to time a great hand gathers the veil on the treetops together like a horse's tail, balls it into a vaporous coiffure that then floats along the walls of cliffs and disappears into omnipresent eternity.

We went to a nearby village. Dark figures were sitting mutely in front of the houses. High above gleamed the snow. Solitude lay in the valley and did not stir.

For a long time we sat in front of the tent. We talked about books. At first it was only a conversation and delight in arguing, so we talked loudly about Wittek, Binding, Rilke, and Carossa, then desire became the theme, that mysterious desire that issues forth from the fissures of this or that poet, that makes the letters so isolated in the printed text gape wide apart. And the desire of arguing about desire rose into whole words that then were uttered, and Siegmund said that one poet's desire was brazen and another's sick, and he suggested the desire of a third, fourth, fifth, who did it alone in the darkness of the shadows of their act. "Alone with themselves," said Utz and grabbed at those around him. The others also grabbed here and there — maybe a new, wild way, I thought to myself, and joined them. "While asleep you don't know whether you're a man or a woman," said the one next to me, and the other one beside me said: "Practice makes perfect." And no one looked at anyone else. As for myself, women shot through my mind like arrows, one and then another, my cousin and the teacher and finally Emma Zocher. And that was my downfall, the rise and the fall, so that then I half sat, half lay next to the others, knowing that the same thing had happened to them — and all that under the secretive, pale moon! Then we men jumped up and ran with Indian yells to the river and tore the rest of our clothes off our bodies and dove into the clear night water and completed our purification.

Afterwards we dried ourselves thoroughly, grinned at one another, boxed a bit, and crept into the tent. Each into his castle!

July 28: Siegmund's wake-up call echoed from the mountains: "Into your uniforms, fasten your belts, take down your tents, pack your rucksacks!" Along the Inn we came to Wörgl. On our way through Brixen Valley to Kitzbühel it began to rain. Gummi left us all behind. How splendid the valley would be in the sun! — One ought to be able to conjure up the gods of weather with ancient Germanic words!

In the youth hostel at Kitzbühel we washed our clothes and bicycles and played ping-pong. Utz and Beilharz continued the debate about this and that literary piece.

I kept to myself. I have enough to do with myself. It's a matter of thinking about Hanno and of following Schade's advice in that regard, which rustles in my innermost ear. And then it's a matter of coming to terms with my homesickness, which all of a sudden came upon me so violently that it almost made me sob. No! it did make me sob, and I could suppress this most horrible thing only with coughing, coughed long and convulsively until it was past, until only a small cozy ache gnawed at my breastbone. And I do know that Mother, Father, my brother, and the house with the street and the light and the air and the noise of home are not lost from the world, that I, quite the contrary, am already on my way back to them.

In the big dormitory the windows are directly under the ceiling. I see the stars go out one after the other.

July 29: The sun shone for us through Salzach Valley to Zell am See. We went swimming. Water fights made the lake overflow. Then we rode to the Luffenstein Pass and then down the Kain Pass to Unken.

Those colorful meadows! Those leas! The senses awaken to all the aromas that drift from the slopes, to the sun, to the blue stillness, to the language of the landscape.

In the youth hostel at Berchtesgaden there was cream cheese, which was devoured on the balcony by some figures in night shirts during a marvelously raging thunderstorm.

After the storm, the wild weather, we were assaulted by questions of life and death. And what had been bothering me slipped out, the thing with Hanno. My friends were surprised. They supposed he was safely in an Ordensburg. I could not confide in them, however, that that certainty is shaken so thoroughly for me. For what if Hanno suddenly appeared today or tomorrow and I had blabbed about such a thing.

July 30: The sky looked down on us dismally when we loaded our bikes to cruise to Salzburg. At Residenz Square we saw a crowd of people. A lot of Hitler Youth had gathered. We joined them. Only Siegmund was hesitant and said he would wait for us at the hostel. That was surprising.

The crowd shifted, the SS arrived. The Führer was ready to appear. Since we were in uniform, they took us to the front. "I'm all aquiver," said Gummi. "For the first time I'm going to see our Führer, the one who has saved Germany from certain ruin."

Ahead of us the Maidens were first. They had to push one another so that they dared step up to the man. "Heil, my Führer!" said one with a picture in her hand. "Could I have your autograph?"

Actually a funny man, I couldn't help thinking, a very, very funny man. And suddenly I had to laugh, very loudly, almost like a convulsive laughter. I was poked from all sides and after a horrible moment calmed down.

"Let the boys come up also," said the man. We strode up. We were standing before the Führer. He asked where we came from, and we told him about our big trip. Then he asked about our travel money. At first we didn't dare say, and then did say: "Skimpy!" and got a big donation.

Afterwards, thanks to the filled-up cash box, we had coffee and cake in a confectionery. Four Hitler Maiden girls had come along. We generously invited them to join us. One, whose name was Inge and who had come especially to Salzburg from Styria, said: "We all looked at the Führer, but none of us could endure his gaze. He seemed to read our innermost thoughts, and I believe that each one of us Maidens in that moment vowed to be loyal to him forever."

That evening I talked about it to Beilharz, whom I like more and more. "Well," said he who has wanted to be a priest for as long as he can remember, "they're like nuns who give themselves to Jesus." And then he was able to tell many a nun story, and I couldn't help thinking of Gabriel and the others and of the whole swindle about race they had talked about, and that the Führer was intoxicating not only the idiots but had also robbed the intellectuals of their senses.

July 31: The next morning we headed in the direction of home. We had seen the beauties of our Reich and vowed to be grateful and never to forget what we had experienced.

IN AUGUST REINHOLD noticed that women were staring at him, looking him up and down, and thought at first there was an oddness about him, a flaw, a weakness, a blotch. Then he combed his hair more carefully, shaved every day, and asked his father to be allowed to go to dancing classes.

"He's growing up," said Magda and laughed and pulled his hair hard.

New pages in my life are being opened, Reinhold wrote in his diary. Hot south winds blow me from glance to glance, from woman to woman. But my longing reaches no one but myself, and I'm also not at all sure whether I want other shores for them.

When school started again in September, Fräulein Dr. Freitag had tied her bun tighter so that not a hair curled along the back of her neck into her collar, where Reinhold's thoughts had often gone in pursuit of shorter and longer hairs.

The "Armed Forces Symphony" by the music teacher was played by the school orchestra. Fräulein Dr. Freitag gave a speech: "We are at war. Our brave soldiers accomplish incomparable heroic deeds day and night. The wonderful strength that enables them to do such deeds they draw only from the healthy body of the populace of our nation. It is the soil in which the German army is rooted. It must remain healthy under all circumstances. Growths and excesses of any sort, however, must be eradicated with inexorable severity. Anyone who opposes the will for victory of the German people, who are ready to achieve freedom by any means, ready to bring the greatest sacrifice for that goal, has forfeited his place in our common destiny. He will be taken out and cut down because he is vermin."

Gabriel! Reinhold had neither seen nor heard anything more from Gabriel, hadn't looked for him, had kept himself distant. — Because of an inner division that threatened me where at many places I already felt myself coming apart, where a murkiness began to hold me fast! Gabriel! I'll find him and confront him with my innermost thoughts and be sure of myself now against his mad lore and rescue him from his murkiness!

"In this war," the woman said, "precautions have been taken that vermin will not develop anymore as they did in the World War. As a defense against that, a special War Punishment Management program was created. So the people can have a sense of absolute security. One of the protective regulations states: Anyone who in any manner associates with prisoners of war, which gravely offends the healthy sensibilities of the people, will be punished by being jailed, in severe cases with imprisonment in a penitentiary."

The woman announced visual instruction for the next morning. The pupils were ordered to be in uniform at eight o'clock on the town hall square.

There a young woman was sitting tied to a chair on an open truck, hands in handcuffs, legs tied apart around the chair legs. Her skirt had slipped up to her thighs. Reinhold could see her garters. She was wearing a slab of wood on her breast: ANNA RITZ, KIRCHGÖNS, HINTERGASSE 4. STORM TROOPERS VILIFY HER AS WHORE, IMMORAL PROSTITUTE, POLISH GIRLFRIEND. SABOTAGE IN BED. A FEMALE WHO FORGETS HER OWN KIND!

The square was full of people. Two SS-men cut the young woman's braids off, shaved her hair to the bare skull, fastened the braids to the slab. The truck started off, drove at a walking pace around the square. "Anna Ritz," someone said through the megaphone, "engaged in criminal intercourse with a Polish prisoner of war. Therefore she is denounced here on our town-hall square. Her bare cranium is now the brand of her dishonorable behavior. Tomorrow she must answer to a special court. She has besmirched Nature, not only arranged for presents for the Polack and accompanied him to his camp, she also had intimate intercourse with that subhuman. She must go to the pillory. Perhaps here a courageous German will be found who will tell the Polish prostitute about her shame to her face."

The truck drove in its circle at a walking pace. People walked along behind the truck. "She was caught in the act," roared the man through the megaphone. "And the prostitute's mother knew everything and did nothing. Nice people! Nobody who spits on her will be liable for prosecution, because whatever helps the German people is right, whatever hurts them is wrong. If our women give birth to nigger, yellow half-breed, Jewish, or Polack bastards, then the flood of mud will engulf us. If a German woman gets involved with niggers, yellow half-breeds, Jews, or Polacks, then she is entitled to no legal protection, nor are her legitimate or illegitimate children! The mixture of the races is punishable, and the preservation of the purity of the body of the German people is the highest duty of a citizen!"

The truck drove slowly, the woman's wedged legs were open. Reinhold saw that her gray woolen underpants were wet.

Gummi and Utz had stood next to Reinhold. But when a troop of Hitler Youth began to yell, they went back to their school. No one said anything. They had their clenched fists deep in the pockets of their short pants.

When they came into the classroom, in addition to Siegmund Eis, who had been missing at the town-hall square, only a few people were at their places. Fräulein Dr. Freitag stood erect before the benches that were slowly filling up, talked about the disciplinary intentions of their forefathers, about knights "who dedicated their lives to severe discipline," about "children chosen for their noble breeding and beauteous being," and said smiling — smiling sweetly! — Amfortas had, in opposition to the command of pure love for his own kind, gotten involved with the bestial female Kundry. "Like to like creates increase," the Fräulein said with a smile. "Unlike to unlike, destruction."

Her face, the body of the most solitary woman! As though she were already outside of herself, as though the great last breath had taken place. And not a sound, only quiet, only the dry tears. Her whole body as though gone, and yet there like that. Death would be a healing, I tell myself, but what in heaven do I know, Reinhold wrote in his diary.

The man, the Pole, they said, is to be hanged. But she must have loved him, that man. Whose business is that? Love is the only freedom of mankind, the only one! Who should bother about that, except that He and that She. An injustice lies established there that just doesn't appear right to me. And then they said the worst thing: that they will remove what's below, what is necessary to get babies!

The hammering of her heart rang in my ears. Muffled drumming, torches, caps, will o' the wisps, eyes of executioners. That seemed to me as though from prehistory, as a simile for the present. It gripped my senses: I held her, held the woman high and firmly in my arms, I took her soul by the hand, I walked cautiously away from the square with her so as not to disgrace her and not to shock her with a sudden movement — my God, my God, I'm trying here with inky fingers to utter what can be only be left within!

It must be a long time ago that I experienced the foundations of my beliefs. But I want to ask myself still: Did I have any at all? Or did the foundations consist, in the final analysis, only of my father and the neighborhood from here to there?

I am looking for my truth. I want to see it naked and exposed. That is a painful thing, even the attempt. Hurt as a solution, a release — but from what? As though I had pressed my chest against a thorn and pulled, pulled, could not get loose from it. And now? The whole time something has been pleading, pleading that everything would last and stay the way it was.

But I must look at it and say: I despise those who despise! And: It's an injustice, however I think about it. But when the injustice here happens in the name of the People and their world-view, perhaps that injustice happens also at other places. And the question about what's going on with the Jews intrudes upon me more and more. But the answer that there are good Jews — those with a wooden leg and the Iron Cross from the War, and bad ones who haggle, who wheel and deal, and are driven by a wicked urge — is absolutely no answer for me anymore, is null and void.

Gabriel keeps coming into my head. And I'd like to talk to Hanno. I can't talk to my father, for starting today I'm afraid that this injustice could grow and spread over our German concerns like a cancerous tumor. And then I would hardly know what to do with myself and my innermost thoughts, then I probably would have lost my homeland.

Does my belief threaten to sicken into superstition? And Hanno, Hanno — why do I hear nothing from him? Here, too, a worry gnaws that there might be something true in the black tale he told me, that in the end it wasn't only overstressed nerves, not only the high, wild fantasy that is so characteristic of my friend.

But what shall I do with myself? I know only one thing: I want to seek and find myself and control myself. I want to be master of myself!

But during the night a dream about the woman and the truck came into my sleep, a dream about her poor, little head, about the crowd with its lustful faces, faces of shame, about her spread thighs and of the release I forced on them, into them, into deepest abandon! Then the woman opened her eyes, and they were blue.

Sinful thoughts that creep here in the darkness of my mind I write in my diary this morning in desperation, completely desperate. And read the words as they stand there after the last sentence of last night, and I'd rather kill myself.

September 16, 1940. In recent days the sky was so heavy that someone like me hardly dared go into the street: Indian summer like a dead day in winter, a superfluity of light, deepest darkness. It went gloomily in me back and forth, tenacious melancholy crushed me. Then chance ambushed me: I met Gabriel — Gabriel, his whole body ash gray, with gray, gray eyes as empty as caves — met him in the library while I was looking for companions in pain among the poets, as he probably was doing in his way. We saw one another and pretended to make laughing faces. Then he said: "The wild animals are ganging up! What do you think?"

"I'm thinking thoughts about resistance," I said, and I was serious about that. I talked to him about Anna Ritz, and meanwhile we walked out and then along the river, and Gabriel said: "When Herr Hitler writes that the fox is always with the fox, the goose always with the goose, titmouse with titmouse, field mouse with field mouse, house mouse with house mouse, then that's a faulty knowledge about Nature and leads to the false conclusion that the urge to racial purity is there as an eternal law. That's just not tenable, Cadet Colonel," he stated, "just the contrary: Natural evolution is characterized through permanent racial mixture, through which the formation of new species is first made possible."

"The blood of thoughts," he said, and had been up to this point so serious that I cheered up at hearing his horrible laughter again. "They feel they are tools summoned by God, my son," he said, and I really felt good being near him. "Each one waits until the other starts — that's the vicious circle. We have to break through it," he said.

We stopped. He opened up his briefcase: a pack of fliers. "The Anti-Spirit Lives," it said, signed "Song of Defiance." "Would you like a couple?"

But I — I wasn't clear about anything. We walked on. "And Hanno?" I asked. We walked along together for a long time. As we separated, Gabriel said: "The germ of ruin is growing rampantly, believe me, my son," he said, and laughed wryly as he left.

In October Reinhold came with Utz and Gummi to the dancing lessons. Beilharz too, who had refused to participate in dance instruction for two whole years, came along. He was head over heels in love, Gummi knew, and his inner priest was left behind.

After the first classes, in which it was exclusively a matter of learning "good manners," the question in the room was, who would become whose dance class gentleman and which dance class lady would say that he could be her gentleman until shortly before Christmas. My cousin, who had also come to the dancing class, stood whispering and giggling with the other girls, and Reinhold believed she was whispering about him and giggling because of him.

When Reinhold, Utz, Gummi, and Beilharz went for an outing in a rowboat to consult with one another on a lonely river island, it turned out that from the start only the cousin had mattered to Beilharz.

"But she's a cold fish," said Reinhold, laughing to hide his shock. "She's just ice and snow. Seen in the sun, she's nothing at all," he said and wanted to tell his friend about himself and the shame he had suffered through his cousin, but he couldn't get it out in front of the others. "She's a bleached blonde," was all he said.

But Beilharz looked up at the clouds and confided to his friends that he had already been thinking about giving up his thoughts of becoming a priest.

Reinhold had decided on Gerda Lang: without great passion but with pleasure. "Ash-blond hair, gray-blue eyes, I like her," he said. And then when each one had named his chosen one, the friends were relieved that no two of them had been after the same one.

"Where is the one who understands love?" and a long discourse ensued that for him it was more a matter of the soul than of the body. And when at a late hour they had arrived at their objectives, Utz said: "Maybe, quite consciously, mellow in a woman, smelling, tasting, with inner eyes!"

Gerda Lang had said Yes. — She's now my lady. I feel like a pair. Someone belongs to me — in the most trivial way, fine and good, but anyway. And it occurs to me that I'll distinguish people from now on. So quickly does pride arise, and it comes before the fall! Reinhold wrote in his diary.

"She's a high-class girl," Heinrich had said. "She's the daughter of a manufacturer, boy," he had said. "A man ought never to get stuck aiming at big things. He ought not to have to look up to a woman, but look down on her a bit. Don't say a word," he had said to Magda, who hadn't said a word at all, who had been cutting handkerchiefs for Reinhold out of Heinrich's old shirts, who slipped Reinhold some money saved from the household budget when he went dancing, "Dance money for the dance king," she whispered and laughed and squeezed his neck.

Reinhold invited Gerda Lang to the movies. "My parents won't let me," she said and went along.

He had already seen the film "Ride for Germany" twice and was enthused about the male lead, Willy Birgel. Gerda Lang put her elbows far over the arms of the seat pointedly into Reinhold's space. But he looked only at Willy Birgel and paid no attention to her elbows.

It was already dark when he took her home. The darkness made her beautiful, he couldn't help thinking, and they walked more slowly. He put his arm around her shoulders, she put an arm around his waist. They walked even slower. They stopped. She leaned her head back with her lips open. He put his mouth against her lips.

Then she pushed him away, closed her lips, and breathed heavily. And when with a hoarse throat he asked what the matter was, she tossed her head even farther back and her arms too, and said with a tremor in her voice that Reinhold didn't like: "That was my first kiss."

And he didn't tell her that it had also been his first, and he forgot that he hadn't liked the tremor and said: "What now? Where shall we go?" And when she said nothing, he jumped at a tree and yelled: "We'll climb the Himalayas!" And when she still said nothing, he ran back to her and kissed her a second time and said: "Movies are nothing compared to that!" And when she answered his kiss, he said: "Now we have secrets."

Then they took a detour, for he thought it necessary to talk about himself: "I'm seventeen. I want to be a poet." He had disengaged himself from her and had walked ahead. "Forgive me," he said, when he noticed it, "but

111

there's a storm in me, a heavenly storm. Also, it's that I wonder sometimes whether it's a storm coming out of myself or whether it drives me, whether I'm being driven by a power stronger than life, by a storm that whips up in me so much that I could burst. Burst the way you think you'll burst with happiness. Maybe that's happiness," he said and kissed her until she wouldn't let him anymore, and he said: "The moon's making me drunk!" And he did a handstand and walked on his hands next to her the last few meters to the gate to the manufacturer's villa and delivered her at the house door, just as quickly as he could, without being able to look into the eyes of her manufacturer father.

I've opened a new page in my diary that has the title "My Life," and there I read with excitement, as though I were reading something taboo, he wrote during the night. I have tried love — it tastes good. And so the woman for that shall be named Gerda. I'm sitting at midnight, and I can't think of a line of poetry for her.

There were no dancing classes during the fall holidays. It rained for days. Reinhold sat at home, played chess with his brother and his father, and he noticed that his father was quiet, and when he noticed that, he began to observe his father. — It seems to me as though a misery were being hidden, hidden away, as though the holes were stopped up through which it might howl — but what?

And he stayed at home and sat with his mother and read to her from his poets. And Magda had to weep listening to him and had to laugh. "It's about love," she said and stood there so alone, weeping and laughing, that Reinhold had to get up and join her.

For protection against the sadness, he wrote in his diary, that comes to a woman because her husband can't guarantee her salvation through love. And that makes me furious. But maybe that's the problem for my father.

October 21, 1940, the last day of vacation. I met Utz and Gummi on the Ziegenberg. We wanted to talk about women. When it began to rain again, we looked for the entrance to the old, abandoned mine, found it, saw light, went through the shafts toward the light, and came into a room with wheelchairs and stretchers piled up in mounds like junk.

"Not mining carts, stretchers" said Gummi and looked miserable in the miserable light that shone dully from the wobbly bulbs on the ceiling. When four National Socialist Peoples' Welfare nurses suddenly came running, we hid behind the equipment for sick people. — We are in uniform, we're Hitler Youth, we bear the braid of the Führer! So we marched through the shaft entrance after the nurses, as though that were normal. We walked through shafts, having to bend over. Warm water dripped from the ceilings. Again some people ran past us, men in overalls — again we hid. Iron doors led out of a large cavelike room. It was still. There were three of us and our hearts pounded. We opened a door, another passageway, higher than the shafts, carved out and built up, doors to the left and right. I peeked through a crack. There someone was lying on an iron cot: little arms, legs, ankles — young or old? The little arms and legs were flopping through the air incessantly. It was sheer death agony. From a side room someone came with a bucket and poured water over the insect. We ran away. But, led by the four National Socialist Peoples' Welfare nurses came a pack of ghosts toward us. We saluted smartly. The nurses looked surprised and saluted back smartly. The ghosts had only outlines, their faces seemed smooth white surfaces. The apparition galloped past us. But I knew the last one and held him fast. I knew him, for his temple was throbbing. I said: "You're Herr Daumer. What are you doing here?"

He had become smaller, or I just bigger. He was pulling another one along. I recognized his brother. One brother laid his head on the other brother's shoulder. The brothers looked at the three of us.

Herr Daumer unbuttoned his shirt. He had small, round holes in his chest, and he unbuttoned his brother's shirt. He had holes, too. And Herr Daumer pointed at the holes and said: "He's lecherous and jealous, the moon monk is, makes angelic grimaces and lets his rotten fruits rain down."

The woodpecker in his temple thumped, and I remembered the fright of my childhood and asked again: "What are you doing here?"

"The river of shame is racing along, and my bridge of comfort is crumpling."

"Do you live here?"

"In the Hall of the Moon, of course."

"But what are you doing here?"

"It's been ten years since the rowan berries were red."

"And now?" I asked.

"Now they are pulling and tearing at my inner oaken foliage."

"And why are you here?"

And when he said nothing more and only held his brother, I thought of the angels. I remembered that the man had spoken to me about the angels that time.

So I said, "Angels."

"I must save the Black One," the man said at once, and the woodpecker in his temple pounded like a machine piston. "But he runs wild and flaps his wings," said the man.

Again a pack of ghosts came toward us, and again we came to attention. The sisters were surprised, saluted us. The ghosts pulled the brothers along, a flood of ghosts!

"Let's get out of here," I said, and we succeeded and landed in the autumn rain under the trees. We ran to my house.

And then I saw my father's shock. And saw my Uncle Eberhard standing stout and brazen beside him. Saw my father get hold of himself and heard him say: "Sickbeds had to be freed up for wounded soldiers and injured ethnic-German civilians from Poland. Scientists, doctors, and nursing personnel are doing their work in the mine by the command of the Research Office of Ancestral Heritage. Inmates from old people's homes, from institutions for the crippled, from nursing homes and community homes find shelter there."

"Say it straight out," my uncle barked at my father. "The boys weren't born yesterday. We're talking about the project Worthless Lives. An Ethnic-German Research Institute has been set up in the mine. In that way tens of thousands of worthless consumers still get their reason for living for the community. The unscrupulous rearing of idiots, the rearing of the children of syphilitics, alcoholics, and the insane contradicts our theory of morality! Those born weak and useless are disposed of there."

My uncle is a beast, I couldn't help thinking, and look at my father sitting inconsequentially at the kitchen table. Thank God that my mother wasn't there!

"Compassion knows only one act: to let the sick die who cannot be restored. Only the healthy are fit to live," said the beast.

Then I walked with my friends for two blocks. We didn't know what to say, but we knew that we had seen another injustice.

At home my father was still sitting at the table. My uncle had left.

"The Daumer brothers," I said, "they're there, too."

"I know," my father said.

"Let him alone, else he'll never be able to bear it," my mother said, who had come home from evening services.

"My red house," said my father, and I knew that he meant the madhouse of his childhood days. "The red house used to be full of noise, now it's become still," said my father. And the man who had learned to help, as others learn brick laying or carpentry, then said nothing else.

There is a trembling in me. Something will engulf me and mine, engulf my people. Something can no longer be contained.

After the fall holidays Siegmund Eis was missing. The rumor went around that he had Jewish relatives by marriage. When Reinhold, in his capacity as a cadet colonel, asked for information from the school principal, he was told:

"Eis has gone to the Country Boarding School for Israelites on the Luneburg Heath. He is only partially incriminated by his mother, and his father, though a Jew by birth, is a holder of the Iron Cross. But he, who's a war invalid, got a tumor from his prosthesis and had to be taken to a transit camp for ill Israelites. His mother couldn't run the shop alone. That's the whole story."

At noon, when school was out, Reinhold went to the fabric shop of Siegmund's parents. It was closed, the door sealed, the display goods removed from the windows. He ran across the bridge to the other side of the river to the Eis family residence. The little house was abandoned, the window panes smashed, the walls burned black.

Reinhold made a report for his comrades. The report provoked indignation and was taken to the office responsible for the Hitler Youth. Two days later Reinhold, Utz, and three other Hitler Youth commanders were invited to SS Headquarters. There they explained to them the whereabouts and the future of the Eis family. In the East, they were told, a new homeland was being set up for Jews and Jews-by-marriage of the first and second degree. Eis, a three-quarter Jew, was staying until further notice in a transit camp on the heath. His half-Jewish mother had found care in a Jewish women's home. His father meanwhile was missing.

"I was faithful to you," said Gerda Lang, who had been with her mother for two weeks on Lake Teger.

"What do you think about the Jews?" asked Reinhold.

"Nothing," she said, and laughed.

"No, really," he said, "are you against them?"

"Anyone who's a friend of the Jew and anyone who supports him, about him I say that he's worse than the Jew himself," said Gerda Lang and opened her lips for Reinhold and swaggered along.

But Reinhold didn't want her lips. "I'll see you home," he said. "There's no detour anymore. I've got stories in my head, do you know what I mean?"

"Oh," she said, "women stories?"

And when he just stood there because he didn't know what to say, she cried out: "Well, is it maybe a Jewish girl?"

And he left her standing there.

And went no more to the dance classes. He had learned to waltz and to fox trot, to tango and to rumba — that was enough, he had decided.

IN NOVEMBER UNCLE FRITZ, the stage lighting technician, came and asked Reinhold whether he would like to be an extra in the State Theater. The Reich's theatrical days were coming up and they were looking for strong young guys. Also, he could earn good pocket money doing it.

And his uncle, who liked to call himself a lightmaker, took Reinhold along to the theater: "They're doing *Egmont* this evening. Elsa Burger plays Klärchen. You'll laugh. When she goes on stage, I need less light. She glows from within." And Reinhold knew that his uncle was smitten by Elsa Burger.

But when I saw her, when I finally saw her, and all around me only polite, gray art lovers, it seemed to me that my uncle had understated her. It wasn't enough that she caused the room to light up, she filled the empty faces that surrounded me, breathed life into the dead ears. So it happens, Reinhold wrote in his diary, that I will fill my need for light from now on with the magic of the theater.

And when, after the performance, following my uncle, I walked down a long dressing room corridor, suddenly she was standing before me, small in comparison to my size. Eye to eye I was standing there with her.

My writing flies away with me: She is a small creature, she was smeared with makeup, light from the stars shone out of her.

A different world belongs to every soul. Hers is wide and high, so that my gaze must hurl itself into her height. I could write poems about her! I can for once write poems only from a burning heart for another and not from a cold one against another. Words would leap and clink apart like icicles.

I could write poems about her, for she is a woman.

On a Saturday in November a direct mail delivery of the *Song of Defiance*, addressed to Reinhold, lay in the mailbox. Heinrich found it when he got the newspaper. "Muddled stuff," he said, "forbidden. Boy, how do such guys get to you?"

Reinhold ran to his room. BREEDERS OF MEN! REPORT BY A MAN, WRITTEN WITH HIS BLOOD, was the headline on the sheets. And further there was: *I write in the night, before my soul breaks free. I am writing with my blood. Little by little, horror has penetrated me, filled me, overcome me. They were trying to get to my soul. They wanted to rip it open and let bleed out what is left of God there, until the empty shell would be open for the angel with the tail. I am writing my last here: I am a cadet in an Ordensburg, from which the diabolical race, a consciously produced mutation of the human being, is to begin its victory parade and make a reality of the thousand-year Reich of earthly origin. How long has it been since I was alive? A year perhaps and a bit more. The way from there to here was long, and I am certain that it ran a long stretch not in this world.*

Here is my report: In the beginning we cadets were exposed to isolation, were tormented in body and soul in such a way that we felt powerless, totally powerless. We were supposed to be containers empty of Self so as thereupon to be filled with the damned. And when the emptiness would be filled so, then the superman would be born. If you are not suited to be such a container, perhaps because your mind is filled with the painful longing for God, then you will be sacrificed as I am being.

I saw it, I have seen it, I am a witness. The consciousness released by the nearness of death led me to that place where until then the order under the death's head, whose masters had appeared before in my unconscious only as shadows, worshipped the trinity of evil, the cosmic Anti-Christ. I looked into faces that had nothing of humanity in them and saw something that damns the past and the future, that prevents any salvation and all forgiveness. My power of memory is unweakened and sharp, but here I can write down only my under-standing or lack of understanding of what cannot be described more precisely, since the events have abandoned the word as a habitation: The beast of Revela-tions has been summoned. The creatures consider themselves to be the creator. The superman, begotten from diabolical knowledge, reared in diabolical cold —he is here!

My blood ceases to flow, and with that I lack the ink to go into great detail. My last wish is that this gets out of here and to my friends. But so that it has a chance to be heeded, I sign it with my full name, Hanno von Wolfsberg.

In addition, and this as consolation for the few whom I count as my friends, in this, the night of my death, in my deepest heart, which in spite of everything has not been lost, I concur with Master Böhme, who wrote: So the piercing and breaking shatters in death and falls into the freedom of the first will before which fear is terrified, death shatters, and out of fear springs a life in joy.

God keep you all!

"Song of defiance," whispered Reinhold, and knocked three times and called softly, "Song of defiance." The priest opened the church door, recognized him, and let him in.

In the room under the church they all were sitting together. Only Gabriel was not there.

"Where is Gabriel?"

"The Reich's Heini set his murderous crew upon him," said Charly.

"What does that mean?"

"They picked him up from the university — maybe another November death."

117

"What about Hanno? That piece of writing is a counterfeit, and if it isn't, how did you get it?"

"The post office brought it to our house," said the priest wearily. "And it's Hanno's handwriting. Gabriel authenticated it. Do you want to see it?"

And Reinhold saw the handwriting, red as though of blood and written not with a pen, perhaps with a little splinter.

"In the sky a great black cloud seems to take on the shape of a swastika," said the priest. "I don't know what to do," he said.

Reinhold ran away, raced through the streets, set the doorbell jangling at Hanno's house.

"Neither Herr nor Frau von Wolfsberg can speak."

"But I must speak to them. I'm Hanno's friend. What's going on with Hanno?"

"The young master is dead," the housemaid blurted.

Then Reinhold ran past her into the great hall. There lay Hanno. There stood candles high as a man, there his parents were sitting in two wing chairs like waxen people.

"What's happened to Hanno?" Reinhold shrieked.

And Herr von Wolfsberg said with eternal ice in his voice: "Your friend fell in battle near Paris."

"Only God can answer all the questions of man," said Magda, after Reinhold had told her, had gone to his room, lay on his bed, and did not want her nearby. "Don't forget Him," she said. "He gives the answer constantly. It stands written in the middle of your chest. You can read it from the inside."

That gave me a little life, the great human face that belongs to my mother, Reinhold wrote in his diary. Then she left me in peace and by myself. A heavy silence prevails in the apartment, after it has now become still.

Only from the distance did I see what lay on the high black bier and had been Hanno. It looked like nobody, just commonplace. So now the world becomes merely commonplace for me, for what could excite me still? From now on I am old.

It's night. A cold wind blows to me from beyond the grave. Hanno! the name, that word, was bound to me with so much tenderness and was bound with that body, which gave its lofty soul such fine expression. So of what interest should mine still to be to me, and how shall I trust it still? I'd like to throw it off and with that be able to understand all that is corporeal as something superfluous, just throw it off and arrive in the land beyond death, to find out about it, to make sense halfway of what is senseless, the only thing that keeps me going still.

Magda had not gone to bed, had remained in the kitchen, had darned and mended, roamed in her Heaven, had put her son's friend up there in a house, on a chair, at a table, had surrounded him with friends and had enkindled God's lights, had stood at the threshold and had heard the cry: "Help me, help me, do help me, Reinhold!" And was with him immediately, who clung to her, crept under her. "Mother, I am the mother, the mother," she had cried out.

Reinhold had sent her away, had gotten up, had dressed, had run out of the house.

His way led to the Ziegenberg. — It's not sleepwalking, it's my path! Something tragic is said to have happened. Hanno, it has to do with Hanno. It's not a daydream: Hanno is dead!

"Hanno is dead," he said to himself with every stride up the hill. Then he had arrived at the springtime place, the summer place, which was the one they had had in common, and he was waiting for his weeping. It didn't come. He sat and shivered. He thought of the Daumer brothers inside the hill on which he sat, thought of Gabriel, was forced to think of the von Wolfsberg house, of Herr and Frau von Wolfsberg, and when the thought of Hanno's sister came to him, he stood up and went home shivering.

I was sitting on the Hill and wanted to think about Hanno, but I was freezing, and my thoughts wandered in every direction. I couldn't stop them, gather them, direct them. Now I'm sitting on my chair at my desk and want to try to capture them in writing with numb fingers. But the cold won't abate. And so my thoughts are directed toward warmth: to creep into the warmth of a woman, to fetch Hanno, to grab him by a corner of his soul and pull him in, to me, into the warmth, into such an eternity. Amen!

The following evening in the von Wolfsbergs' house the funeral service was to be held. Reinhold stayed in bed all day long. His friends came, sat with Magda in the kitchen, crowded together there. Reinhold gave them the direct mail *Song of Defiance* with Hanno's report, went back to his room, left them with the terror that he had.

The friends went together to the open house for grieving guests. The house was airless because of the scent of flowers, candlelight, mourning crepe, from throat clearing, hand clasping. Many SS members there, stretching from one onyx sphinx to the other.

Black walls around a black cradle, Reinhold couldn't help thinking. And would the guardians of grave and temple now open up their maws, he now

119

couldn't help thinking, and lisp through beautiful, full lips with the loveliest of voices: "The glorious mortal here, he was chosen to be a ruler. From the days of his childhood on we kissed every stir of his heroic soul!" — and would a hissing mix with that soft lisping, he had to go on thinking, would they stretch up their wings, their eagle wings, and with them mightily cover the ceiling, would their steer flanks quiver, their lion claws grow, and would they crouch to leap, a great leap of vengeance on the black men of the wall, then in jerks through the hissing would come: "How did the one born for springtime, who was just now standing under the arch of victory, how did he lose his life, and for what did he suffer death?"

"In proud grief," the voice of Herr von Wolfsberg interrupted Reinhold's images, "we have assembled here, the parents and siblings, the relatives, teachers, the friends and the comrades of our son, Hanno."

Reinhold saw the priest of the *Song of Defiance*, saw Charly, Gisèle, and the girl with the red mouth. He did not see Gabriel. Saw soldiers and sailors, saw Hitler Youth comrades in uniform, and himself stood in the black suit that he had borrowed from his father.

Reinhold had asked his father for the suit, and he had not dared to ask why he did not want to wear the uniform, and his mother had also not dared to, nor did Mechthild, Utz, Beilharz, and Gummi.

Reinhold stood at a distance from what was lying in state on the dais between the sphinxes, surrounded by standing parents and siblings, screened by the black wall of men.

"We have assembled," the voice cut in here and there, "in order to celebrate my son, the dead hero. He died for the German people's soul. No priest is required to honor him.

> So do let the Church sink deep down
> Like a ship sinks with man and mouse,
> What is not of its spirit must drown,
> New in Gothland God builds his House.

"Our God is the Chosen Father Woden, his rune is the Eagle Rune. I place it on your breast, dear son, hammered from purest gold. I place it on your I-hood, on your I-Rune. Chosen Father Woden, who vanished when His oaks fell, Chosen Father Woden has sent us a new Savior, and in humility my son has brought Him, to Whom all must be sacrificed, the greatest sacrifice with his life.

"One day our Führer, the Law-Giver of coming humanity, will bring down the New Tablets from the Holy Mountain, the peak of the Elbrus. And perhaps he will some day, in order to complete his mission totally, die a martyr's death in great service. Probably not until then will we understand that he is the Savior of this world and the next. And so the Edda proclaims: 'But one day another will come, even greater than he, never would I dare to pronounce his name, and what he works will eternally preserve you.'

"I beg your composure. We will not plunge down into the dull despair of an abandoned community. We honor the young warrior by giving expression to our faith that the German God is the God of the Germans."

The icy voice clinked, threatened to break, stopped for seconds, froze together again. "And so I speak the magic words: Woden, Wili, Weh!"

"There's an alchemistical wise saying," Reinhold heard someone next to him say: "*When a converted man uses the right means, the right means works conversely.*" Charly's mouth was grinning, but terror stood in his eyes. "We're going to hold the wake," he said. "Will you take part with us?"

"Silence," the icy voice could be heard again. "Bestow now a mindful silence upon the departed."

Storm the stairs, Reinhold couldn't help thinking, destroy the black wall, seek the last of Hanno, find the last of Hanno, save the last of Hanno, and up and away, go with Hanno's last!

After the silence, Hanno's father announced that all the comrades who wished to hold a wake through the night were welcome to the dead boy and his family. The burial would then be tomorrow morning at eleven.

A lane formed, the von Wolfsberg family came down the stairs, strode through the lane. Behind them the Death's-Head SS came toward Reinhold, walked past him. Everyone followed them.

Only Mechthild and Beilharz remained, Utz and Gummi, the priest of the *Song of Defiance*, the redheaded Charly, Gisèle, the girl with the red mouth, two Hitler Youth, a naval officer, and two of the Death's-Head SS. An old gentlemen also remained, the priest knew him. He was Professor Geilfuß, Hanno's godfather.

The great hall is too big for those who are standing around by themselves, Reinhold couldn't help thinking. The man-sized candles, which a moment ago were flickering in the draft from those who were crowding outside, are standing still. Implacable flames from the implacable angel, the most dangerous one, lit by his blazing armor. Implacable angelic song prevails, comes upon us as a silence unbearably burdensome and overwhelms us. Here I am and am alien to myself, for lying there is what was best known to me next to my father and mother and has become alien to me! Reinhold went past those who were standing there singly, went up the stairs, approached the bier.

And then had to look at it: Hanno with his much too black hair! The face distorted as though something were missing or as though something too much was there, and on his uniform two entirely different hands!

"Something's wrong," Reinhold heard himself exclaim, "they've hurt him!"

Then two of the Death's-Head SS men were beside him, but his friends were also there, and the priest. And the old godfather took up a position before him: "By reason of my being his godfather," he said, and with his aged hand ordered the Death's-Head SS-men out.

"The black escorts," the godfather cried out, "the shamans! They tormented him and murdered him. And added on to him!" The old man gripped the brown hand, which lay under the white one, pulled at it and had a hand in his hand. Everyone screamed, flinched. "What is luminous lodges in the cold light," said the godfather, "and the alien spirits that have come into them carry on wherever they want, and they keep carrying on, nothing orders them to stop."

"God is the way He is or He isn't," said the priest, white as Hanno's other hand, which lay there dead before all of them.

As the only reality, as my old reality, Reinhold couldn't help thinking, it's past now, he thought and watched how the godfather examined the dead boy. Watched him as he took the false hair off of a bald skull, as he lifted the eyelids, saw that the dead eye stared from only one, saw that under the other was just refuse, watched as the godfather unbuttoned the uniform, saw the white, smooth chest, the tattooed rune.

"That is the realm of the dæmon," said the godfather, "it is the victory rune of the SS, but the lightning symbol runs from right to left and not from left to right. It's the diabolical reversal of the light rune. They all wear them on their chest. It creates the magical connection that binds them. And here, over the solar plexus," he cried out and unbuttoned the jacket completely, "here," he cried out, "I knew it: the threefold 6!"

"Hanno," said Reinhold loudly and against everything that had taken hold in his friend and on his friend, "Hanno! You will dwell in my soul."

"Six hundred and sixty-six, that's the numeral of the Anti-Christ. The Aryan Lodge draws its shadowy power from it," the godfather exclaimed. "I beg you to follow me, beg you to support me with your love for him, if I now celebrate a ritual against the diabolical powers for my godson Hanno, so that his soul, free and unbound from all darkness and all terror, can go forth wherever it will."

Reinhold saw the old man, the fragile man, the man white of skin and hair, put aside his ebony cane with its silver lion's head knob, saw him lift his arms with difficulty over his head and place his hands together, heard him call out to the Number of Numbers and the Light of Lights from eternity to eternity, and sink into those eternities.

When the pallbearers came to get the coffin with Hanno's corpse, the man-sized candles had burned down only a few centimeters.

The godfather said adieu, gave Reinhold his address, and the dead boy was carried out past them.

The weeping came at the grave.

"Where there are graves, there's resurrection," whispered Beilharz. But when the hymn sounded in a minor chord, Reinhold ran away.

He ran across the cemetery with its bare trees and stiff angels, found a place between gentle marble women bending low, and there wrote in his diary: This is the stillness of death. It cannot be disturbed by any cawing of crows. Those are the cypresses. They've become thicker. The comforting angels have crept into them, because they are weeping. They are ashamed. That is the sky, which is empty. There is the whole view of Nature. That He comforts everything is asserted. But if Nature has died her death, who then can comfort? What comforts a man whose outer Nature corresponds to the November of his inner one? And so, as I sit here, trying to capture my thoughts in writing, so that they will lead me off to something, to even a small bit of animation, it seems to me as though something were listening to me in my trouble and comes nearer as though from above and rises in my senses. I would like to call it Hanno, Hanno.

That evening Reinhold found himself in front of the municipal theater again. Elsa Burger was playing *La dame aux camélias*. He saw himself buy a ticket, looked for and found himself on a standing place in the balcony, and during intermission remained in the balcony. "Sleep standing up, not sleep walking," he said to himself. "This is the day on which I ought to die," he told himself. "Willing to die means willing also to love. Willing to love means willing also to die."

"Though she's an actress, she's natural," said someone who came onto the balcony after the intermission.

"And still she has a hundred faces in her face," said someone else.

"But the ambitious ones, the actors, they pay tribute all around her," said a third.

"Not interesting," said the first.

"I'll write to her," said the second.

I will write to her. She'll answer me! Reinhold went his way home.

The maiden Mechthild was sitting with Heinrich and Magda in the parlor.

"Boy," said his father, "we were worried. Why are you coming in so late?"

"Mechthild told us about it," said his mother and didn't know what else to say.

Magda and Mechthild were holding one another's hands.

Reinhold remained standing in the door: "Once, in the Middle Ages, or sometime earlier, the dead were laid, tied, and gagged in the ground, so that they did not speak, so that they did not come with their vengeance upon the living. I'll avenge Hanno," he said.

"Himmler's in charge of that," Mechthild blurted.

"And I'll write the letter!" said Reinhold, turned around, and went to his room.

He was sitting on his chair at his desk. He turned on his lamp, took a piece of paper and a pencil, and wrote:

My dear Madam, today my best friend was buried. Last night my suspicion was confirmed: He was murdered.

As children we had a feeling for divine omnipotence. That probably led me this evening to you in the theater.

And through you something like Faith and Hope came over me.

I will avenge my friend. That's one thing. And the other is that if you were sick like the one whom you depicted so wonderfully for me today, if she were you, I would heal you with my life.

Explain my words to me, answer me, write soon, since your silence should not last too long. Reinhold Fischer.

P.S. I am still in high school.

The next morning in the city newspaper it said that the student Gabriel Ellerbeck, mentally confused, had taken his life.

"Song of defiance," Reinhold whispered and knocked on the church gate in the twilight. No one opened it.

Something is happening, and something must happen, he consoled himself, as he waited hour after hour in the darkness of a building entrance opposite the church, to see whether someone would come out or go in there.

When it struck eleven, he ran away, raced through the streets, stopped in front of an old town house, found the name Geilfuß, set the doorbell jangling. The godfather opened the door.

The frail old man in the silken housecoat invited Reinhold to enter. At Hanno's funeral the priest had said that he was a German scholar who had lived in Chicago for a long time and written books there. At the age of eighty-nine he had returned to die in his native land.

The apartment was large and high-ceilinged. Old books were standing in tight rows from floor to ceiling.

"It smells like knowledge," said Reinhold. "I need knowledge so that I can act. Can you help me?"

"Yes, maybe," said the godfather. "You're a Jungvolk commander," he said. "How can that go on?" He prodded a table leg with his silver-knobbed ebony cane.

"They killed another friend, too," said Reinhold. "I found that out in the newspaper today. And maybe they killed all the others who had anything to do with him."

"They didn't," the godfather said and struck the table leg with his ebony cane. "I have a message for you: You are not to go to the funeral, no one is going. You are not to go to the church anymore either. You are to keep quiet, be quiet." He again struck with his cane and again: "Silence!" he said and would say nothing more about it.

And wouldn't talk about Hanno and not about anything concerning his death. But he did talk about the sacred books, in spite of his frailty climbed up ladders and took books down, opened them for Reinhold, explained words and symbols to him.

Night fell.

"The visible world," the godfather said then, "is penetrated on all sides by another world. It is inhabited by spiritual beings, whereby the first, insensitive to good or evil, can be instruments of either. The second, living traces of incomplete men, are driven by insatiable greed. And the third, finally, are our ideas that there act like real beings.

"The driving force by which one can have an effect on the powers is the will," said the godfather and held Reinhold fast with his gaze. "The will of mankind can exert influence on Providence, when it resides in a strong soul and the help of Heaven is at its side. Will and freedom are one and the same. Will that proceeds decisively is faith. It submits to all things, if it wants to go with God. But if it wants to go against God, young friend, listen to me, then it climbs over the boundaries of darknesses and doesn't find its way back, unless a great angel reaches out his hand."

The godfather stood up and lifted his arms, as he had done at Hanno's bier, and it seemed to Reinhold as though the man grew, as though he filled the room with himself. And he heard the old man speak words that he did not know: "Eheieh, Jahib, Eliah, Adonai, Iobel, Iaho, Iod!"

Reinhold had fallen asleep. The godfather was sitting in his easy chair, looking at the youth's sleep. He waked him up, when it grew bright, and gave him books that he had written years before. *Fire under the Earth* was the name of one, *Flood*, the other. Love stories. Puzzled Reinhold accepted the gifts.

Again the godfather demanded that Reinhold should stay quiet, and he poked him for that reason on his chest with the ebony cane. Then they separated.

Reinhold kept quiet, lay down on his bed, lay under the winter blanket. Wrote nothing, read nothing, and no reply came from Elsa Burger.

Christmas passed by, and then the first days of January. Sometimes he lifted the blanket a bit to talk to Schade: "Although you've grown fainter to me, even fainter, I can still feel you, friend. Hanno is somewhere else, perhaps so near that it might overwhelm me, and also so far away from here and black that I become dizzy and terrified. But the latter is perhaps only the immense terror that goes on within me. That arm is long.

"Oh, Schade, however safe and sound a man may be born into this world, however well installed mind and spirit and soul, and however imbued with body and network of nerves, still somewhere cracks in the structure do occur, from which then like lava the primeval sadness wells forth, the unavoidable certainty that I and you and everything, in the end, are merely meaningless. And if that condition lasts long, then comes the yawn, nothing else.

"Sometimes I creep out of the house like that sick man who, shut off from reality for years and years, wonders whether it even exists. Creep my way to the godfather, Geilfuß, who sits over books, over the greatest and most splendid ones, and still himself has written merely hardly more than coarse kitsch. How, in God's name, is one to understand all that, and why?

"And there's one last thing I want to tell you: I had seen in her a higher being, but now I consider her a woman and assume that my letter landed with a mild smile in the wastebasket in her dressing room. All right. With that, what's supposed to be my life would be plain and simple.

"And the last thing of all: Gabriel. I dream the worst dreams. But it would be my dream to see the three of you over there in your Beyond smirking with one another.

"And in the final analysis, my little one, you three all died of the same thing, and maybe I'll be the fourth.

"The Hitler Youth was a good thing, but now it's past. In good faith we served a bad master. I have laid aside the aiguillette in spirit and wear it on my body only so that no one will recognize that I carry a dagger in my clothes. Adieu, wherever you are or aren't."

At the end of January came a letter from Elsa Burger: *I had no performances over the holidays and through January, and traveled up to the Rhineland to my mother and sister, so your letter did not reach me until today. I would like to sug-*

gest we meet in the Café Deibl at five in the afternoon next Saturday. Should this not be possible for you, please leave a short note with the stage-door man.

REINHOLD WAS IN the Café Deibl at half past four on Saturday. The chair he was sitting on seemed to him to tremble. A reverberation of something inside, he said to himself and calmed himself, saying: "The only thing that a man has is the present!" and was startled when the same waitress who had served him and Gabriel at the same place at about the same time came and with the same words asked what he would like, and he vowed to himself, after he had said he was still waiting — for someone, he had said and blushed — vowed to himself not to forget Gabriel in spite of the present time that at any moment would approach him.

She came right on time. He jumped up, walked toward her, stood before her, bowed, didn't know what to say, and led her to the table.

Then the words came. Elsa Burger said them softly so that Reinhold had to lean toward her: "Was your friend a Jew or was he a Communist?" She looked at him. She had a frank gaze.

And he told her about Hanno, told her everything that he knew about Hanno. And the waitress came, and Elsa Burger ordered cream cake, as Gabriel had done, and when Reinhold continued to speak about Hanno, she also ordered a cream cake for him, as Gabriel had done, and Reinhold talked and talked, and Elsa Burger listened.

"We're closing," said the waitress.

"Will you accompany me home?" asked Elsa Burger.

Reinhold walked with her and walked next to her and kept talking to her about Hanno until he was through. Afterwards they said nothing, just kept walking.

"What do you want to be some day?" asked Elsa Burger.

"A poet," said Reinhold. "I want to write poetry in the old, sublime languages and invent new ones for myself. I want to create my hope and give expression to my longing by writing."

"Longing for what?" asked Elsa Burger.

They had arrived at her door. "I have to go up," she said. "It's gotten late. We'll see one another again." She held out her hand. He held it tightly. She withdrew her hand and left.

She was gone, and I sank, I drowned, Reinhold wrote in his diary. I wandered helplessly around her building and didn't even know which was her window. I still felt her hand, still smelled her fragrance, to think of which, to describe to myself I hadn't found enough time because of my wretched talking — a fragrance of such sweetness! Then the door opened again. There she was again, Elsa, again! Came back to me, said: "I hoped you would still be there" Said: "Forgive me! But, I..." she said, as though I had contradicted her, "I wouldn't have forgiven myself," she said, and said: "Come!" and opened the door up wide for me, so that, like the sleepwalker over the roof, I went up the stairs without falling. "I sublet from a piano teacher," she said. "Her practicing is sometimes bothersome, but I'm beginning to get used to it. She still has pupils this evening," she said and pointed toward the back part of the apartment, from which piano playing came.

Mutely I entered her room. I remained mute now, and now she spoke. My feet were standing on the ground and my head towered up to the stars.

"In our time there is much — much that won't let me sleep. People disappear," she said, "Jews and others."

But then I had seen the picture of a man that stood on a small table next to her bed. "Who is that man?" I had to ask, and she laughed because the question came blurting out of me. "My father," she said. "He was a Communist. He's dead."

We sat at a round table. She had brought salt crackers and glasses and a bottle half full of white wine. And she started talking: "My family came from East Prussia at the turn of the century with the migration from the country to towns that swept maidservants and farmhands, for ages without justice and without possessions, to the Rhineland. There they became factory workers, went in the morning to the large factories, stood at the conveyor belts and lathes, and by evening had earned just enough that it was sufficient to stay their great hunger. Their children followed in their footsteps, for they had no choice."

Elsa! Her nails were drawing patterns on the tablecloth. She talked and did not look at me. But I looked at her, heard her, filled myself with her, heaped this Elsa up in me.

"I grew up at my grandparents with my parents and a sister two years younger," she went on with her story. "They had a small row house in the workers' settlement. They lived downstairs, we lived upstairs. But we were rich: We had a garden with pear and cherry trees, rabbits and chickens, sun and shade, and my father knew every flower and every kind of grass, and knew stories about everything. He worked in the paint factory, which makes that famous titanium white up there where we lived. Every morning, singing and whistling, he jumped on his bicycle in his blue work clothes and came home in the evening, white with the paint, with stiff hair, singing and whistling. But sometimes he stayed out, remained away all night. Everything was too confining for him then, and he had to lie outside in the forest under the sky and breathe, and came back freezing to his women the next morning .

"At noon I went to him and took him his meal in a lunch box. In the gigantic workshop the hammering and pounding and stamping and screeching was so loud that there was no place left in the air for him to sing and whistle. He was standing at the conveyor belt, and I saw how it ate up the work and brought it up again and again and heard it cry out: 'Here I am, grab me, don't sleep, take hold!' But my father stood thoughtfully in all the rush, and his gray eyes were as though absorbed in each piece that he took in his hand. And sometimes from one corner of the great hall the *Deutschlandlied* sounded and from the other the *Internationale*. My father sang the latter often, out in the forest, out by the water, when on Sunday we rode on our bicycles away from the noise and the bustle. And when at school we were asked: 'What is your father,' then we said: 'Free thinker,' and were proud.

"But then the strike came, for weeks no wages, hunger at a thousand tables. My mother went cleaning. 'In the houses of those who are sucking our blood,' said my father. The pawnshops were full of clocks and winter coats, the streets in our neighborhood full of cops. There were protest rallies. They marched through the streets with red flags. My father was a ringleader, and I was proud of him because he opposed the injustice of the world, and I ran everywhere that he spoke, into the workshop, into factory yard, to the marketplace."

Elsa stood up — she is an actress and she must act! — got up onto a chair and portrayed her father. And the longer I saw her, the longer I looked at her, the more I saw myself in her.

And so, standing on the chair, she spoke, shouted and argued like she had done as Egmont's Klärchen, and, thank goodness, nearby the piano practice was still going on, one arpeggio after the other so that the content of her speeches could shock no one. "Comrades," she shouted, "we'll not yield by one step! Fight is the watchword! Long live the solidarity of all laborers! Comrades, some fight for international solidarity, others fight for their spoils. Comrades," she shouted, "and should we therefore feel ourselves a part of the nation and do without six percent of our wages? And what does part of the nation mean here? Does it mean we should see our enemy again in the English and French worker? Maybe we should soon sing again 'Victoriously shall we strike France'? And should we also then, again in the name of our nation, march off to war for the masters of big industry, so that they can make a pile with war materiel? I ask you, comrades, is that what you want?

"He was magnificent. I respected him," Elsa called to me "Can you understand that?" she called, and did not notice that she had used the familiar form of address to me, and jumped down from the chair and came to me in her enthusiasm and took my hands in her enthusiasm and pulled me up out of my chair.

I kissed her hands. She laughed and let me do it and kept talking and talking as her father: "'They had ignored the stipulations of German worker's rights, comrades, but we will show them that we're not without rights, like slaves, that we're there, that we're keeping watch. Keep watch,

comrades, and down with all who wish to make fools of alert, working people! Long live the German Workers' Movement! Follow me!' my father
shouted, 'each man has the right to live!' And he walked in front and sang
and carried the flag, and I walked beside him, and the cops drove along behind us, and I thought I was the daughter of the king.

"But fathers no longer brought the meager amount of money home, and
mothers could no longer buy the meager food. So, distress, so, battle. There
was a revolt, just a small one, one entirely unimportant for history, but one
that decided everything for me!" the woman cried out and flared — flared
away from me, I couldn't help thinking and was afraid for her. But the pian-
ist had completed the practice, and so I begged Elsa, for goodness' sakes, not
to go on acting Klärchen.

"Yes, yes," she said, and then whispered on and sat now on the floor, her
dress pulled up over her knees, her knees pulled up, her arms locked firmly
around her knees, and spoke up to me, sitting on the chair and not daring to
slide down to her because then all that I felt within me would perhaps, and
in the end certainly, have overpowered me, while she was speaking with no
idea that I opened my heart so widely to her that I would never again be able
to close it — I, a high-school boy, with nothing in my hands except myself,
ridiculous!

"It was the revolt against hunger," she went on and on. "The settlement
was sealed off, light and water were turned off. And sometimes suddenly —
and without regard to the rubber cudgels that guards were shoving — a
hoorah for the Soviet Union rose up — it seemed to all of us the Red flood
breaking all dams, the Red dawn of a new age, the morning light of freedom:
free people on free soil, following their own laws, united against the hand of
international finance with its people-throttling hand. It could easily have
happened at the time, and our spark could have lit a flame.

"But sometimes the rage broke through: Life is after all futile and wasted.
Let it go to the devil! Resentment had become hate. It took root and was like
dynamite. But you didn't touch it. You went into the woods, lay down on
the grass, looked into the sky. And sometimes a shot was fired. 'They're
shooting against hunger,' my father said, 'but they're not hitting it!'

"Then it became known that the concern would hire cheap Polish workers, if the employees did not show up again within ten days. After weeks of
strike without wages, everybody went back to work for the sake of their
wives and children. Even the Communists had capitulated. Only my father
remained staunch. He packed his things and said: 'I'm going to Russia. The
proletarian has no homeland, he's got nothing to lose. When I'm there and
have found work, you'll follow me.' But we, his women, we clung to him
and cried and screamed — so the man stayed.

"He and the other ringleaders were not rehired. The concern foreclosed on our house from one day to the next. My grandparents found shelter with their daughter, lived there in a small room, and didn't live there for long. We four got a room next to a movie house, where my father took a job as a janitor. My mother kept on cleaning for the factory owner, and sometimes, at night, my sister and I heard her reproaching our father. She had been a good pupil and had had a good teacher, a woman, and would have learned something from her to no purpose, she always said, and said then: 'What do you know about factories anyway, what do you know about those that are being built in Chile and Argentina, in China and India? What do you know, Adolf Burger, about the big concerns? Who tells you why this has all happened so that you are now sitting there without work? You know too little about this world, and so you burned your mouth and our skin. You don't know what's behind things, lurking, what drives them and stops them.'

"But my father kept on dreaming his dream and kept whistling and singing and drove with us into the woods. And I watched all the movies that ran in the movie house next door to where we lived, and my sister did, too, and we acted them out: Lilian Harvey with Willy Fritsch, Hans Albers with Käthe von Nagy, and when my sister fell asleep, I kept on acting alone, acted men and women, acted all the roles, acted myself out of the life into which fate had forced us."

"And then?" I urged her, for I was afraid that, now that the clock next to her father's picture showed three o'clock in the morning already, she would send me home.

"My father was without work for ten years. But he never lost his courage to go on living and never considered himself too good for anything that brought in a couple of marks, chopping wood for the priest and working in a field for a day's wage. Two years ago they rehired him, again at the conveyor belt. The young men had to go to the front, so they needed him again.

"And then — I had my first engagement in Neuss — I heard him calling for me at night in my dream, and I knew that something had taken him away from me. I got dressed, drove home — my mother and my sister, they said, were at the hospital. When I arrived there, my father was dead. During the night shift, no one knows how, he had gotten caught by the conveyor belt. There had been a blackout, no one could have seen him, no one could have heard him. The conveyor belt slammed him against the wall again and again, there where it disappears into the wall. There it had slammed him and not turned him loose until his chest was smashed."

She did not cry, but she was quiet and small next to me. And I had grown tall and powerful next to her. I took her in my arms, and she accepted my protection. I felt her life, I held it. Then she saw me to the door.

Twenty-one pupils of the graduating class are being drafted at the end of the month for the defense of the Fatherland! Fräulein Dr. Freitag read the names, Beilharz's was among them. A celebration was to take place in the gymnasium.

Reinhold's devotion to the Fräulein had turned into a slight dislike. — She's too loud, and the metal in her voice stings. Her walk, her hair, her clothes and shoes: She's lost her femininity! And when the Fräulein said to Reinhold that he was chosen to recite Hölderlin's poem "Death for the Fatherland" at the celebration, he declined.

My soul is burning me, Reinhold wrote in his diary. He's my poet. But he never created love, he only wrote poems about it. But my longing has overwhelmed my writing poetry, stripped me naked, divested me of words and towed me out to the open ocean where I must love or sink.

I should recite his battle poem, take my place before my comrades to prepare them with those glorious verses for their sacrificial death. It's impossible for me. Especially the word "sacrifice" echoes for me eternally and horribly from the mouth of Herr von Wolfsberg like the worst lie. Of course, I don't doubt that that greatest of all poets understood his poem entirely differently than it is to be understood here and today. But I no longer understand him and me and the world.

That evening Reinhold went to godfather Geilfuß. He seemed to be glad, invited him in to talk, offered him cognac. Brightly printed silk cloths hung over the lampshades. "Old age needs soft light," said the godfather. But the walls of bookshelves and the great white ceilings that merged through the French doors were as though set in motion by the patterns. — Like dreams that light here with Hanno's godfather, Hanno's dreams deposited on the inside walls of the rooms in which his godfather resides!

"Hanno's childhood was full of longing for a different world," said the godfather. "Sometimes his gaze frightened me. He seemed to me to see through the borders between here and there. He was predestined for the ecstasy of cosmic experience, and therefore he was also destructible. The dark men probably knew that," he cried out, and thumped his cane on the floor, "and they would like to have made use of that great talent, and misused it," he cried and thumped his cane, kept on thumping it. "But they were unable to break the wings of the boy's spirit, his spirit rose up, be consoled by that, my young friend."

I would like to have spoken to the godfather about Elsa, Reinhold wrote in his diary, but I didn't have the courage. I would like to have asked whether I might be sinning against Hanno here in seeking happiness secretly so near to his death. Instead of that, I left early and ran through all the streets that I have in common with her, and stood in front of her building and stared up at her black window.

She told me I should wait, she would get in touch, she said, and so she took any action out of my hands. So now I, unworthy, just wander around.

She's not in the theater. She's not acting there, not today, and not in the next few days. Where is she?

> You come, oh battle! already young men
> Descend in waves down your hills to the dale,
> Where boldly upward press destroyers,
> Sure of their art and their arms, but surer.

Utz was standing before the whole school, Reinhold wrote in his diary, stood there in my place and read the words that to me, who could have recited them freely, suddenly sounded pure and divine. And, although yesterday my senses supported me firmly against their meaning, their sound today swept me away, onto the mountain of language, where I would like to have stood free and dazzled by that greatest of poets, merely his tool. Still, my good Utz read line after line, droning and staunch, moved by the high tone and not by the words. And a rage arose in me, and I would most of all like to have taken my friend from his speaker's podium and set myself up there on duty.

> The souls of young men engulf them all,
> For the righteous strike, like sorcerers,
> And the songs of their Fatherland
> Lame the knees of the dishonorable.

And so, for the length of that high hymn, I was pulled back into the enchantment of what through Hanno's death I had had to experience as horror.

> Oh sweep me, sweep me up in the ranks,
> So that one day I will not die a common death!
> To die in vain, I do not wish, but
> I do wish to fall on a sacrificial hill.

And yet, Fatherland that had so completely possessed me before could not completely take possession of me, for the hill on which I want to sacrifice myself now is called Elsa. And this came to my mind, while I was standing with my comrades and looking into Beilharz's eyes and hearing that Utz had bitten off much too much with the poetry.

> For the Fatherland, to bleed my heart's blood
> For the Fatherland — soon it is done! To all you,
> You treasured ones! I come, who taught me
> To live and to die, come down to you below.

And as I was overcome by the fear that perhaps I would look Beilharz in the eyes for the last time here, it happened that amidst all my comrades, in full sight of the whole faculty, I suddenly broke into tears. This had steadily been growing in my depths with the recitation of the stanzas, until it threatened to overcome me. But Utz droned heedlessly and unmercifully on. And when he got to the last stanza, I had control of myself again.

> And heralds of victory descend: The battle
> Is ours! Live above, oh Fatherland,
> And count not the dead! Love is
> Yours! not one too many has fallen.

Everyone was probably compelled to think that my agitation had been provoked by the content. But I'm sure that it had more to do with anything else but that, more with my inner farewell, with the pain and the knowledge that much that is German, well felt and well thought, was colored contrarily, distorted, and turned from brightness to darkness. And, of course, it also had to do with the great assault on my heart that happened to me through the woman, that had assaulted me so that my whole house stands in flames, and all that I have is consumed.

On each of the evenings that followed, Reinhold visited Geilfuß, the godfather, and they talked a lot about Hanno and Gabriel, about good and evil powers, about war, and about things German.

"Longing," the godfather said, "that feeling of solitude and infinity, is the most German of all emotions. Just think of Tristan, my young friend. Close your eyes and put yourself into the place of that solitary man. You are standing high above on the cliff, infinity above you, eternity before you, your body aching, your soul full of torment. In that respect you are close to timelessness. Your soul longs, as does Tristan's, for something infinitely distant, an idea that for Tristan on earth means Isolde. And now into your desolation come strange tones, and to those tones you sing a song that cannot be captured by any words born of reason. The song grows out into the solitude, out into what infinity means to you. Sing, young friend, sing!"

And then Reinhold began to tell him and didn't stop until he had told Hanno's godfather everything.

"You're starving to death from your expectations, young friend," the godfather said. "Don't lose your way. Maybe the woman has had a man for the longest time, and she was intent only on tasting very young blood."

And when Reinhold was about to say something in protest, the godfather said: "Psychological confusion has its laws. Sleep on it well two or three times and entrust your pangs to your diary. *This sickness will go with the wind.*"

Reinhold had left the godfather, had run to the theater, had told the stage-door man that he had to get to his uncle, had hastened along the dark dressing room corridor — the song of the operetta from the stage had been exaggeratedly revolting to him — had found the dressing room with Elsa Burger's nameplate, had thrown open the door, seen her makeup gown on its hook, seen a picture of her father on the mirrored table, the makeup containers and the powder, the pencils and brushes, the hair she had combed out on the floor, her hair! Had brushed it together, picked it up, stuck it in his pocket, and run off, raced off as though he had stolen something.

It is February 17, 1941. I've gone crazy. I hold a few hairs in my hands, and that makes me rich. All the live-long day. And now it is night. I think constantly of nothing but her and don't want to sleep so that I can think.

February 18: She has drawn me into a maddened waiting. At evening doubt rose up, set his horse's hoof on my heart and stomped it. Not a sound is in me. I am a dark house without her. I have put out the night light and lost hope.

February 21. This morning her letter was in the mailbox: *Come. I need you. Will you be so kind as to pick me up from my rehearsal tomorrow at 9 o'clock? Wait for me with the stage-door man. Elsa.*

February 22: Carnival costumes romp through the streets already. I don't feel like wearing a costume. I just want to be me and no one else.

She came. We were both somber. We went to her house. We didn't talk. In her room we didn't turn on the light. We sat at the window. The light from the street fell on her face, and I saw the tears. We reached for one another's hands and climbed a mountain range beyond this world. Her mouth was salty from her tears.

I returned only late at night. My mother was awake, but she asked me no questions.

March 7: We see one another every day.

At noon the waiting begins. I stroll through the city, wander around. Is that you, Reinhold? Are you still the one you used to know? She possesses my soul, my spirit, and my being. And I want nothing more than to be with her and keep her.

Only sometimes do I worry. Sometimes it seems to me she is brooding over some sorrow, and I don't know how to help her and me, for I don't know about anything. The reason that she's not entirely frank with me is a puzzle to me and a secret to her.

March 19: It began while we were walking through the streets. She was laughing so much. Boundless body, I consoled myself, heartless body, for it wanted more from her than merely this closeness. We kept on walking through the streets, and she laughed more and more. We walked until it got serious. And then we kissed one another until our swollen lips were sore. And then we climbed up to her room. It was like an ache. The fabric burned on our skins. She asked me to, and I left her slip on. I set upon my beloved, and as a man did her no harm. A whole night long we were bride and groom, and at morning we returned hand in hand out of the land that lies beyond death.

"Why did you let me get so old?" she asked when we were in the world again. And when I didn't know what she meant, she said: "You should have come along earlier!"

"But you're still young," I said. "What do the six years that lie between us mean?" And I said the phrase solemnly that has been said so often since the first human beings.

"Anyone who loves has himself to blame," she said.

And I could no longer understand her, but believed it must have something to do with the secret that was becoming menacing, now, that morning.

I put my head in her hands and asked for her thoughts. I pleaded for her secret, but she couldn't give it to me and was tormented and said: "When war and this madness are past, then I'll try." And then she put her hands over her face and cried so that I thought she might drown in her own tears.

And then we embraced, and that was like a faith that we began to believe in, one in the other.

On March 21 Reinhold had to take his physical examination. On March 30 came the call-up papers.

He made his round of farewells, to Uncle Fritz and Uncle Otto, to Mechthild, Utz and Gummi, and to Hanno's godfather. His mother didn't stop crying, his brother played soldier, and his father asked whether he maybe wanted to know something about women, now that the seriousness of life was beginning. And Reinhold said that he already knew everything, and would like to have said that he knew the physical structure of a woman, along with its functions, more than only from the Brockhaus Encyclopedia, from the life-sized, folding illustrations in it that he had often studied again and again. "Of course," he would like to have told his father, "I love her very much, the woman, but otherwise I don't want to know anything at all. My head is chaotic, and so adieu."

Reinhold went to Elsa. Nearby the piano playing began.
"Come again before you die," she said.

Magda and Mechthild had come to the train station. Elsa was there, too.
The train arrived.
Elsa was standing apart from Magda and Mechthild. — They don't know one another! If they only knew one another now!
Reinhold looked at Elsa, looked at Mechthild. — Don't look at one more than the other! Or less! Prefer neither in my heart! To see enough of each! Oh! all the tears that the women of this world cry! You could drown in them!

3

"**Y**OU SHOULD LOVE peace as a means to new wars. And a short peace more than a long one. War and courage have done more great things than love!" One-eyed, noble, the major stood in front of the cadet officers and called out the words of poets as the sacred truth of the new world: "Friedrich Nietzsche, Hölderlin, and my George! You must read them," he exclaimed, "they are your lords and your masters. Devote your souls to them! But your bodies belong to the Führer and the People."

Since Reinhold had been a Jungvolk commander and a high-school student with a graduation certificate, he had come to a war school in Werdohl in Westphalia.

Before that he had been shaped and drilled for two months in the basic training camp for recruits near Altena. There he had had to share quarters with ten comrades, had been able to get to writing only at night, had taken a letter to Elsa every morning to the camp post office, and never received an answer.

The discipline here holds me together. My comrades do me good. The racket seems right to me, because from Elsa I hear only silence, Reinhold had written in his diary.

I search my memory, recover every glance and every word. I look in the green meadow for the yellow blade. Sure, I knew that a secret was behind her brow, and it was like a wall that repelled me.

I wanted to leave her my longing until, having come home, I could have been able to stand beside her as someone. But her secret separates us. She, who moves within my innermost being as though she were plowing furrows in my field, as though she were stripping the veins from my flesh — she guards her secret and is silent.

At night I hold her as a small creature tight in my arms, but during the day darkness creeps into me and is a morass within me into which I want to sink.

After six weeks without a reply, he had written his brother and asked him to go to Elsa Burger's apartment, there to deliver a letter from him, to look things over carefully, to look around there, and then to report to him.

Are our worlds drifting so quickly apart? he had written to her. *Will you allow that, Elsa? Full of yearning and heavily I turn to you and must surely make an impression on your soul. Or has something happened to you? God! I would demolish this world and the next! Elsa, answer me, so that I don't have to drift past you, so that one day I don't turn around to you and say to a beautiful figment of my memory: Your being echoes within me like a distant turmoil, to be sure, however the yearning faded away in me, the wound is scarred. The pain is gone, but within me my heart is so hard.*

His brother had answered him that Elsa Burger had told him off at the apartment door. She had said that they should leave her in peace, in the name of God, in the name of her father, that was what he should tell his brother. He had heard piano playing from a room at the back. It had been pretty dark in the foyer, and so he was unable to study her face, but he had noticed that she had stood there at noontime still uncombed in her dressing gown. — *She may be a flighty, fickle creature, I can hardly say, but there was something tremulous about her,* his brother had written, and: *What is that woman to you?*

For two days and nights storm and fire roared in me, Reinhold had written in his diary. Now someone can come and sweep me out, for here there are only ashes.

But who are you anyway, Reinhold Fischer, I wondered on the long marches with my comrades through the Westphalian forest, and step by step I resolutely cast out what was still within me of guilelessness and stupidity, of weakness and venom. You see more deeply into yourself, when you're so empty, and you hardly miss a will-'o-the-wisp.

Others had entered into my feelings, that much is certain. I had turned away from myself and to them and in doing that was almost lost for the Fatherland. Had let myself become lost in myself, had let twilight into me, had in the final analysis believed the godfather and the priest and Gabriel with all his *Song of Defiance* more than myself.

And the stuff with Hanno? They had injected me with their insanity, I had eyes full of terror, ears full of magic and mean enchantment, and smelled the bloody breath like a dog. Of course, my friend fell in a natural death, and like with many another soldier his hand, and his eye, and the skin on his head were lost. I don't know how to explain what the tattoos signify, but even there, seen in the light, there is certainly an explanation.

And now Elsa and the nature of her soul. Does she have one? If she does, then something happened to her that took it away from her. If not, if this one woman has none, then women have no soul. Then never mind.

Of course, more and more often the thought of her overwhelms me and lays me low, but I have lighted the extinguished lights again and put them back at their accustomed places, and a song has again been planted in my heart, and its refrain is Fatherland. The marches here are long and the training exercises hard, and my heart, although too big, too fast, is ready.

Old thoughts and goals arise in me again, old friends cheer me again. Comradeship lifts me, a lost one, up again, and everything that lies between the old and the new homeland, even Elsa, seems to me like summer light-ning. The godfather and the priest and Gabriel with his *Song of Defiance*, all of that, among men of war who set a firm foot here on the soil of their home-land, is like an elfin leg.

When the recruits had time off, they had swarmed out to dances, had in-vaded inns, and anyone who couldn't hang a lady's panties on the hook in his room the next morning was mocked, his manhood called into doubt.

"Shall we go into the woods?" Reinhold had asked the redhead when he was dancing with her, leading her, bending her back and forth. "You look good," he had said, when she had gone with him.

They had sat on the forest floor, and the redhead had snuggled up against him. "The night rustles so dully, so wearily in the dry foliage. It's seen the story too often that we want to have ahead of us," he had said and had moved away a bit.

But the redhead had snuggled closely to him, and Reinhold had gotten mad. Emotional faux pas, he couldn't help thinking, and then had given in to her a bit. And that made him even madder. Revenge on the whole sex, he had thought, and said: "Then just undress."

And the redhead had undressed, had stood whitely before him, freezing and shivering in the July night and said that she was still a virgin.

To hurt someone whom I can't stand, he found himself thinking. And had thought of Elsa's underclothing that had been between them.

And because the redhead had still stood there naked and trembling, and because her panties had fallen onto the moss, he had stolen them anyway.

Had laughed a little and then had not been able to look at the redhead any longer, had told her to get dressed again, had picked up her dress, pressed the dress into her hands. But he had kept her panties.

The redhead had put on her clothes again and looked for her panties and begun to cry. And Reinhold had been ashamed of himself and acted as though he would help her search. But he had put the panties in his pocket. "You'll definitely have a lot of children," he had said, "five or six."

Then the redhead had cried all the more.

"Probably you'll marry a rich man," he had said, "who'll put you on his horse and take you to his palace."

Then the redhead had run away, through the woods and back to town. And Reinhold had followed her so that no harm would come to her.

That night, after he had hung the panties on the hook in the room and had been exonerated from all doubt by a unanimous "All praise to what makes you hard!" from his comrades, Reinhold wrote in his diary: An incident happened to me, as though fabricated, for which, hardhearted as I have become, I'm not blameless.

But then when Reinhold had arrived at the war college in Werdohl, when the major became his teacher, he forgot women.

It is April 11, '41. And I feel like shouting, wrote Reinhold in his diary. For a long, long time I had the feeling that there was no one left for me here in this world, to whom I can turn in my search for truth and greatness, except for those who brought me into this world, and Mechthild, maybe Mechthild! Then fate puts this major in charge of me!

"Since our soldiers are already before Moscow," he confided to us, "a special force of Alpine troops has set out on a march to the Caucasian Mountains with the highest command to climb to the peak of Mount Elbrus, the magic peak of the holy mountain of the Aryans, to plant the consecrated flag there. The consecration of the flag on Elbrus will then be the sign, the symbol for the start of a new age."

Admittedly, the word "magic" is imbued with black and terror, but I can forget that in the face of the totally pure stateliness with which the major gave us that announcement.

As an officer candidate, Reinhold resided in a monk's cell of the former monastery in which the school was situated. He did not have to share the cell with anyone, could write whenever he wanted, wrote in his diary, wrote to his parents and to Mechthild. He no longer wrote to Elsa.

It is my yearning to be alone that I call my chief emotion at this time, and the happiness of experiencing it so often now because of the new circumstances. Being alone with myself! Only in this isolation do thoughts come to me that make my humanity appear to be meaningful and dignified. I withdraw into myself, I march into my most distant reaches, which are perhaps true infinity, and there I am able to wrest myself from any pain. So somewhere in my inner landscape the thought also came to me that it really never ever matters what we wish for ourselves in life, simply only what life wishes from us.

When a night-time attack, probably an English one, forced us into the bunker, I happened to be sitting next to the major, and he began a conversation and asked me whether I wrote. And when I said yes, astonished and also flattered, the major said that he agreed with Nietzsche: "Anyone who wishes to be a creator must smash what is old, along with its values. Free of tribulation, he has to act like a fool or a madman according to what urges him on. Also old formulas," he continued, "that once had value and endurance, cannot further be made use of unquestioningly, for the eternal truths will again

144

and again and for every age of man be driven from the depths of the soul into the light."

Above us flew the bombers. It was a great hour.

Reinhold received his marching orders for Russia. Heidelberg was his place of deployment. The second Heidelberg, in the middle of the Ukraine, a hundred and twenty kilometers from Odessa. On the way he was supposed to stop over in Kiev to deliver to the commander in chief there a personal letter from his major.

It was July. He had a week-long train ride ahead. He wrote a letter to Magda: *Mother, I'm off to Russia! But not to the front, though right into the middle of the country that, as our own originally, we'll get back with God's help. My major has sent me on special assignment as an officer candidate, and now I'm awaiting my duties full of expectation.*

"You will reach your unit the end of August," the major told him at departure time. "You won't get caught by the winter. The German troops will storm on, and the cold will retreat before them: The spirit has made a pact with Nature. You don't have to worry about winter clothes."

As an officer candidate, Reinhold Fischer set out on his journey on July 17th of the year 1941 with five kilograms of smoked sausage for rations in his pack. Russia was his destination, and his task unknown to him. His route led via Warsaw and Kiev to Russian Heidelberg near Odessa, Reinhold wrote in his diary. The guy was precise in body and soul, manly discipline and Fatherland in his liver, heart, and brain — and here follows a little laugh à la the erstwhile Gabriel. No, I don't think I'm lost, I'm letting myself be quiet and look out of the windows.

In Werdohl before his departure, Reinhold had bought himself a new diary, black and bound in oilcloth like his first one. He had titled it *War Diary*. In his old book there had been only two empty pages left, and he had sent it to his mother with the request that she keep it in a safe place — its contents belonged only to him.

When more and more people had gotten off the train and fewer and fewer on it, when Reinhold had long since traveled beyond the old German border, he took his new diary out again and wrote: You experience only yourself, in the final analysis. Time has streamed away to the left and the right on the railroad embankment, one stream flowing forward and one backward. I forget myself and much else in a condition similar to sleep for very long days. I look deeper into myself and deeper still, there into my bottomless being where no stone would land. But I'd like to press forward farther and farther, and this trip can't be long for me, for I want to travel into my innermost being, and there I will greet my God.

Anyone who has time to himself is raised above everybody and starts talking to himself: I look forward to the twilight, the fissure between the two worlds into which I want to slip, even if I must force myself. I wait for weariness with owls and sunset, wait for the trees of wild forests to become black and merge like a mountain range, wait for the gigantic blue sky of day over the endless swamps and moors, over the reaches of meadow to become colorful and oppressive, for the first red fires to glow from the dark horizon to the east, for blue ghostly lights to dance to the north, for farmers and laborers on the land to sink into the soil, and for everything to be right and find order.

So day by day I swallow the sweet drug of solitude and write, read, watch.

I have only one book in my rucksack, the field edition of Rilke's *Cornet* — perhaps I will need his example. Perhaps you must really know only one book in your life. If it's a sacred one, maybe that's enough. Mine is twenty centimeters long and twelve wide, and it's thin — it has only seventeen pages. I read it twice daily, so that I have it in my head in case someone shoots it out of my hand.

I write letters, and when the train stops, I put them, with no hope that they will arrive, into mail boxes. The train stations look devastated, the towns abandoned, stricken like the forest by war. Stomped crops, dead fields, wiped clean, shattered, farmers with wooden carts and bed clothes — Father, Mother, compassion overcomes me! And it seems I'm getting closer to the front.

"Comrade," says someone in the night.

Had the train stopped? Reinhold looked at his watch. — At this midnight you can well believe in ghosts!

"Did you hear about the prisoners? Did you hear the rumor going around that they hang like monkeys in a cage and we let them go hungry until in the end one Russki eats the other?"

Reality is fragile. Maybe I dropped it. Maybe I'm sunk in sunken Russia, Reinhold told himself. They've evacuated individual people out of time. They now can look into the empty trains of eternity, beyond good and evil. "I haven't, comrade," he said, "and can't believe it, either, comrade."

"Did you hear that the Cossacks slit open the living bellies of pregnant women and sew hungry cats up in them?"

Why should everyone you meet be a creature of flesh and blood, Reinhold said to himself. "I come from back home," he said, "and where do you come from, comrade?"

"From Jassi, Romania, from the slaughterhouse."

And then even more came down the train aisle into the compartment, past the compartment into the next. The field flasks were passed around, and war songs resounded.

> When the golden evening sun
> Sent its last rays down,
> A regiment of Hitler
> Marched into a little town.

Outside a red moon flew over a barren, gray plain. The one who had just spoken sang along.

> Sadly keened their song
> Through the little quiet town,
> For they carried to his grave
> A Hitler comrade down.

"But I, comrade," Reinhold cried out against the song, "haven't seen a Russian yet!"

> When the golden morning sun
> Its final beamings hurled,

The regiment of Hitler
Marched off into the world.

From the east a glow of light crawled pale and flat over the land. The train stopped, the soldiers got off.

The next morning Reinhold wrote to Mechthild: *For eleven days nothing but flourishing grass, swampy meadows, stretches of moor, stalwart poplars, red pines, white birches — now I can sing my Russian song about vast skies and clouds that drift.*

Mechthild, maiden, you are a good comrade to me. And so I want to admit to you that I have been startled two, three times from my sleep by the thought that came like a bullet through my dreaming skull: I'm in a foreign country, in the land of the enemy. May be that the front has moved, and I'm rattling around here in the middle of the Russian beyond.

No one put in an appearance. Not for days. Just tonight German ghost soldiers were suddenly there in hordes busy wanting to tell me that not everything that glistens is gold.

Fear of the front? Fear of death? Certainly, there's something in that. But maybe only those are brave who don't allow themselves to imagine things, to form impressions. I also don't know where I'll be when I get there and what I must do there. I have decided at any rate to shoot into the air and terrorize the enemy by roaring.

I notice that I think of Father and Mother a lot. And the sausage is almost gone. Greetings, Mechthild.

After two more days the train stopped in Kiev. Before the city the German army headquarters had been set up on a princely estate, in the middle a courtyard, a chapel with gilded onion towers, stalls, the lord's residence, and servants' quarters. No Russians, only Germans.

Reinhold was standing before the commandant to whom he handed over the major's letter, and he said no more than Yes and No to his questions about back home, about the major, about his trip, about his destination and his needs. — My voice has gotten hoarse from being silent. Language is familiar to me still only as thought or writing. And this seems to me worth striving for: the silence of the mouth and, from that, silence as a song among the words written down!

A private first class showed him where he would sleep, took him to the officers' mess that was in the former banquet hall of the estate, kept him company while he ate and ate. The private first class reported that he had taken part in victorious battles at the front, that Moscow would soon be taken in an attack, that the new wonder weapon was about ready to go, and therefore the eastern and southern regions of Russia would be conquered in a few days.

A good mood prevailed in the officers' mess, the food was abundant and tasty. "Tonight there's a big to-do," said the private first class. "They've flown in pop singers from home."

After Reinhold had equipped himself with provisions for the rest of his journey, which was to continue the next morning at five o'clock, he went out into the courtyard. In front of the chapel a rostrum with a loudspeaker had been set up.

There was then a gigantic roar, Reinhold wrote the next morning in his diary, again in quiet and after traveling for a short while. Two women came out of the chapel door. Where once Russian incense had wafted before icons, the two ladies had applied makeup and hiked up their skirts, the musicians had donned dirty tuxedos, they had begun shouting their heads off, had shrugged off all restraints before the sacred eyes and ears of that old world. Germans behave barbarically in the land of the barbarians, and I don't feel good about that.

But then they grabbed me and hauled me along into their world with their impudent songs and with yearning ones and depraved ones, and I could no longer control my behavior and roared just like the other twenty thousand troops who had gathered there. And in its whole irreality the spectacle seemed wonderful to me: Right in the middle of Russia they're whistling, they're singing, they're playing, they're dancing the war into the background! The roaring came to all of us as though from a single mighty maw. We roared out our fear and our hope, we roared out the shots we had fired, those that had hit us, roared them out along with homesickness, roared like lions and bulls. And all of a sudden the women had moved into the row of saintly icons, stood appropriately on the podium in front of the chapel, and bestowed foolhardiness upon us.

The following night the forest was in flames. A summer storm had broken loose. Incessantly lightning flickered through the loose blinds in Reinhold's compartment.

There is no thought of sleep, he wrote in his diary. Instead, memory rolls on, wished-for and unwished-for memory, a sorrow buried alive rises up and overwhelms me: Elsa, and again and again, Elsa!

And when the lightning had set the forest afire, when the old forest with a groan burst into flame and began to burn, the certainty came to me that it had to have been a serious problem, a matter of life and death, that brought silence upon Elsa, that had driven her to pretend to my brother. And I, I have felt only my pain! But you have to look away from yourself, if you want to learn to love.

Meanwhile it has become hot in the compartment from the fire, the odor of wood and resin penetrates with the smoke through the closed windows. The spectacle outside is large, glorious, and dangerous. The fire rages around me. Hanno, Schade, Gabriel — it's into the fight!

THE TRAIN WENT on without stopping. In the gray of dawn appeared stations whose names, lit by station lights, were standing in the twilight: Rohrbach it read in German script, Speyer, Sulz, Katharinental, Josephstal, Karlsruhe. And then came Heidelberg.

Reinhold was ready to go, stood at the window holding onto the window grip. — The ground of reality under my boot-shod feet is slippery in the early morning after the flaming night, and with every new light in the land of the enemy a name from home stands before my eyes. Russian Heidelberg in the gray morning — it's enough to make you lose your senses!

Reinhold marched through the city. — I'm a German soldier with Russian eyes on me! He struck the nail studs of his boots on the pavement. The ground under his feet remained slippery.

A small river flowed through the Old Town of Heidelberg. — The Neckar must be broader. I've never seen the Neckar. Will I ever see the Neckar?

Then he met German soldiers, who gave him directions to his company.

At a street closed off with barbed wire he found the headquarters: a stone building, a courtyard on which grass was growing, next to it the police guard house.

It was already hot in the morning. In front of the guard house were chairs and tables. A couple of fellows were lounging in the shade. One from the army offered him schnapps, said that the company had moved out and would not return until in the night. Another man in civilian clothes, one of the Gestapo, showed Reinhold his bed in the stone building.

"I've been underway for two weeks," said Reinhold. "Where does the front run now?"

"Five hundred kilometers farther in the direction of Siberia," said the man in civilian clothes.

"And what do we do here?"

"You'll see! Give me your papers and fill out the questionnaire. Then come down to the guard house."

In the office men were standing together in black uniforms.

"Ah, he was a cadet colonel," said the man in civilian clothes. "Great! Boy Scout, you can lead us here on new bloody paths." He gave Reinhold a mimeographed piece of paper: "You can read? Then sit down in the shade and have a good day. Nothing's happening here today for you."

Reinhold sat down at one of the tables that stood in the street in front of the guard house.

"Cup of coffee?" asked someone.

"Go on, coffee!" mumbled someone, "he'll get blood to swig."

Laughter on the street.

"If you run over there," the mumbler pointed to the barbed-wire blockade, to the empty streets beyond it, "you'll get blood to swig. The Jews draw off blood and give it to their brats with water and rye meal to eat as soup. The blood from the Red Sea!"

Laughter on the street.

The sunlight had become harsh. — Excited light, light over a place that seems to be there for nothing more than that you leave it behind you, vanquish it! Reinhold drank the coffee, read the mimeographed scrap of paper: *We are fighting a battle against the Jew. And we will allow no more Talmud turning, and no Talmud turning will help him anymore. For if with the help of his Marxist creed the Jew is victorious over the peoples of this world, then his crown will be the death wreath of mankind, then this planet will move void of people through the ether as once millions of years ago. Signed: A.H.*

Reinhold saw the light shimmering over the blocked-off street. "Where does it lead?" he asked.

"Into the Jew hole," mumbled the mumbler.

"WHEN YOU WRITE, you don't die," Hanno told me. And so I have written down a nightmare from which no one who has dreamed it will ever awaken.

I approach the street. I lift up the barrier.

"Let him go ahead," someone calls behind me. "He'll be coming back when it stinks enough for him. The Jews stink," someone calls behind me, "like when new wine is fermenting, like cow piss."

I walk along the street. Light is dim. Quiet, in the middle of the day.

"Mange eats away at Jewish hide," someone calls behind me. "Gangrene and scabies are infectious, Comrade."

A wet dog with a bleeding eye and a rabbi's hat tilted on his skull runs across the street. The dog face is nasty and caustic. Has the dog gone mad?

Tones come from a house, rise, fall. A trembling creeps over the dog's body. The dog eyes well over. Two other dogs come, also wearing hats, also have bloody eyes, are also wet. — They aren't wet! They been skinned alive! SS guys are there, break out laughing.

I follow the tones. The house has no door. It is dark. A boy comes to me, asked me in German: "Are you from the Hitler people?"

The tones are being sung by people who are sitting together on the floor. I sit down with them. They move away. They go on singing. "El male rachamim," I understand, and again and again the same "El male rachamim."

"What does that mean?" I ask the youngster.

"God is full of mercy," he says. "They're celebrating."

"What are they celebrating?"

"A child has died and been carried to Abraham's bosom by an angel. In Abraham's bosom the trees grow, the heart of God beats."

Outside there are shots. They keep on singing. I run outside.

"Schnapps?" one of the SS guys offers me a bottle.

"What were those shots?"

Wind is rising, stench, sweet and sharp.

"Why does the chicken have to cross the road! Can't it wait? Tomorrow it's off to Jerusalem anyhow one way or the other."

Laughter. They walk on.

I see gray, thin legs in the gutter. I've never seen a human being so thin. His head lies turned completely to the side, as though he wanted to hide his face. The coat has a red spot.

I run back, find my bed, fall asleep. The smell of blood sits like something runny fast in my nose.

In the middle of my sleep comrades pound to the left and right on their cots.

Toward morning someone yells: "It's time! Get up, comrades. There's a dance presentation. The piece is called the St. Vitus' Dance."

Twenty, thirty troops hang around the windows. A man comes into the courtyard, a truck catches him in its headlights. The man lurches, hops. Someone shoots, the man hops. The shooter aims next at his feet. The hopper cries out. The shooter has a fool's clapper, he claps and rattles with his left hand for the dance and shoots with his right. The hopper screams, takes gigantic hops, his body lurches, the fool's clapper claps.

Then a shot hits, my comrades howl, now the hopper still hops only halfway, falls. The twitcher just twitches. The headlights switch to high beam, brains pour out of the skull on the ground. The headlights go out.

> Old Heidelberg, divine,
> You town so rich in fame,
> On Neckar and on Rhine
> No other is the same.

My comrades are sitting on their field cots and singing! Outside on the square lies the fool. Blowflies, bred in the swamps, not accustomed to human things, sit in black clumps and devour the fool.

I run into the courtyard. My comrades are singing.

> Town of fellows of good cheer,
> With wine endowed and wise
> The river's waves flow clear,
> With a flashing blue of eyes.

It is already hot in the morning. There's already decay. The fool as a last defense rolled up the pupils of his eyes and left the flies only the whites.

Three trucks are parked in front of the guard house. A fourth comes, bringing its load of women, white, faces down. Naked flesh wobbles like jelly back and forth. The truck stops. They drag the fool up, crumple him, toss him over the tailgate onto the women. The truck drives on.

I report to the company commander. He is wilted from the night. "We're a small, dedicated company here, are dependent on one another in the midst of our enemy," he explained to me and said: "Your turn comes at noon."

Men in black uniforms are sitting in front of the guard house. I sit down with them. I receive a breakfast egg.

The one from the Gestapo, who during the morning showed me my bed, comes, holding up bloody hands: "I harvested before breakfast. The blueberries are ripe!" He disappears into the building. Water rushes.

When he comes back, he sits down at my table. "The Jew," he says, "is a principle, the Jew is pious, the Jew is crazy." He laughs crookedly and continues speaking earnestly: "That melancholy race stretches its faith too far. Its God floats in Jewish blood. He gasps for air, does God. God drinks to the dregs."

"Too late, you'll never rescue that God now, so take the life of His children," someone at the next table roars and whips up his pistol.

"Under the bombs of the Jewish terrorist pilots our women and children at home must lose their lives," says the man from the Gestapo. "Anyone who is still sentimental," he says, "will not accomplish our business."

Two more trucks arrive. People gather on the square in front of the guard building.

"Curiosity seekers from the Old Town," says the man from the Gestapo, "they need a few movies in their backwoods."

The barrier goes up. Those who live on the street come onto the square. They form lines, are quiet, line up as though for tickets. Groups are assembled, names are called out, those called climb onto the trucks.

"What'll happen to those on the trucks?"

"They'll travel to Jerusalem."

Laughter.

The trucks are standing in the sun. Those on the trucks are standing, are tired. Their faces become too heavy for them. They can't raise them.

Someone hands me a rifle. I climb onto a truck. The trucks drive off.

Next to me someone moves his hands as though he were wiping dust from his chest, from his brow. When the trucks turn into the lanes of the Old Town, he tears his clothing, slowly, without an outcry.

The trucks drive along the river, past the train station and for a long time on a straight road next to the rails. "That's my way back," I think. But then the road comes to an end. It gets lost in sand.

Then we're off into the Russian forest. Carnivorous plants bloom, thistles, red poppies.

"Brother Body," the one next to me says to himself, "it's off to Jerusalem," and then he strikes his wiped-off, ripped-bare chest.

The forest grows thicker. Warm, dry light and twilight. The man next to me says: "This is the path to death, isn't it?"

But my mouth is dry, my tongue sticks.

Then the truck stops, then we climb out. Then we go on our way on foot. The crane flies are humming, the woodpeckers hammering, the jays jabbering.

Ahead of me the long line of those who are on the path that leads into the thicket. A malicious, stony path that crunches under our feet. Out of the long line, out of the weary stream, out of its breath, a mist comes, creatures turn and wander off among the trees. Does a human being release his spirit like that?

A moaning runs through the line, from the front far ahead of us, backward toward us. The stream comes to a halt. A whimpering, a soft howling tone presses into me.

My throat is burning, my mouth is screaming, then I am screaming, then our own men catch me and tie me to a tree.

The sun has set. Grass and fern are damp. A coolness comes from the forest. Naked people are lined up beside ditches. A high piping is in the air. Those are the minutes of death piping, time plunges. There's piping.

They stand up at the edges of the ditches. No one bends over to look at the bottom before the shots sound. I didn't know that shots make such a loud noise. I didn't know that there were four, five seconds before the blood comes, as though the flesh would first take fright, only then bleed. The deeper the shot, the nearer to death, the longer the fright — I did not know it was longest of all with a shot to the heart or the head.

It endures, short or long doesn't matter, for such a thing doesn't pass, it endures, in the midst of creation, like lead, presumably forever.

Vapor over the ditches. They pile on dirt. Dirt rises from breath, floats down. Dirt is piled on. Dirt moves. They grasp, grab, still breathe for life!

Then I am untied from the tree. My feet start to run. They shoot at me. They laugh.

I'M SITTING NOW in a clearing in the sun and telling myself what I cannot grasp. I must describe it to myself, must seize it with words. It must be put into words, so that I can grasp it.

"When you write, you don't die," Hanno told me.

I am eighteen years old. I've run away. They shot at me.

Am I a deserter?

I am a deserter, for I've counted the days seven times and the nights eight times now. It must be September already: scorched earth, bent grain, broken clods of earth, rock-hard stones, sultry heat, no bird song, nevermore this year.

The corn has been eaten up. The rest that I couldn't eat dried up in fields all around. No farm trucks came. I have collected dried clustered flowers for days. — You can make a fire and cook corn soup! You build a shed in the forest, you collect the cracked grain, and put provisions under a roof!

The Robinson in me takes shape. It seems to be a rule that you maintain yourself. It seems that life is natural and death against Nature.

As I am here, I have nothing outside of myself. I can think and survive. I have nail-studded marching boots, I can walk across the landscape.

Hanno and Schade, Gabriel, Father, Mother, Brother! Under the immense sky, in the endless swamps, in the deep, deep woods no human being is with me. It's as though I'm the one who has survived. There's no sense in looking for sense, in climbing a hill, in digging into the earth — this is the world, and its sense and my sense must lie outside us, over or under or near us. Here it's the way it is, and it will stay that way, whatever you want. Or think, feel. It doesn't matter how you control yourself.

You must know that I spend the night with open eyes. No sleep, no courage to sleep. I stand and sit and lie down on the human earth, on earth that is made of human beings. And my lost ones grab me with their poor arms.

At night you also see deeper into yourself. You see in yourself what has passed away, what has passed away from yourself, and what has passed away of those who belonged to you. So deep inside of me then, when the trees of night grow closer together, your face flashes, Hanno, and yours too, Schade, flashes, and I see my past with long Hitler Youth strides run toward the dark bride who becomes ever darker. But your faces, friends, have become brighter.

In the Russian forest, in the forest of death. It must be October. I have a beard. There are still apples under the trees. The earth is cool now and the forest still. The black birds are gone. I ought to dig myself in, become a root man, hibernate.

For a long time I was not my own master, at times didn't know whether what happened took place, whether I remember really or whether it was told to me. But now I know my way around in my four walls quite well, so that I can let one or another thought of remembrance rise up without immediately stomping it into the ground.

And here I know, too: Not everything is dead that lies without breath under the earth! That is not a fear of ghosts, certainly not. It's my new knowledge, born out of the long time with myself in the forest, that the Being is not illusion that comes upon me, enters, flashes, that it's Being itself. So why fear ghostly shapes, when I will not fear shapes of memory in me that are just that. Whatever! After all, they are friends who belong to me.

But when the nights are deep and dark, when the nights become nights of death, when the grave toads creep into my dreams and with gaping maws tear out what I hastily buried, when I think of Hanno, and when I must think that now I must believe what I didn't want to believe! And when I think of my German people! When I lie flat on dead branches and rustling leaves and the only thing that still matters repeatedly is what happens at the beginning of the forest! When at morning the mists overtake me and I stare into the day with the gaze of an animal and my ear roars: Look for it, look for your life! — Then derision comes over me, then derision knocks me down, then I surrender myself.

Days later. I had forgotten to write and want to start again.

It's getting cold. No freeze yet, but rain, pouring rain. For days I've been wet. My provisions are running out, for nothing is growing and ripening now. I must ration my food. And that's ridiculous, since I certainly don't know how I can get through the winter in my thin German uniform. But my inner disciplinarian is victorious: I get two handfuls of this or that daily. Mostly the food is raw, for when the brooks pour down from the trees, the fire won't light. My face must be that of a dried-up corpse. I get an idiotic delight from counting my ribs. Ought I to eat the last gray grass?

Autumn. Autumn is all around, wherever it is ending and disappearing. The hills don't give a damn what happens to what remains of creation. Nocturnal storms shake me and with their howls deafen me to the last mouse that squeaks because I step on its hole.

I am a wild man of the forest, and it seems to be that, except for myself, there's no other animal here. I talk to myself about home, I entertain myself as well as I can. I gossip with Mechthild. I pull the pins out of Fräulein Dr.

Freitag's hair. I balance in January on the ice-slick bridge rails over the river of my hometown. I become younger. It pulls me back.

To my mother! When I was little, Mother, my thoughts of myself were contained in those of you. Then came manly things, and my selfhood and being myself seemed so vital. Not that I would have thrust you away or parted from you. I merely set you out of my center into a nice corner on the edge. You accepted that without complaint as your place. And now, at the end of the world or life, I'd like to get out of my center and would like to share that small place with you.

Mother, I've gone along on one path of death and have at least one more ahead of me. Soon I'll have been in the forest for three months. I still had the birds before, and the mosquitoes, and now and then a fox — now I have only my watch. I take pains to hear it tick, want to think it's the heartbeat of something alive with me, a small piece of life, Mother! And in addition: Wherever I am and remain and wherever I get up and go, there follows me a black bulk. But it's only fear and nothing more. I should make a list of my fears, but the leaves of my good book would not suffice, and I must save them, for they are the only reality that I have.

And now to my father! Our soldiers are demolishing this world and the next. They have slain the human being within themselves and the one in us, if there was one in us and one in them.

If I look back, I get dizzy, for I have to look into the abyss into which values plunged me. It's war, it's war, Father! I'm a soldier, Father! But any-one who obeys, Father, doesn't belong to himself.

So now I'm here by myself, Father, and obey only myself. And my heroic death will belong solely to me, in a week or two. But that my body will not rest in German soil, which is still a painful quintessence of my homeland, is to me bitter in spite of all swindle and abyss, in defiance of all horror, truly!

One more thing, Father: Did you really not know what is happening here and there, what certainly is happening where you are? Do you still not know it? They promised us light, and now darkness prevails, and it opens up its jaws, swallows, swallows God and His world. And Father, Hanno was right: The cold has spread. What is quintessential has hardened for many, and those too many now perform their work of butchery on the instructions of darkness and cold.

There's war, Father, war against mankind and against its God. But if it's man who wages war, what then is God?

And one last thing, Father! I am in the land of Dostoyevsky, who wrote: *I am afraid of one thing: not to be worthy of my torment.* I want to tell you this, Father, for the torment will come over you, if you just listen and know. And so I would like to stand beside you once more so that I could speak the Russian word for *dignity* to you, since I no longer wish to use the German word for *honor*. My brother must now do it in my stead, and he must grow up quickly.

And so, to my brother: You were always too young for me. That's my fault. When I could still go along my paths, I should have taken you on this and that one. That's my failing. I have accepted you as one who is there and for whom I remain. That was my mistake.

My world is shattering, and perhaps yours still has an aroma of happiness. But I warn you, Brother! You can't be peaceable, being peaceable is base. The trashy Gothic novel that is called Germany is firmly written, and if you read it and then don't reach for your knife, then you have been a human being in vain.

Until recently you were two heads smaller than I. Now I beg you, Brother, grow taller than I am quickly.

And now to the woman whom I don't know what to do about: Elsa! I read in my prized possession, in the *Cornet*, which I've been carrying in my pocket up until now as one carries one's prized possession, with my hand on it, even at night. After all, it contains only the thoughts of another that, with me being so alone, reach me and lift me up here. And, Elsa, in many a sentence the other's as well as my own seem mine, as when I read there: *They will give one another a hundred new names and take them all back from one another again...* And then when I read on, it says: *God, Thy will be done.*

But I don't want everything just to fade away and nothing to become strong and to resist that Away. Elsa!

And again days later. My inner emaciation has gained in extent. Hunger begins to howl and lures wolves and fantasies.

I look for memories, for streets and squares. I don't lose my homeland. I see my street. It is my street, but I don't see the houses. I can see up to the forest, to the Ziegenberg. The sun shines there, but here a sign is formed of smoke and gaslight in the sky. Earlier the buildings were tall, now they've collapsed. Maybe the gas works exploded. Its black boiler stood two blocks away, before. The sign of smoke and gaslight is forming in the sky! Did they all lose their lives, or did it happen at five in the afternoon, my father on his way here, my mother there, my brother somewhere else? I enter my street. A few façades are still standing. They fall over because of the vibration my steps make. The sign is forming in the sky. There, where formerly the house with the greengrocer's store stood, I hear whimpering. I look for the whimpering. I dig with my hands in the bricks, I reach into a hole and pull small human beings out. They seem familiar to me. Perhaps they are people from the buildings on my street. They're very small. I collect them in my arms,

160

but can't hold all of them. The sign of smoke and gaslight is forming, but I can't read it.

So my brain shilly-shallies to itself, it drivels along. Or is there war in my town, are my parents threatened? Will I die here, they there?

It may be days later. It may also be that I continue to write on the same day after a pause.

I'm tired now, and it would be good to sleep. Also it hardly gets light. When I'm not running around with aimless steps, I huddle under two fallen trees that offer protection from the rain, in the last dry moss and leaves. Here I associate with the dead.

Today I met Gabriel. He's really cheerful, and his bleating laugh brings up whole herds of goats. Near him I also saw the red shock of Charly's hair. I joined the two of them. We walked through nature here and talked about the dull sense of those who look for the dead man in distant emptiness, whereby they could have looked only into their own inner selves to find him there.

"And if you find him there not whole," said Gabriel, "did you find him whole when you had him outside before you?"

We walked, and it became a wandering. Having become familiar with earth and air, myself soon air, myself soon earth, I could keep up. But in the end, everything proved to be a guided tour, and it ended with Hanno and Schade.

Then the earth stirred.

"But the earth does stir," said Gabriel and bleated away.

"That it still can stir!" said Schade with astonishment.

Hanno took my hand and walked farther with me. We didn't have to talk about anything. I surrendered to the happiness of walking at his side.

When we heard sounds of the Ave Maria, Hanno turned my hand loose, and I let him turn it loose, didn't hold on, in the certainty that he would come again and again.

I followed the sounds and was then alone. I came to a village. I saw a small church, but its steeple was broken off.

"Is that sound my death dream already?" I said to myself. In a death dream all the bells toll, and all the gates open wide! Or who has tolled which bells here?

I stood and listened to the deep: Probably a lake is in me in which I would like to sink, and the bells may be tolling from my sunken landscapes, from the towers in the reservoir lake, in the moor lake. And the howling that is just beginning, is that howling coming from me? Is a dog howling there? Have I ever heard a dog howling like that? In times of violence and war wild animals increase. Bears, wolves, hungry boars — isn't that what they say?

I went through the church door. The small church was desolate and plundered. I sat down on a wooden bench. I was very tired. Next to me sat a dried-out harvest doll with a crown made of stripped willow branches on its oat hair. The cold rose from the firmly trodden clay floor.

I slept until twilight. Then I woke with a start. Then I ran through the village. Abandoned yards, charred wooden houses. Trees broken by the storm, bleached by rain, scorched by fire. I climbed over a wooden fence, I walked to a house. The door was locked. I crawled through the window. I called out: "Does anyone live here?" I waited for an answer. It was cold, it was still, there was a smell of salted hides. Skins were hung up to dry, dried fruit was there, potatoes, rutabagas, garlands of onions.

I ate, then I slept again. None of my friends came, not even their images, not even their names. I lay on straw, and the sheepskin stank.

Wind around the house, horns of night watchmen, church bells in the night. But no one tolled, and the steeple is broken off behind the seventh Russian forest, I said to myself bravely in my sleep. Rustling in the wall. The wind tore at the roof. A shingle fell to the ground, two.

After the night, morning came, the first freeze, the first snow. The last barriers that were put up for my feeling for reality are snowed in.

In front of the door I sank in to my knees. I had trouble pulling my boots back out of the snow. I grabbed the snow, molded it, aimed at the nearest roof. A flock of pigeons flew out.

To Elsa, to my elders! You both begin with *el*. That seems holy to me. I beg you, fill me, nourish me with your thoughts, for my inner emaciation is taking control. I am tired and would like to lie down on my fresh snow here, would like to close my ears with snow so that I don't have to hear the silence anymore.

Russian winter. And my comrades? The whole army in thin German uniforms?

The freeze makes the tree branches crack, the freeze increases. Frozen ravens fall from the steep shingle roofs. The freeze creaks in the ice. The icicles hang from the roofs of the black-charred houses, which are sunk in the white snow. Aren't heads peering there out of the window frames?

But there was only my present time. I was with my present time alone. I crawled into my hideaway — only I against the stiffness and the stillness. I crawled into the sheepskin, forced myself into half sleep, wanted to keep fear in bounds.

Elders, Elsa — the images won't turn me loose that we Germans had thrown here against the walls of the houses. Who else threw them, the images of conflagration, the images of devastation, ravages of war! And the dead that we have killed, the dead come closer and closer to me in the deep Russian snow. Do the dead walk barefoot? I can't remember how Hanno and Schade walk.

Now it's afternoon. I have broken off the letter. I can't write any more letters.

I wandered again out into the whiteness, the purity, the inhuman, for in the walls here the spots of mildew are growing before my very eyes as though the slain inhabitants of the house were crowding from their Beyond unmercifully into my world, as though they crowded unwaveringly through my entreaty that I had nothing in common with their murderers and despoilers but just being German. Dry rot grows sticklike, and the mildew puffs up.

I wrapped rags around my feet, stuck straw into my boots. It had stopped snowing. The wind was cutting, the cold stuck needles into my eyes, on the roofs the shingles cracked.

And then I saw tracks. Other feet had walked here in the snow. Human feet? Or is the snowman making his rounds? The wind had blown over the tracks, and so maybe it had even been a stag.

I'm sitting beside the fire in the stove, which I started after it finally occurred to me that I can warm myself with it. The fine threads that had bound me still with what was outside, the outer part of me, my own flesh during these last solitudes seemed now also to rip.

The night is bright. The stars are hard nails. Perhaps this will be my last diary entry. I won't turn my diary loose. I'll put it in my breast pocket with the *Cornet* and carry it with me through the night.

And what if the tracks do come from humans? If the Russian finds me, he'll kill me. It probably does little good to change my uniform for farm clothes out of the dresser here. And if our own troops find me, then God have mercy on me just as much.

And what of the wild animals that are ganging up to devour the last human being here? But if it's none of all those and not a fabulous creature either that has set its large foot with a step from the Himalayas to the Ukrainian forests, then perhaps it's only the hungry stag that has come into the village to die?

I remember that my grandmother told me that wild animals when dying seek the proximity of humans. The proximity of humans, she said, was more settling then to a wild animal than the nearness of death. "The animals from the forest," my grandmother told me — and surely knew what she was talking about, for the farm on which my mother had been a child was surrounded by woods and meadows for miles and miles — "they know that man knows more about death. They believe that man can ward death off, since he knows." She had even seen, my grandmother said, how a hedgehog that had eaten rat poison had not moved from her door sill and for hour after hour had licked her hands until it fell over.

I douse the fire now. I creep under the sheepskin and let the light of the sky through the window. If I hang rags over it, it's not much warmer but is shut off from life and dark as death. If this should be the night of my death, then I'll die as a fragment, then I was only a line in my stanza.

Hanno, Schade, Gabriel, keep watch! It can be that I'm coming.

But I see this bright morning after an awful sleep, during which it lay on my neck like a hand that turned me incessantly.

Freezing storms that raged around my hut put boils in my dreams. Frigid buzzes that came over the ice crust entered my ears: Frost sirens, those women! And they all came over me in my sleep. And all were Furies. And even Rachie Neumann, the innocent child, whom I had forgotten long since deep inside of me for nothing but Elsa and Elsa, for nothing but Russia and war, slung her thick black braids around my neck and slowly tightened them. Her ribs yawned open and I saw her heartless breast. Great God, where do such dreams come from?

Now snow is falling again. The heavy winter sky is pressing me with every step deeper into snow banks. Winds whisk and lash the ice crystals. My face is sore from them. And so I stay in the house beside the stove and forget myself here and there.

Under a few boards of the floor I have found a meter-deep cellar hole. There is sweet and sour canned food, enough for me and this winter. But even if I eat and drink, the fantasies will finally do me in long before the first thaw.

Tonight I saw faces at the window, faces of devils, grimaces of angels, and thought I was again having a dream in my sleep. Now I sit and write it down so that I don't have to lie and watch how Heaven and Hell perform their mystery play before my window. But maybe life ends just this way.

THEY BROKE THROUGH the door, broke in upon Reinhold, fell upon him, threw him over, knocked him down, rolled over him, lay on him, ripped the buttons from his uniform, ripped his torn uniform into tatters. And were still just a boy and a girl who shrieked, roared, tied him, bound his hands to his feet.

Reinhold laughed because he saw human beings, heard human beings, language, words, Russian words, laughed, couldn't stop. "Hitlerist," they screamed, "Hitlerist," he understood.

The boy was holding a fence pale to strike. The girl screamed until Reinhold stopped laughing, until he screamed back: "I'm not a Hitlerist! I ran away, deserted, went underground, half dead from the forest, half crazy from the snow!"

The girl and the boy turned him loose, stood before him, looked at him. Reinhold lay bound at their feet.

"But you're German," said the boy. And then they were silent, looking at Reinhold, and the boy held the fence pale ready to swing.

When morning came, they were still standing, silent, not taking their eyes off Reinhold. The wind blew dry snow through the window.

And then when all three were shivering with cold, Reinhold said: "You can make a fire in the stove. You can hang rags over the windows." And then he said: "Here is a black book. My diary. If you can read German writing, then read in it who I am."

The girl took the diary, held it out to the boy. They leafed through it, read, spoke Russian with one another. The boy put down the fence pale, took the diary from the girl's hand, read on. They were in rags, covered with scratches, disheveled.

"You probably have had bad experiences," said Reinhold.

"We have dead people," said the boy. He put Reinhold's diary in his coat, untied his feet, pulled him up, pushed him out into the snow, pushed him along ahead. Cold descended upon them. The wind whirled between the houses. The sky hung low over the white roofs of the black-scorched houses. The outlines of the houses were erased.

A man was standing before one house. The boy spoke to the man. The man stared at Reinhold. Then he opened the door. The boy pushed Reinhold into the house, the girl entered after them.

Two old people were sitting by the hearth. The woman was startled, jumped up, took a few steps toward Reinhold. She was lame, bore her weight heavily, was wrapped in cloths and furs. The man didn't look up, stared at the clay floor, pulled a hair from his beard. The one who had been standing outside the door had come into the house.

165

The boy spoke Russian, much and quickly, pulled Reinhold's diary from his coat, showed it around. The old man at the hearth sat still, listened with hairy ears, reached his hand out for Reinhold's diary, read. Gave the diary back to Reinhold and again stared at the clay floor, pulled a hair from his beard, and another one.

"God helps the Jews," the old woman said.

"I'm Asriel," said the boy and untied Reinhold's hands.

"Drink a cup. It'll warm your heart," said the old woman and poured tea.

"My sister Golda," said the boy. The girl had remained standing at the door and did not look at Reinhold.

"God helps the Jews," the old woman said and cut onions from chains that hung from the ceiling. "There'll be onion cakes," she said.

"She's crippled," Asriel whispered. "Her brothers carried her on their backs." Asriel was speaking in German, but his tongue tripped over the consonants and the words at other places in the sentence.

"Are you German, then?" asked Reinhold.

"No, but we are speaking the German, too. We're all from the German church towns near Odessa. We're from Karlsruhe. We survive," said Asriel.

The one who had stood outside the door was now standing at the window, scratched a hole in the layer of ice on the pane. The hole closed up again.

"Is that your father?" asked Reinhold.

The old man at the hearth stared at the clay floor, the man at the window scratched a new hole in the ice, the old woman was baking the cakes.

"They thought they were to die, when they got lost in the forest. When we met them, these three were thinking they were going to die. They're not relatives and not acquaintances. We met them in the forest," whispered Asriel.

The warmth of the hearth fire went through the room. The ice on the window melted. Everyone sat down around the hearth. Only the girl remained at the door.

"You precious child," the old woman called. "Come and eat!"

The girl remained at the door. Then the old man asked: "What does a grave have in common with a womb?" And when the girl didn't know the answer, he answered: "Just as the womb receives and gives back, so also does the grave receive and give back. But if the womb, which receives in joy, gives back with suffering and cries of woe, then how much more should the grave, which receives with cries of woe, give back in jubilation?"

Then they ate the onion cakes that the old woman had baked.

It had stopped snowing. It had grown dark.

"We don't need candlelight," said the old woman. "God's stars shine more brightly than ever. God helps the Jews."

The old man at the hearth had fallen asleep. Asriel stared at Reinhold. Then he, too, slept, all of them slept. Only the girl did not. Motionless, unresponsive she stood there, apart from the others lying around the hearth.

During the night Reinhold woke up because he heard weeping. Then he crept to the girl. He crouched next to her. She did not look at him. He took her hands. They were cold. He put her hands under his armpits. "Tell me," he said. "Telling means stepping across the threshold, means overcoming fear. Tell me," he said.

"From the beginning?" asked the girl.

"From the beginning," said Reinhold.

"Born in Karlsruhe near Odessa," she said, and then she wept again.

"Tell me," said Reinhold.

"Ask," she said.

"About Karlsruhe," whispered Reinhold, "tell me about Karlsruhe."

"As I remember, about ten Jewish families were in Karlsruhe, and it was a lovely village with three thousand farmsteads, as I remember," whispered the girl.

"Tell me, tell me," whispered Reinhold.

"But in Soviet times we were, you know," she whispered, "and so no Jewish education we receive. But I still remember the father, when on holidays he prayed, and then the mother I remember with the cloth over her head." The girl began to weep again.

"You must tell me," whispered Reinhold. "Whenever you tell a story, it gets better than it is."

"They died the death, you know, the parents. That tore my soul apart, and the pains which are from that do not sleep."

"Is your brother Asriel younger than you?"

"Two years difference. I remember still when he was born."

Both looked at Asriel, who lay sleeping at the hearth.

"We would have needed little to die," the girl whispered, "but we didn't have enough."

"Tell me," whispered Reinhold, when she was about to cry again.

"One other brother I had, and he died because the parents were Jews. And no help was there."

"Tell me about the brother," whispered Reinhold. They were sitting in the darkness next to one another, not looking at one another.

"I tell," said the girl. "The parents they put in a jail in Odessa. We children hid, traded clothes for a piece of bread, and the brother mine, twelve years old he was, found a hole and went through the jail wall eight times and took food to the parents. And then he got typhus. But some Romanians had come, and Germans, too, and to the Jews no doctor was admitted. When the parents were out of jail, the brother had already died the death. Men came, on a sled laid him out, wrapped in a blanket, and took it to a cemetery, and where they buried it, I don't know, because no Jew has not a right to that."

"Tell me," whispered Reinhold, "when you tell, you can't cry."

"About Karlsruhe?" she asked.

"About Karlsruhe," he said.

"Fine," she said, "I tell. Very pretty place, with very many good people. In the village everybody spoke the German language, the Jews as well as the Christians, German language and Russian language. But there was a guy there, Johann was his name, and bigger than I am he was. He always hit me. And I asked the parents: Why? Said the parents: Because you're a Jewish girl. And I asked: What means Jewish girl? And the parents answered: We pray at home, and all the others go praying in church. But I go to church, too, I said to the parents, for I always went with the girls from my school and dipped myself in the holy water and crossed myself and crossed myself, really, all five fingers, first the right side and then the left side. And more than once I afterwards saw the Christian Lord as a lamp over the altar. And I sat with the other children in a row, and the priest stroked my head. The priest always stroked my head, and I felt in church the same as all the others, you know? I remember still when all the paths on holidays were strewn with flower blossoms, were the girls dressed so prettily, had the boys candles in their hands, and I very much wanted to be one of all of them."

"Tell me," whispered Reinhold and wrapped the blankets more tightly around her.

"Yes," she said, "I tell you what I remember. It was the starvation year of '33. The father was a mechanic of threshing machine and locomotive. Until then, times had not been bad, but with the death of Lenin Stalin began, and the fanaticists came, and with them came hunger. Everything easy had disappeared, and what was hard became very hard. The Stalinists had made laborers of serfs, and the kolkhoz had taken away everything from every person and had burned up the farms. Big monk's hoods of straw they made and lighted them until there was terrible fire in Karlsruhe that burned and burned. Everything they took away from us down to the bare walls. The father no longer had job, and the mother worked here and there for a bit of bread, for a little soup."

"Do you want to rest?" asked Reinhold.

"No, I tell," the girl whispered. "You can call me Golda," she whispered.

"I want to tell you about the one named Johann, who made me feel like that any second he'd take me by the throat and choke me, such eyes did he have for me. And before the war began, I went from Karlsruhe to Speyer to my aunt. I saw Johann before he let me see his knife flash. And then I was with the aunt and the war was there. The aunt was like a mother, and she wasn't a Jew, and she said: 'Golda, you have to go home, even one second more you can't stay in Speyer, you've got to go to your parents, what will happen to everyone will happen to you!' I didn't understand why. In the streets one was happy, one laughed and sang, shouted hurrah that Germany has taken over in Germany. Speyer and Karlsruhe and all the other places were paid for by Germany, all the buildings, the school, and the hospital, and the poorhouse. Germans had come a week before as liberators from the Soviet, and they had been received with bread and salt.

"'Be quiet,' my aunt said, 'sit in the apartment, don't go outside!' And then she brought a young fellow who had taken two horses and a small wagon from the kolkhoz and put me in the wagon, and my aunt kissed me and hugged me and said, You all shall live, you all shall live! And the young fellow drove me home.

"But when I came home, the parents were already in jail, were there just the two brothers. Those were the first days that they rounded up the Jews. And when the parents came back, he was dead, the brother. You know?" whispered Golda and wept again. "But I keep telling you," she said, "and in the end I tell everything good.

"One night they called us, it was already wintertime, already cold. It was called out: All Jews! All Jews! And the father, because once he was in the army of the Czar, had there learned to make shoes for the officers, packed up his handtools and thought that his handicraft he can do anywhere. Took the parents a sled and food, and they led us away. 'Where does this lead, where does this lead?' it was asked. Romanian soldiers they were, and German soldiers they were, and we were all Jews, and they drove us over the fields. They drove us into a village and put us in the houses there. There weren't any Jews there, there were Ukrainians. We came to a woman. The woman's husband was a Communist, a chairman of the kolkhoz. He had gone away into the forest. All the Communists had gone away into the forest, all were afraid of the Germans. And soon only the children were left, and the old ones. Old ones and children. All prayed, all. And the woman, long may she live! She gave us food and drink.

"And then there was shouting again all through the night: All Jews! All Jews! And all of us, all went outside. There were probably two thousand people. No one hid. Where to hide? Germans and Romanians said: 'The Russians that hide Jews will be killed.' Do you understand? Of course, people had been telling around that the Germans are killing the Jews, but nobody didn't believe. You know, every person thinks, That will pass me by, that won't touch me. But it did touch.

"Hush," she said when Reinhold wanted to speak, "hush, I'll tell! It was a long way. We went outside at ten o'clock in the night, at four o'clock in the morning we arrived. One felt something terrible is coming, but one said to oneself it will a camp be. Some people claimed to know something about a camp, it is called 'The New Path.' And the Romanians and the Germans, there were maybe ten, fifteen, no more soldiers than that, they were drunk. Jokes, laughing were there, merriness. What's happening, what's happening, it was asked, and one did feel that it was coming nearer, the bad thing.

"Then there was a ditch, dug out, long. Said they: 'Stand with your face out front!' And one heard laughing and talking, Romanian and German. The parents didn't understand what is going on. The father, he said: 'I know German. One won't touch me.' He understood that it was against Communism. 'I'm not a Communist,' he yelled. 'I know German,' he yelled.

"Behind us shooting began. It was the father, the mother, the brother standing there like that. I was in shock, in shock you don't pray. But I felt: All two thousand we are here, we returned to God, all! I'm not an Orthodox, but in my heart I went.

"The shots were coming closer, were there. I hear the brother saying: 'Golda, fall, Golda, fall!' Understand I didn't, what. 'Fall!' he says and pulls me by the hand. And I, I see, the father has fallen, the mother has fallen, so I fell, too.

"And then all got quiet with laughter. No more shooting. See I blood, want I to scream. 'Quiet, say no word, say no word!' says the brother. Understand I didn't, what. I checked the mother, the father. One heard their last heart, one was bloody from the parents, one felt it beat out, one smelled and tasted the blood of the parents, one felt, it's sticky. The parent feet were already cold. 'Do nothing,' says the brother, 'quiet!' We laid beside the parents, we didn't move. A silence the world doesn't know.

"It can be that one lay one hour, it can be two. One waited until no laughter anymore, no voice anymore. It was already dusk. 'We climb over the bodies,' says the brother. And he took from the father's hand a little box of iron, and so we got out, up out of the ditch, into the forest.

"And still more people came there, other Jews, there were more than fifty. But the old had no more strength, and we young ones kept walking. Walking in the night and hiding in the day. And it was snow and cold. We have had the little iron box from father's hand. It was an apple in it, some pieces of bread, and a cup. One found in the field potatoes, out of the snow one dug them, carrots and red beets that one hadn't harvested in summer,

170

and at night in the forest one sat and cooked them. One was in the abandoned villages and found flour here and millet there, and by day one was farther and farther away from the ditch. That's the whole remembering," said Golda. "I've told," she said.

And when Reinhold said nothing, she said: "I did read your diary."

Then he held her tightly, and she held him. "We're holding on to life," she whispered. "Don't be afraid! It was an other ditch," she whispered. "It was an other forest, it was an other time. Say your name," she whispered.

And he told it to her, and she laughed, and so they laughed. And she repeated his name with her slow tongue, and they laughed at his name.

"And the three old people?" asked Reinhold.

"It's the cantor with his sister and his brother. They're from Josephstal. They weren't at no ditch, not at this one and not at no other either. They buried their possessions at home and fled into the forest. They were hidden in a village, and the brothers had gone out, and the sister was alone in the house. There came a Russian patrol, there she heard words of a commandant, a Russian, he said: 'Why only the Germans can do that? I, too, can do that! I want shoot all Jews that I find here in my country.' And so they shot her through the foot and threw her into a stall. There she lay, and trembled and heard how the Russians got drunk and forgot her. Three days and three nights she lay there, until the Russians are gone from the village. But the foot was in a boot, and it was much below zero. There the blood froze in the boot, and that saved her, a bandage it made. Half dead the brothers came out of the forest, had had to watch all from the distance. Then they went on, deeper into the forest. And the brothers took turns carrying the sister on their backs, and then we came upon them. We've been together now for long days, but until today she suffers from pain, the woman, and the foot is shorter, and the wound opens up again and again, and little bones stick out. But she didn't tell no one nothing about that, not never. I know it from the brothers.

"I've told," Golda said. "Will all be good now?"

It was morning. Reinhold was asleep. Someone pulled his nose: "But you have a human face!" Golda was sitting next to him with the blanket over her head. She let him find her face. "I'm fresh," she said.

Reinhold was about to laugh, but Golda didn't laugh.

The cantor was sitting at the hearth, his hands on a book. The cantor's brother was lighting candles.

"God helps the Jews," said his sister and retired to a corner and laid the shoulder cloth over her head.

"Come, my Kaddish," called the cantor, and Asriel, who had still been asleep, staggered up, and joined the men.

"What are they doing?" asked Reinhold.

"They have lighted the candles for the dead," whispered Golda.

Asriel and the two men began to sway to and fro.

"What are they doing?" asked Reinhold.

"They're filling in the open graves," whispered Golda. "Angel, now the angel is coming," she whispered, "I feel it, my soul gets bigger."

The cantor began to speak.

"What is he speaking?" asked Reinhold.

"He's speaking the holy language," whispered Golda.

Asriel and the two men had closed their eyes, were swaying to and fro.

"What is he saying?" asked Reinhold.

"He's leading us into the Land of Israel," whispered Golda.

The cantor lifted up the book and read.

"What is he reading?" asked Reinhold.

"He's reading: *Say this to the children of Israel. 'I am the Lord, I will rescue you all from the servitude of the Egyptians and will release you with outstretched arm and through mighty courts I will bring justice. I will bring you to the land that I promised Abraham, Isaac, and Jacob, and I will give it to you for your own. I, the Lord, say this!'*" whispered Golda.

The cantor pulled a small sack from his pocket and held it high.

"What's that? asked Reinhold.

"It's a little sack that white sand from the Land of Israel contains," whispered Golda.

The cantor let the book sink, looked through the window out into the snow, and continued speaking.

"He's saying: Moses leads his people through the Desert Sur," whispered Golda. "The cantor sees the Levites move through the desert with the Tabernacle, the column of fire ahead of them, behind them the cloud," she whispered and scooted closer to Reinhold. "He's singing the song of the sea of reeds," she whispered, and sang along.

The cantor's voice was raised. Outside the window raged the snow, snow banks, snow hills. The blizzard blocked the window with snow.

"Jews, save yourselves, Jewhews," came the cry from the old woman.

"I fear nothing, only God," the cantor's brother cried out.

Asriel swayed faster to and fro but watched Golda, did not let her out of his sight.

"Trust, like Job the holy man, in your Lord, the Keeper of this world," the cantor said quietly, "trust and know: Even if all the Jews and all the Torah rolls burn, then the flesh will burn and the bones will burn and the parchment, but the letters, they will fly away from the flames."

And then they ate. The old woman had made noodle soup. "If God lets us live," she said, "we will eat more of it tomorrow."

It had stopped snowing, the sun was shining. Reinhold, Golda, and Asriel ran over the snow, sank in it, laughing, charging about, built a snowman. When the sun grew pale, a new storm arose.

"Soon it will be dark. Then it's Shabbat. Mamme will light the candles, Tate will pray, we'll eat meat and fish," said Asriel.

When they went into the house, the old woman was passing out dried fruit, two pieces for each one: "Shabbes-oyps," she said. "God helps the Jews," she said and lighted two candles.

With the night came the cold that turned the old people's lips blue in spite of the hearth fire, and a wind came that blew out the candles even with the doors and windows closed.

"The storm walks over the graves of Russia," whispered the old woman. "In such nights you can encounter those who were and those who will be. For twelve months the body of the deceased is preserved, so long does the soul ascend and return. And the unborn walk for seventy years over this world with tempestuous strides before they form a heart, take courage, and plunge into the world."

"God is swimming," the cantor's brother cried out. "God is swimming in our blood, in His blood does He swim, for our blood is His blood."

"Now all the angels are on the loose," whispered Asriel and laughed and pulled his sister to him anyway and shifted close to Reinhold anyway.

"The angel of death," whimpered the old woman, "the angel of death is at the door."

"It is the angel Metatron," said the cantor. "He guards this house."

They sat and listened to the storm. Now and then one of them laid on a piece of wood. Then they slept, lay so close to the hearth that one side of them burned and the other froze anyway.

Reinhold was awake, looking into the hearth fire, listening to the storm. He leaned against the warm wall next to the hearth, pulled his diary out of his pocket, and read:

Tonight I saw faces at the window, faces of devils, grimaces of angels, and thought I was again having a dream in my sleep. Now I sit and write it down so that I don't have to lie and watch how Heaven and Hell perform their mystery play before my window. But maybe life ends just this way.

But it was no sleep, he wrote with fingers hard as ice, but a dream maybe? Maybe the dream of a dream, whose name is perhaps Golda. I surrender to this dream, I let it happen. For during that night, that will soon be two nights ago, one time ended, but not life.

During the stormy night to my father!

I'm now in another world, Father, and I'm astonished that there can be so many other worlds in this world, and that the most desperate human beings can so desperately exert their faith to understand God's fearsome ways.

"Not even sin," says the wise man with whom I am allowed to be here, "can separate itself entirely from its divine origin," for I asked him about the sin that in your name and mine and all Germans is taking place here. And for the wise man, Father, and for all who are here with me, the earth, under which its dead lie and keep breathing for it, still moves, and the earth is lighter than that breath, it rises over the breath of those who more and more and without end die there, for those who survive here. Father, what do you know about it? But the wise old man says, "Not even sin can separate itself entirely from its divine origin." I must therefore question purification through suffering. Some get the sin from God so they can commit it and so that the others, against whom it is done, can purify themselves from their own through suffering. And the children of God get it from grace most plentifully.

Father, Father! Your uniform, and the boots, from my childhood they stood for honor and decency. And now, my blood, it stops when I think that you, Father, you singer and helper, could have known! You were involved early, Father, and when I can't help but think that you could have contributed to this plan, which destroys…

Reinhold put on more wood. The old women screamed from a dream. Golda woke up.

"Sleep," said Reinhold, "I'll watch." And wrote further:

To my Mother!

I put on more wood. I see the light in the fire. I'm now in the middle of a moment, Mother, in my inner space, in the middle of the inside of me.

Let me tell you about the Jews, Mother, tell you how they hear God singing and how they sing to God. Let me tell you of the man of God here, how he sings and speaks and shows the way and all follow behind him, how they follow him through their own expanses, as the children of Israel followed Moses through the desert. And Mother, they saw the desert, saw the Levites moving through the desert. And when the man of God spoke the song of the sea of reeds, did they not raise the hems of their heavy robes so that the rearing waves on the right and the left did not douse them — I would almost rather have written the rearing worlds to the left and the right,

Mother, for I have discovered already that one world stops, but life doesn't, rather it goes into another world, and I'm discovering here and now that the other worlds, the different worlds, really tower around you and me and everyone.

And so let me tell you more: They wandered through the desert and around Mount Sinai. And when the man of God spoke blessings, they really saw their Lord climbing down.

Mother, I'm here now and would like to send you an angel.

Asriel had turned away from Golda in his sleep, and Golda had turned to Reinhold in her sleep. The old people were sleeping loudly, the young softly.

I am the night watchman, Reinhold wrote in his diary. I can't sleep. Asriel said, 'Now all the angels are loose.' I can believe that, for first of all there lies beside me, at my feet to a certain extent, a sleeping cherub's face that belongs to the girl with the black hair — Golda is her name, and her hair reaches to her waist. She loosened it and combed it twice already and wove it again into braids since we've come together here. And second, I hear rustling in the air, and third the air sounds a though there were flying. Wings are probably underway.

The barrel organ builder of the Black Forest comes to mind. Did he not speak of angels to us, to Mechthild, Utz, Gummi, and me? Didn't he say that music and dance were the same for the angels, so that dance brought its music with it?

Mechthild, now I think of you! Mechthild, if you knew, maiden!

When Reinhold asked the cantor the next morning about the angels and about the sound of angels, he said: "Brother angels are leaping flame, and that has its sound, and their wings flap, and that makes a sound. But the angel of death flies loudly and closely and so is heard by many."

And during the night yesterday Reinhold was asking.

"Every night the angel of death flies over what is far from God ever since the unholy one has reigned, since he practices magic and demands the living body of the children of Israel for his ritual. The angel flies without pause. Woe to the one and woe to his soul, for it weeps."

Reinhold had taken up his daily writing again: As though I were about to eat again after a long fast, I cautiously taste the colorations of every word and write it down only when I have tasted it and enjoyed it to the full totally and completely,

The words that the old man spoke, he spoke so deeply that it overwhelmed me: "The Führer, a black sorcerer!"

Hanno, my friend, what do you say to that?

175

There's a lot I have to think about. And next to me the child who's always looking, with eyes so wide open, who says she was seeing the dead who did not rest, who climbed out of the ditch, marched toward us, marched over her soul. She says it like that, and her beautiful child's mouth splits from it.

But when she said she had remained alive for Asriel, just for him, but for herself she had been dead since, then I wept. She wept, and I wept. But the dead don't weep. And she, she looks for my glances. And then I lost myself in hers, lost myself in my own after her.

The old people were sleeping deeply, and Asriel was having dreams.

"How could that happen?" I asked.

"We live," she said.

Every breath of air between us since that night is full of expectation and need, Reinhold wrote in his diary, when Golda in one of the following nights was asleep beside Asriel.

"He has the pictures of father and mother," she had said and was away from Reinhold over to the brother. "I'll be with him now," she had said and had stayed beside him.

And Reinhold wrote: We tell one another everything during these nights. She knows everything about me. I talked about Elsa, and also that I had thought I was much too singed by thoughts of her. But now: I quiver like a shivering cold for her whose name is Golda. But no way leads over the Jordan and the Rhine that flow between us: I don't believe in her faith. And even if I did believe it, I was born wrong.

"Disturb not love and do not awaken her until she wishes it herself," said the cantor.

Earth came out from under the snow, moss turned green on the roofs.

"We still live," said the old woman. "God helps the Jews."

Buds, birds, sunshine, mild rain. The sky lay in the puddles.

"In springtime you can hear the stars. They sound," said Golda.

"And I can think only of German songs," said Reinhold, "but I must sing them."

And Golda laughed and found the songs pretty.

And here begins an Oriental fairy tale, or we're already in it, Reinhold wrote in his diary: Introduced by German song, two have found one another, two have joined together.

"The forest is a cathedral of death," said the Prince.

"The forest is a wedding church, and we're getting married," said the Princess.

The forest grew up during that spring and grew closer, and the two found their springtime hiding place. Face in the grass, nothing but her face and the grass, alone under the trees and the sky!

When two are together, time cannot pass for them. When two are together, death cannot happen to them!

And still the moon rose and wrote messages on the earth, signs that only lovers can read. And they read that it was time, and went away from one another back to the others.

In the house the cantor read from the story of Creation: *Be fruitful and multiply and fill the earth.*

Then Reinhold had to get past a fight with Asriel, who couldn't help beating him and pounding him, against whom he did not want to defend himself.

"Good, good, may they multiply," said the old woman and set the soup on the table. And with lips pressed together the cantor's brother imitated a fife, cymbal, and bagpipes.

"Light the lights for the dead," said the cantor, "for they have come and wish to celebrate with us. For all who ever belonged to you, even those who wandered far away, who left this world long ago, are here and sit here with us and taste the aroma that rises from the soup. That's why we have but one word in our Jewish language for tasting and smelling," he said to Reinhold, "that's why, because we think of our dead. Now you must think of your dead, too, for now you're one of us."

"My precious child," the old woman cried and did not want to let Golda go.

"Foolishness," said the cantor and pulled Golda away from the old woman and pushed Reinhold and Golda out the door and out of the village and into the wheat field.

A single being are we in an abysmal land, Reinhold wrote in his diary. And yet, we are still alive, still are. Time falls away from us. We are in the forest.

Asriel had run through the forest. Asriel had seen tree-high Russian tanks. Asriel had run behind the tanks to a village, had seen someone in a German uniform on the gallows in the marketplace, had seen red flags, and had heard that the Red Army had won the war, the Germans were beaten on their retreat, the front ran far behind the Dnieper. Asriel had run back through the forest and had seen more Russian tanks.

"You're German," the cantor had said to Reinhold. "You must leave."

"But Golda," Reinhold had said.

"Is Jewish, must stay."

"But there's the hole in the cellar," Golda had said, "and before the door the forest, we can hide, then no Russ will find him and no German neither."

"If you stay with her," the cantor had said, "it will cost you her life."

It's become May in the year '44. I haven't written for a long time. I was with her, of course. Now I press my head between her knees and want to press it there forever. And then again I feel her life, hold it, and promise us eternity.

If a Red Russian finds the Jewess with the German, then the Jewess has committed not only a Jewish sin but a German one as well, then the Jewess and her kin will be rubbed out by Red Russians in a German manner. So the German has to leave.

I'll walk away backwards, Golda! I'll see you, Golda!

"But leave the light burning," Golda said in the night.

"But it's not tomorrow yet," said Reinhold. "It's still today," he said.

Golda got up early. It was cold and dark. She got dressed.

"But we still have our whole life perhaps still before us," said Reinhold.

"We don't know what life is, nor what our death nor what God is, nor what we ourselves are," said the cantor.

"Be well, be well," said the old woman.

"You must go westward, always westward," said the cantor's brother.

Cold and deaf with departure, I left Golda.

Walking, standing, waving, waving, walking, standing. Asriel walked along a piece. Then he ran away.

I went westward. The forest rustled. I cried aloud.

Then I found myself in a clearing again, terrified. Wasn't there a stony path running there, over which they had come? Wasn't that the tree stand here on which they had tied me? Didn't fresh blood ooze there out of the incurable earth?

It was perhaps the place, or it was another. Many ditches run through the Russian forest. I go westward. I have no choice.

At a swampy stream lay gunned-down Russians, ten, twelve. What kind of sense is it to count corpses? They looked like they were made of dirt, clods of dirt, sandmen. Blow flies were feeding on them, thick black clumps gnawing them.

But how beautiful the forest is! And how familiar to me the earth and air!

Oh, Golda, reality floats like a delicate bubble over the world. Shall I take a little stick and prick it?

REINHOLD WALKED DAY and night.

The forest was burned, the fields devastated, the villages destroyed. After two days he arrived in a city.

German army, artillery, engineers, news units, battalions of riflemen, antitank and antiaircraft guns, Romanian cavalry divisions blocked the streets.

"What are they waiting for?" Reinhold asked the man ahead of him.

"For a hero's death," he said.

A company of old men trotted past.

"The last conscription," said the man ahead. "Strew ashes at evening around your bed, then you'll already be able to see the footprints of those ghosts the next morning. Back home they're pulling the old men out of their deathbeds and the babies out of the cradle now."

Reinhold joined the man ahead of him. They made their way through to where they had to report. He showed his I.D., said he had been with a reconnaissance group, had been separated, had fallen into Russian captivity, been taken to a camp, had for a long time done forced labor there, had finally been able to escape.

At the report office commotion and overwork prevailed. Excitement and confusion was rife among the soldiers who crowded there. No one listened to what Reinhold said, no one asked him about it.

"The front is too close for questions," said the man ahead of him.

Reinhold and the man ahead of him were assigned to a holding battalion, received an emergency pack, rifle and steel helmet, ammunition, and leather belt.

Field kitchens distributed schnapps and cigarettes.

"Special distributions. That sounds suspicious," said the man in front.

The procession left the city, moved westward, wheeled into the steppe. Combat marksmen cleared the way, antitank weapons drove on both sides of the armyworm, Romanian cavalry divisions joined it.

As far as my eye can see, nothing but stunted growth of grass, plain to plain, dust to dust. A gigantic armyworm crawls over the end of the world.

We set up for the night. Together with the man ahead of me, whose name is Willi, I dig a foxhole. He has a small shovel in his combat pack. We take turns digging, we shovel with bare hands. They say attacks can be expected during the night.

I'm writing with the last light: The forest of death, the wedding church are far from here. Officer candidate Reinhold Fischer, who is really through with the war, lets his thoughts go — they run eastward. There the sky lies on the trees.

The night was loud, fires as beacons of the retreat all around. The warriors here are not in a milder mood on account of the lost game. The command is: Scorched earth. And they torch and shoot about them like encircled gangsters, Reinhold wrote in his diary.

In the gray of dawn I experienced a great shock in my anguish: "Cossacks!" Yells, screams: "Cossacks, Cossacks!" The terror that seizes you at this name, and the terror at the sight of the gigantic cavalry on the horizon of the steppes! Even to see it with your naked eye, to hear it! The steppe boomed under the hooves of the galloping horses. Fearful roars of hurrah swelled in the air. Sabers flashed in the innocent morning sun. — Cossacks slit open your stomach and sew hungry cats up inside. Cossacks tie you to horsetails and gallop through fields of thistles. Cossacks pull your skin slowly and in strips from your body!

In great haste we formed a defensive wall of fire, while the mass of horsemen rolled up on all sides. We estimated about two to three thousand Cossacks. The command roared: "Don't shoot! Firing will begin only with the leading machine-gun column."

An uncanny tension was in the air, left you breathless, pulled your feet out from under you. After all, everyone knew that a failure of our weapons would mean brutal destruction.

The horsemen raced toward us side by side in several wedges. We could already make out details, their hats and their beards! They were shooting from galloping horses, swinging their flashing sabers. There! When they were about three hundred meters away from us, our machine guns barked. Our artillery, the infantry marksmen, antitank guns and antiaircraft guns roared all together. The machine-gun barrels glowed.

After a second of terror in which I saw no one fall, in which I cried out: "Nobody's falling!" the front rows collapsed, the mass of riders pressing behind raced at a gallop with cries of hurrah into our exploding grenades. Men and animals flew through the air. Scraps of men mixed with scraps of animals. But the horsemen kept coming from the horizon, came in waves, pushed forward, more and more new waves rolled on, ran over, were man and horse, were torn limb from limb.

The last ones stopped a hundred meters from us. But we could not be restrained and attacked the last ones. With hurrah we rushed over horsemen and horses torn to shreds. The last ones fled from us.

A great, deep groaning, a haze over the earth, the mass of men and horses! We pulled Cossack sabers as souvenirs out of the mass.

The one whose saber I took was a real fellow and opened his eyes, and had Hanno's eyes, and was Hanno, and I screamed and screamed until the man in front of me, whose name is Willi, woke me up.

They moved for days through the steppes, cut off from all the world, without contact with other troops, without contact with the commanders of the procession.

They moved for weeks through enemy territory. Battle planes appeared, dive bombers. Fighter planes attacked at low altitudes. They marched only at night, took cover during the day in the reeds, in the corn, in fields of sunflowers.

It turned hot. Food was rationed, gasoline became short. Vehicles were left standing along the wayside. The officers, too, now went on foot. Only vehicles for the wounded were still driving along. Supply trucks were burned. The spare horses were shot.

It turned hotter. There was now only canned sausage, corn, and cabbage soup. There was no more cigarette paper. Tobacco was wrapped in sunflower leaves. Many men were seized by pappataci fever.

It turned even hotter.

The heat is causing agoraphobia. The grass is withering under our feet. Devils seem to be playing with fire here, Reinhold wrote in his diary. Dust storms — often I can no longer recognize the man next to me, the man ahead of me, whose name is Willi. Then we hold hands like little girls so that we won't get lost.

On an endless dusty road a column of louse-ridden Nibelungen move westward. Dust has eaten into their faces, dust is eating their faces. Dust penetrates to the skin through bootlegs and through uniforms. Dust weighs down on the trees, bends the branches, forces them down until they break. Colors are faded, birds are suffocated, the Nibelungen move on.

Marching, marching, standing still means waking up out of impending death and foot ache. My feet begin to suppurate. But when we stop, we collapse, let ourselves collapse, remain lying until we get up again. Again and again low-flying planes appear. We hide, spend idle days in cotton fields. We walk past countless graves of German soldiers. Their decorations haven't withered yet. Willi, the man in front of me, asks: "Who will weed them after us?"

Heat strokes begin to afflict us. We vomit from the heat. It's probably close to 120 degrees Fahrenheit. In the shade we struggle for air. But sometimes we find no shade. And yesterday the sun scorched through the grass onto the face that was lying to the right of me. Then the face became flat and broad. Then the man died.

We can't bury each one. There's already a sweet smell on our way, a sweet odor wafts after us.

The land is so wide and so empty. No one has a map. The officers are no longer officers. Each one thinks only about himself. We march at random, know only that we've been going southwest for a long time, since the Russian sharpshooters bark at us from the north.

More and more often I think it would be best to stop and to die, but then the thought of Golda, Father, Mother twists into my mind and shoves me on.

Willi, my man ahead, is faithfully at my side. He can tell stories, has lived a lot, and seen a lot. Yesterday we camped on swampland. The frogs were croaking as hard as they could. There was no thought of sleep. Then Willi told me a Ukrainian fable that the Russians tell as a parable for the beaten Fritzies. Fritz, that's what Ivan calls our like. And the fable goes: A man went hunting and killed a bear, skinned the fox, brought the rabbit home, the mother slaughtered the duck, and made a pudding, the man tried it, it tasted bitter.

To Golda! I live my life for you, even when I go away from you, for death comes nearer with every step. I live my life for you, for you are my wife. Being man-and-wife is now my Homeland.

That miraculous word — I know very well that you Jews mean the name of God by that, but for me every word performs miracles, saves me, rips me out of my human helplessness and lets me be active. And so I can at times even write off to you, Golda. And you may read me in the air and laugh.

I associate again daily, furthermore, with my dead. Hanno and Schade stick up for me here. So outer conditions melt away, sink in the day-to-day dust, and inner ones gather in new ways. And in the middle you stand, Golda!

Ankle-deep sand, knee-deep sand, the armyworm dodges over the fields. Hundreds of thousands trod down the harvest. Plundered villages, burning wooden houses, howling dogs, brambles that proliferated over the paths.

The gray yellowish day opened up its maw, and now follows a long yawn, Reinhold wrote in his diary. You sit, you clean your rifle, you delouse yourself, you listen for the barking of Russian machine guns, always from the right, always from the right. We are being pushed more and more to the south. And the plague of lice takes control. You can't keep up with your scratching.

It will get hot again today, but we can't hide in the fields anymore. What isn't eaten up there has been stomped down. Autumn seems to have come. We can't hide out of sight anymore. The nights are already cold. What will happen? No one knows. We don't even know where we are here exactly or inexactly in God's wide world. We've survived, but now winter is coming. Russia, land of German longing, what do you have planned for us?

At midday a Russian fighter plane comes in low, light antiaircraft guns shoot, the plane catches fire right over us, the wings wobble, the plane crashes. The pilot lies before us with twisted limbs and smoking legs. Willi and I put a little dirt on him and think up a biblical phrase.

Shortly afterwards the whole sky is full of pilots that hang over our heads but don't attack, come down in dives, turn away, avoid us sideways. Willi and I throw ourselves down onto the field, dig into the furrows. I feel like an Indian, exposed to the superior power that can come only from the sky.

We run, crawl, find a small woods. The dive bombers howl, the antipersonnel planes roar, bombers and war planes are covered by fighter pilots — fighters with the Red star block the sky from us. A sky full of red stars.

And then: a high whistle in the air, a rushing sound, men and horses scream in fright. It sweeps us off our legs. The howling and the crunching explode over us in the tops of the trees. The airborne explosions boom nauseatingly, whistling the fragments arrive and smash down. The sky dissolves in fire. Phosphorous grenades burst in the air, giant flames rain down. The earth is burning, fire devouring fire.

And then quiet, trees burning with a low crackle, trees crackling, men crackling, the odor of blood, the haze of gunpowder, and sunglow through the scalped trees.

My man ahead of me whose name is Willi lies beside me, his face down.

"Are you still alive, Willi?" I roar. The vapor of the human victims mixes with the gun smoke, rises. My roaring is a croaking: "Are you still alive?"

"I pretended to be dead," Willi croaks and stands up alive, "I thought, just in case."

There are no medics anymore. There are no vehicles anymore. Anyone who can't walk has to lie there. Those who can walk, walk as fast as they can, away from the odor of blood, away from the throat rattles, groans.

We've dug ourselves a foxhole, the man ahead of me, whose name is Willi, and I. I've sat down next to the foxhole in the evening twilight. Perhaps it's my last light — who knows whether tomorrow's light will shine for me.

Just blood and fear, the true essence of matter! The masters, the racial masters, lie there covered with blood, lie violently beside it. Blood is nothing, just garbage, human garbage, without regard to race. And the brainless brain, without thought, that sprayed up next to me at noon today is no more than a most pathetic substance.

But the air trembled over the dead. There it sits, there it rises! Truth rises with the day there, our soul, which we still clutch to us with bloody hands on coarse flesh, rises up and away. And afterwards they are just more corpses.

Death is contagious. The weariness of death already has us all. But then you run again before there's trouble. And now my ears ache from the shooting. And the nights get colder and colder.

Before I go to sleep, I want to reflect about whether every comrade thinks of a woman when grenade splinters whistle a lullaby.

And I want to tell you, too, Golda: I had the beginning of a poem under the grenades. To bleed myself to you rushed through my mind. But I survived and canceled my lyric. And now please appear to me in my sleep as something or other, even though it be only a tiny spark of Golda.

The southern flank of Russia was bypassed. The armyworm had left Russia. The Romanian allies had withdrawn. Partisans tried to prevent the retreat over the Balkans to the north. English fighter bombers appeared.

The marching took place at night. In the daytime hiding places in the mountains were sought out. There were mountains everywhere now. The road was a gorge.

They had to walk at great intervals, for it was said the road was mined. They could not go far into the mountains, for it was said the partisans were there. They were not allowed to make fires at night and smoked in the hollow of their hands, for the English made their reconnaissance flights also at night. Once a week jagdwurst was distributed, twice hot coffee. Many were wounded: bandaged heads, arms, legs, suppurating wounds, gas burns, tetanus.

It had become cold. They had wrapped around them everything they had and what they could take from the dead along the way. No one argued anymore about signet rings and wrist watches — now it was only about jackets, pants, and shoes. When the birds of prey shrieked, nobody listened to them anymore, and when they settled on the dead, no one scared them away anymore.

So I'm getting acquainted with the nightside of Nature, Reinhold wrote in his diary, but there's night also in the daytime.

Today, because the cold was clinging, I slept with my good Willi in a heap of straw. It was a bottomless sleep, and something in me pleaded for it never to end, until I dreamed that my teeth were getting loose. And I awoke with a start and felt them with my tongue, and they seemed to me really no longer to be tight.

185

"Now winter's coming," said Willi, chattering beside me. "We'll dig our-selves in," he said, "feed on rotten worms and cold mice." And all of a sud-den he gave a start and screamed and roared about whose and which idiotic nonsense we had to thank for everything, whether I might know, whether I had ever heard rumors about a certain Hörbiger, an uneducated fellow who had tried to explain the history of mankind with the eternal battle between fire and ice. But I didn't know the name, and so my good Willi went on, talked to me about the World Ice Theory, the chief work of Hörbiger. But since I had never heard about that either, he explained the theory to me: Since our forefathers grew up in snow and ice, the belief in world ice was the natural heritage of the Nordic man. But he, the superman, had once climbed down from the mountains — I couldn't help thinking of my old Nietzsche, there I hear a heavy step — summoned to rule over the earth and the heav-enly bodies. But between ice and fire there has existed for eons the battle in endless space. And, my good Willi hollered, now completely beside himself: "The idiot persuaded the other idiot that he didn't have to furnish his troops with winter clothing — a little cap and a scarf would suffice. World ice would give way to the German army of flames!"

"And where does my good Willi know that from?" I hollered also and laughed as well.

"You won't want to laugh," he hollered back and was already at my throat. "I was there when they planted the sacred flag on the Elbrus. I was there, do you understand? SS Mountain Trooper, Seventh Company, do you understand!" He struck his chest and soon would have smashed his chest in two. "That was the sign, it was said," he roared, "the beginning of absolute power. Winter would now give way before our legions."

Then my serious major in the Werdohl War College came to mind, how he had spoken of the magic peak, how he had cried out — yes, then I heard him still yelling: "When the flag waves on the holy mountain, the new age will begin!"

"I was there!" my man in front roared and stuck to my throat. "The fire would conquer the ice from now on and for centuries, it was said. The sea-sons would be subjugated to mankind. And in spite of the warning of mete-orology about a bad winter, in spite of all the menacing signs, the idiot rushes his troops to Stalingrad!" My man in front, the good Willi, howled: "Bitten by the wind, burned by the ice, you must end up in cold desolation just to prove that the mysticism of that idiot is truer than Nature!"

Willi, my man in front, mountain trooper, daredevil with the edelweiss in his button hole, howled like a wolf, got control of himself, came to atten-tion, and said to everyone: "Gentlemen, with my promotion to lieutenant I received the old edelweiss of my father, who in his time was also a mountain trooper. But now I know that I can no longer wear it with German honor. Gentlemen, at home crazy men who have gone wild sabotage the accomplishments of front-line soldiers. I herewith take my leave, gentlemen!" And the good Willi tore off his edelweiss and stomped on it, completely beside himself.

Winter is here. The white gets whiter. Before me wraiths of fog totter, stumble, slip on the ice-covered ground, help one another up, totter again, will soon lie on the wayside frozen stiff. No one will bury anyone anymore.

But between sleep and death on and on, along past those dead at last on the wayside, on the edge of bright madness where you have to do a balancing act, something supersensory, hard and alert, says to me: "Don't sleep, even when the images of home become firmer! Pinch yourself, scratch off your lice, don't sleep, else you'll have had it!"

The snow falls so thickly that for hours we can't move ahead. Rations reach us, if at all, only in a frozen state. We put the rock-hard frozen stuff between our thighs until we can bite it. Repeatedly we try to make fires. Some still have cooking utensils, others use their steel helmets. They say that cannibalism has broken out among our comrades. You take a close look in the cooks' pots.

Many throw away their machine guns, for they are frozen up and, in the knee-deep snow with the burden of total exhaustion on your back, can no longer be carried.

Chilblains, foot blisters, everything hammers softly and harshly, bores and gnaws on what is human.

Wolves howl, the snow lies peacefully.

Willi says: "Your nose is frostbitten off." Willi is always at my side. I can't feel whether my nose is frostbitten off or not. I don't feel anything anymore, and I don't know whether Willi is grinning or snarling or whether his false teeth are broken.

I don't know anything anymore, and I don't feel anything anymore, and soon I won't be able to hold my pencil. And Golda? Is summertime, saga, the age of fairy tale.

Fields of snow, walls of ice, mountains of ice. The enemy could be everywhere, everything was the enemy.

Reinhold and his man ahead stepped out of the forward march, out of the column, out of the herd. A path led into the mountains.

"Where there's a path, there must also be a house!" said the man ahead.

They had turned the safety off their rifles, wanted to eat and sleep. They walked and climbed, the path ended, they lost their way. And then a man was standing there in the snow, and the snow was falling harder. The man waved and called out, but they did not understand him. But the man waved and walked, and waved, and led them, and took them to a light. A flock of black crows flew back and forth above them, rustled over their heads, and it seemed clear to both that the light could not be human.

In the board cabin the snowy wind whistled through the gaps. Around a fire sat men and women in straw.

Partisans? Ambushers? What can they take from us but our lives, Reinhold couldn't help thinking. What can they have from us except our deaths?

Pictures of guardian angels and saints were nailed on the walls. The flickering of the sanctuary lamps under them animated their faces.

Two women and seven men were there. They talked, cooked, with open arms and large hands invited them to eat. There was milk and rice. Reinhold and his man ahead ate and did not understand what was being talked about. The wind blew out the sanctuary lamp under the picture of the Madonna.

Straw was piled up. The open arms and large hands invited them to go to bed. Broad, bearded faces laughed. Teeth were missing in the mouths. Dirt seemed to have been stuck in the wrinkles of the young faces for hundreds of years.

Reinhold and his man ahead agreed: one would sleep, the other keep watch. And in doing so appeared ridiculous, for the others were already asleep, and no one was keeping watch, and no one had a rifle.

The man ahead was asleep, then Reinhold slept, too. He was aware of the roof over his head, he was aware of the sleep of the others. — What kind of people are these? Strange angels? Maybe angels look different from country to country, clothe themselves with the apparel of the natives and speak the language of the country?

When Reinhold woke up, his rifle was still there. The men were gone. The women lay sleeping. The man ahead was kneeling before the Madonna. It was morning.

Under the overhanging eaves stood a wooden coffin. "They can't bury their dead until it thaws," said the man ahead, "and it's a long way from thawing. Day after tomorrow is Christmas."

They found the path to the road. The armyworm was days long. If they had not returned until days later, it would still have been lumbering along.

There was a loathing in me, Reinhold wrote in his diary. I would like to have remained in my big sleep up there with the good angel people instead of again diving into the army of the vanquished, the rotting, the stinking, of those who no longer hear or see anything around them, who consider themselves to be dead and gone. I am arrogant and await my punishment.

The following night Willi shot himself to death. Reinhold remained standing beside him for a while. At morning, after he had walked on for a long time, he wrote: In deep snow waking is so muffled, life is in such a white distance. Well, now he is dead, my comrade. He put a bullet in his head so that the numbness vanished with a loud bang.

My comrade bloodied the snow red. A trembling came crawling over his body slowly, started with his feet and then came in a heart rhythm as blood out of his ears. And because the wolves were howling so, I made a blood-red snowman out of him.

Since then I've marched quite a bit again, that is, somehow I've set one foot in front of the other. When someone stopped ahead of me or collapsed, I came out of my numbness for a moment into the light and felt the new abandonment.

Now I'm alone among hundreds of thousands and am afraid of my own thoughts but can't escape them. The snow sets limits that no one breaks through.

During the day English fighter bombers flew their forays again. We hid in side paths. Later, partisans shot down from the mountains. Now it's Christmas Eve. I'm standing under a bridge. I've hung my steel helmet on my rifle barrel. I'm writing in the moonlight. My diary lies on the steel helmet. Later my head will sleep there. I don't know why, but I've got hope again. I will survive!

But during this night my comrades are falling to sleep all around me, lying down in the snow to sleep, find, since they've stopped fighting to surrender, that they are like the animals. Their life stinks in the snow, and it is bottomless and eternal.

I am gripped by a sympathy for their bodies, which must fall to earth like that, without a sound, like a coat from a hook. And I have to think that now they are thinking of their wives, they, whose bodies they have left now somewhere deep below them crunch and freeze. I have to think that now pictures of their parents and their friends come to them, which they hang in that hollow lane through which they all must pass, and one after another they fall from the wall. Many will want to have them again, the dearest pictures of life. They raise their heads a bit, their brows, but then their brows become too heavy.

Mechthild, maiden, and in the middle of this night you come to mind: What would your good, human heart say to this? And while I think of that and of your long braids, and when, doing that, I find their beginning and their end, and when I begin to undo them to make the Holy Mother Mary out of you on Christmas Eve, I do see — or I no longer see or no longer stand

189

or no longer lie with the others in the snow, lose my mind and receive pictures — that from those who are still standing or walking shapes come forth, many of them, more and more, a stream of hovering, fluttering, whispering creatures whirls, twists up into the empty air. Faces, bodies, yellow, black, red, stream up, as do cities of fire, spired cathedrals, streets, paths, dark villages. And my comrades become more and more weary with every shape that streams out. The snow grows toward them, sure and lethargically it grows toward them. Then strangers appear, large, white, blow at the pictures until they blur and scatter, put their arms around the empty comrades, whisper, warm them, lean toward them, fill them again.

It is Christmas '44, Mechthild. What can I say. I believe in miracles. I'm still alive.

THE NEXT MORNING came the news that they were standing at the outskirts of Sarajevo.

Days passed before Reinhold went into the city. There the scattered troops were gathered and registered. He had to enter a delousing facility, was ushered through shower installations. His feet were festered, he had a fever. Blood poisoning was diagnosed. He landed in a hospital.

I fell into a feverish sleep and knew nothing about myself. Now they say it is already February, Reinhold wrote in his diary. I'm getting stronger with fat and sweets. I smell the sick men, whose odor of herring hangs stickily in the air, hear their groaning, croaking, their last bad breath, watch how their worldly possessions of blood and excrement, urine and sperm and sour death-sweat collects on the gray beds here. And my homeland is farther than ever and Golda lost forever.

In March, when the fever had faded away and his feet healed, Reinhold received a two-week leave to go home.

Ethnic German refugees and German military columns massed on the train platforms. The trains were overcrowded. Reinhold rode through Belgrade and Vienna, through Munich, Nuremberg, Frankfurt, rode through bombed-out, burned-out cities, fields of rubble.

At night he arrived in his hometown. The train station was still standing. The houses and the churches were still standing. The city had remained undestroyed.

"But I wasn't afraid," Magda said. "I knew you would come back."

Reinhold and Magda were sitting at the kitchen table, holding hands and arms tightly, and laid their heads on the tabletop for one or two hours.

"And now I'll get your father," said Magda.

Then Reinhold had to report. And then he had to ask his father: "What do you know about it?" And then he had to exclaim: "What did you know about it?"

But Heinrich seemed to have grown older, smaller, and Reinhold stopped his questions. And Heinrich left the house, for it was already morning.

And then Magda said that his brother had been called up by the home militia on March 5. And then Reinhold told her about Golda.

Today is March 23, 1945. I am at home, Reinhold wrote in his diary. I walked through my father's city, mother's city, Hanno's city, that was once also my Elsa's city. The city was sleeping peacefully. The city has remained untouched. No signs of smoke and gas light in the sky like in the terrible

Russian dream. The city took me up again, gave me shelter again, enwrapped me with its old walls.

And then my mother and then my father and now my bed! Shall I lie down in my bed, disappear in my bed, and cut down the Russian forest and burn its wood for me until I don't recognize the ashes? What shall I do? What can I do? I have survived, and what now?

I had to tell my mother about Golda, for here and now everything about Golda seems to me just a dream. So I have to talk about her, make her real by talking. And my mother, she supported me fully.

I read back in my diary and find: Being man-and-wife is now my homeland. And now? And now? It's as though there were a hole in me out of which the best of me has fallen. The hole was shot in me by the war.

And Golda, what may she be thinking about me, and how do I appear to her? Maybe she returned home to Karlsruhe or now lives with her aunt in Speyer, and everything that had been between Speyer and Speyer is only a bad dream in which a lovely one is hidden. She dreams it sometimes, perhaps, then maybe cries it sometimes.

Reinhold slept until noon. Magda waked him, said that Uncle Fritz and Uncle Otto were coming to eat, and gave him a letter from Mechthild. The girl had often been with her. They had sat together and talked about Reinhold. She has been transferred to the capital as the regional women's area leader. "She's a good girl," said Magda, not looking at Reinhold. And he would like to have talked about Golda again, would like to have had Golda rise up resplendent before his mother.

Mechthild's letter was from January 10, 1945.

Reino, you should know that my thoughts have gone with you daily, now for all these long years, and that's why I'm writing you this letter, which I will send to your dear mother, so that she can keep it until you return as a hero.

Oh, Reino, how often do I sit in front of the map of the expansive Russian land and imagine to myself where you are wandering and roaming. I hear terrible news and see gigantic fields before me, soaked with the blood of our brave soldiers. But I always believe that I know for sure that yours hasn't flowed into it.

A few weeks ago was Christmas Eve. Sorrow and pain lay heavily on humankind. How many cities lie in rubble, how many people had to lose their lives! When the candles were burning on the tree, all of those appeared to us whom we had lost, my father and my brother along with the many comrades. They quietly communed with us, and their essences filled our own, and we who are alive enclose them deep in our hearts, so they would never be dead. And so again we felt the invincible power of our faith and the might of communality. Never before did

I feel the warmth of a German Christmas celebration so much as this year, that deep meaning of Christmas, the certainty that after night and darkness will come light and new life again. None of us will probably forget the sixth Christmas of the war.

I spent New Year's Eve in the capital. There were a few happy hours with comrades, male and female. We stepped into the New Year with both feet on the ground and heard the voice of the Führer. His profound faith in victory gave us new strength. Whatever may come, we will stand by him, and the reward for our loyalty will be victory. But first of all we all want to work hard, as well as each of us is able.

Who knows when this letter will arrive at your dear parents' house. But in your Russia you're surely in no hurry to be reading anything.

And I give you my hand, Reino, over all the trenches of this frightful war, and wish you a soldier's luck. Mechthild.

P.S. Utz asked about you on Christmas. He's really a fine fellow! He was on home leave only for two days and still came by. In recent weeks he was sent to take courses, is now first sergeant and waits eagerly for his call up.

When Magda's brothers came, Reinhold had to report. Heinrich was sitting with them, said nothing, ate nothing, went earlier than usual back to work.

"The horror will end soon, young man, the war is almost over," Uncle Fritz cried out after Reinhold had told everything. "The Russians are in Pomerania, the French are on Lake Constance, the Americans and the English on the Rhine. But you must speak, young man, everybody must know what happened in your Russian forest.!"

"And I must know what's happened to Elsa Burger," Reinhold heard himself say.

"She's still acting."

"What do you mean, she's still acting?"

"They say that the Gestapo is after her. It's said she has contacts that are contacts, but she's still acting," said his uncle.

Reinhold ran to his room and wrote in his diary:

What am I? Am I a stud? Golda is my bride, and I know it and want it, and still, a flash went through me when I saw my uncle, only because he brought me around to talking about Elsa.

And in addition I talk about those whom I ought to be silent about, if I'm not staking my life on their deaths.

But what am I to do? What can I do? Stand up at the city hall and tell the truth so that no one will believe me? So that none of those will believe me, who go around like Mechthild so unbowed on their false path through the present, on which I was a pathfinder, which I took with them myself? Shall I climb onto the church tower and cry out the truth until they shoot me in the face, finally to lie with those who are silent under the earth of this earth?

During the afternoon Reinhold went to the cemetery. The trees were bare as four years before, when he stood under the stiff angels at Hanno's grave. He went from Hanno's grave to Schade's grave, also found Gabriel's grave, walked from one to the other, walked an hour, two, between the graves, back and forth.

When it was growing dark, he stopped at Hanno's grave and spoke loudly from his heart: "Hanno, I have survived. That has destroyed the life in me. Now I'm merely a hollow tooth, do you understand me! You've been dead four years, friend. I wanted to avenge you, and here I stand with empty hands, and the dagger I carried in my clothing — first it rusted on me, then I lost it and didn't even notice. You'll probably not forgive me for that.

"Hanno, I found the best thing that one can find, that child who is my bride, do you hear? But as a person I have sunk so low that it will drive me here and there until I go to the other one who left me as well, do you under-stand that? I can't really find my way back to myself. And when I think, be-sides, that my home leave becomes shorter with every day, I'd like to step off of this stage."

The cemetery gates were already locked. Reinhold climbed over the wall, as he had climbed over the wall for Schade's wake, and walked to godfather Geilfuß's apartment.

"Who's there?" asked the godfather through the locked door.

"Reinhold Fischer."

"Reinhold? Well, come in!" The godfather opened the door and stepped back and let Reinhold stand in the large door opening and observed him and prodded him with his cane and said finally, "I admit, I'm a bit stunned."

He had grown still more fragile, more frail, with whiter skin and hair. "You'll be amazed, my friend, who's come to us snow-covered in the middle of this cold winter," he called into the dark rooms.

There sat the priest. And probably because the priest was just a priest, Reinhold fell into his arms.

Then he had to talk. The night grew long. The godfather brought one bottle of wine after the other, and the talking and questioning never came to an end.

"What happened in the Russian forests is happening also in the extermi-nation camps all around," said the priest. "Thousands of combat-ready sol-diers are lacking at the front because they're entrusted with the extermination of human beings. And since the extermination camps lie far outside of the cities, our leaders give the German people the possibility of not wanting to know about them."

"The gentleman with the funny mustache rules," said the godfather and struck his cane with its lion's head hard on the parquet floor, "and back and forth and back and forth the angel with the tail thrusts into him. Then he takes the history of this world and the next in his claws, winds it and turns it, and so good becomes evil, and evil is declared just. Then he talks and talks, and when the angel with the tail has talked, he flies away. What remains is only the gentleman with the mustache, bathed in sweat, with a glassy stare."

"But a desperate devil is the most fearful," the priest interrupted the godfather, "and the devil is now desperate, for his thousand-year Reich is going down in firestorms from flamethrowers, rocket shells, fire bombs, and phosphorous bombs. You can hear how distorted his voice is, when on the radio he talks about the retreat from Russia, as he did recently. 'If the German people are no longer strong enough and ready to make sacrifices enough to risk their own blood for their existence, then it should fade away and be exterminated by a different, higher power. I will then shed no tears for the German people. I will despise them.' "

"Certainly. So the circles close," the godfather took the floor again. "And the inner staff of leaders, the Thule murderers, the Death's-Head SS, now sits in hellfire under a rain of hail in its wolf's den and on its Blocksberg, pulls in its head and, since the devil desperately threatens to leave his earthen shell forever, tries to conjure up the devil with the devil."

After midnight, when they had already drunk too much, Reinhold said: "Maybe no German ought to survive the war, maybe the name German must become the inexpressible opposite of the name of God, and perhaps only in that way can the dead under the red Russian forest floor be dead in peace."

"*Through pity knowing, the pure fool*," bellowed the priest deeply out of his easy chair in a muffled minor chord.

"Only what once stood high can fall, young friend," said the godfather. "What is evil is only the reverse of what is good. But the devil loves luxury and always looks for the best lodging. If he had entered the French, the Frenchman would now be a German, for the Jew is hated there just as much."

"*Faith exists, the deaf man hovers*," roared the priest.

"Red Charly is dead," said the godfather.

"And the *Song of Defiance*?"

"Lives," said the godfather. "So, and now go home, young friend. You are brimming with such terror and knowledge that even your youth, as strong as an ox, is overtaxed." And he prodded Reinhold out the door with his cane.

Uncle Fritz and Uncle Otto had waited that evening for Reinhold, said his mother. Uncle Eberhard had come with them, and they had sat with his father around the table and conversed heatedly. And when they had begun to talk about the Jews, an argument had broken out, and Uncle Fritz had talked about Reinhold and the Jews in the Russian forest, and Uncle Eberhard had yelled slander and accusations of slander and had asked his father where Reinhold might have been in the time between Russian Heidelberg and the retreat. "Your son is a deserter!" his uncle had yelled, and they feared the whole neighborhood would wake up. He would get him punished, his uncle had yelled. And his father had shown him the door "Get out!" his father had said. Then his uncle had left, and that caused her the greatest anxiety. Her brothers were of the opinion that Eberhard Gottschlich was capable of anything, and that she should go to her sister so that she could influence her husband.

"And so I'm going," his mother said and tied her head scarf on and left the house.

I wanted to go to the Ziegenberg, wanted to clear up my head there and empty my heart by writing, for my mother's going to her sister for my benefit goes against my grain.

On the way someone calls my name. A woman in a beaver coat. She gets out of a BMW, approaches me, looks neither left nor right, cars honk, brake. I stop on the sidewalk, smell her perfume, don't know her.

"Hey, young man, on home leave?" asks the woman. "Oh, no medals on our hero's chest, how come?" she says. "But you've made good strides," she says, "you've gotten dashing."

I expect her to worm something out of me, to twist a button off my uniform, grab me under the chin and turn my head. But the gotten-up female just laughs, and with that I recognize her as Hanno's sister, for who else could manage to pull down the corner of her mouth laughing.

"Well, and where have you been?" she asked further.

"In Russia," I answer, still being polite and stunned.

Then she says, "Oh," she says, "then do come today for tea with me, young man," she says. "A few gentlemen from the Party will be there, friends of the Party. Tell us about your Russian winter fairy tale!"

"What's Hanno up to?" I ask, so as not to lunge at her throat, not to blow my top.

"Are you ill?" she asks.

"I haven't seen him for some days now," I say, "and that worries me," I say, and leave the creature standing there. But after a couple of steps, I walk back to her. She's standing there thunderstruck, balancing on the curb. "Hanno told me that you have a run in your stocking and a spot on your skirt!" And then I left. And Hanno's laughter lay heavy on my stomach the whole way to the Ziegenberg.

And now I'm sitting up here at the place I had with Hanno and can't picture myself as the one who sat up here with Hanno.

"Writing means waging war," Hanno told me. But this war seems as senseless to me now as the one lost.

But as I write this, Red Charly appears out of my moody torrent, the dream shoots through my head that had led me from the Russian forest to my village: Red Charly had let himself be glimpsed back then with Hanno and Schade. Red Charly is dead, and now my dream at least makes sense.

When Reinhold arrived home, Magda was sitting stunned at the kitchen table. His uncle actually was going to lodge a complaint, against his father and his father's brothers because of slander, and against Reinhold for desertion. And when she had asked her sister to put in a good word, she had gone down to the shoe store and had urged his uncle to listen to Reinhold at least. And now his uncle expected him that evening.

Reinhold went to his room and wrote a letter to Elsa: *It seems I'm being forced to put my affairs in order, Elsa! And so I'm writing to you as I did so often before. After long years I'm here in the city for a short time, and since the way things are it is possible that we won't meet, I want to tell you once again that I loved you and want to thank you for being the one who awakened that emotion in me. Afterwards, I want to say, too, there was a great desolation, and even today I would be glad to find out what prevented you from sending this forlorn one a greeting. But that should not burden you, for it doesn't carry weight anymore. Reinhold.*

It was already dark when he went to Elsa Burger's apartment. On the street a piano could be heard playing. Reinhold turned up the collar of his uniform, as though doing that he were more protected, more hidden. And as he was standing there and freezing and listening, he became aware that someone else was standing there. A few steps ahead someone was standing, looked at Reinhold, looked away, walked back and forth, but did not leave.

Reinhold held the letter against the wall of Elsa Burger's building, wrote on the back of the envelope: *If you need help, perhaps you can reach me still at the old address*, and tossed it in the letterbox. Then he went to his uncle's house.

From the apartment above the shoe store in Schönstraße light came through the cracks of the blackout curtains. The old orchard was black and bare.

"And I had to laugh, dear godfather," said Reinhold, "how everything just begins and goes on and now perhaps ends already, for in that old orchard I first became aware of my masculinity. So now I stand there again, on the one hand a man, on the other reduced more and more to a boy by those who were sitting up in the light behind the blackout curtains."

"And actually, all of them were sitting around the big table, staring at me. My uncle rolled up his shirt sleeves. 'Hi, there!' said my cousin, and had stuffed herself into a dress, the neckline of which seemed to me to be far too large for her new abundance. And so — childhood never ends — I thought of the photograph that a certain Herr Butz had: a woman with a cow and a gigolo. And somehow I was already furious."

"My male cousin was also there. Because of a muscle weakness he hadn't had to go into the military and helped now in the shoe store as a junior partner. 'And how's your heart?' he asked with a grin in greeting. 'Campaign in Russia, shooting down Jews, and so forth. Does it go along with that?'"

"'My heart,' said I, 'do I have one?' For you must know, dear godfather, I had promised my mother not to let myself be carried away by anything, and to recite well an appropriately invented story about Jewish uprising and Russian captivity."

"'Do come and eat first,' said my aunt and drew me to a chair and said how strong and manly I looked now and how many enemies I probably had done in."

"'I'm engaged,' said my cousin and held out her ring finger under my nose."

"'Eat,' said my aunt and shoved me a plate with hard-boiled eggs. And, dear godfather, you'll laugh, for all the childish torment, all the insults and degradation came over me at the sight of the eggs, and I looked at the egg in front of me, which they had once offered a hungry me, and the laughter reverberated in my ears that had clapped over me when I was about to eat the egg and it was one that had been blown out."

"'My fiancé plays the piano,' said my cousin, and I heard her laughter from before, when she had called me a *have not*. And then, I don't know — I don't know. I grabbed the plate with the eggs and threw it against the wall. And paid no attention to what happened then and walked away. I was simply driven to you, driven with giant strides."

"Now there's danger," said the godfather. "Calm down, have a good drink, and then go home, pack what you need, and come right back for a while to me."

"But it makes no sense anymore," Reinhold exclaimed. "As a person I have become meaningless. There'll be punishment for my going around bursting with significance. But what, dear godfather, awaits me as punishment for not taking in my hand the dagger that was given me, that had become so sharp through Hanno's death?"

"Consider your stubbornness," cried out the godfather in reply. "Forget the public spirit that has marked you. *Steal the light from the jaws of the snake*, young friend, and bring it stubbornly with your words into the new age!"

"There will be no new age: The sun will rise mornings and set evenings, horrors will happen, the stars will not fall from the sky, and in the end horror will even become familiar to us. I have lived twenty-one years and eleven months. It seems to me that's enough," Reinhold cried out and started out the door.

"*Not until the extreme is reached will anything become its opposite!*" The godfather blocked Reinhold's way. They stood for a while facing one another as though for battle, until the doorbell rang and the priest arrived.

He brought the news that men of the Death's-Head SS had been handed over to the municipal insane asylum. The nurses there had turned to the Church, since they did not know what to do in face of what the new admissions might entail. He had looked into it, said the priest. The leader of that Ordensburg in which Hanno von Wolfsberg had been was among them.

"Well, that was to be expected," said the godfather, and advised him to keep his distance from it. "You won't rescue the enemy anymore," he said. "Anyone who has allowed himself to be made the seat of that power down here can save himself only beyond this life. That fate is not to be envied, Father, for repentance and atonement cannot be accommodated there. Power will avail itself of them. They'll be found, hanging from window bars, and it will be said it happened in a state of mental derangement. And night is truly around them, and darkness will further be around them, and still, in the end, up there their poor souls will be received in grace. But our young friend here, Father, in his total death-weary desperation, resolute in the face of death, needs your words of encouragement now."

"Trust, like Job the saint, in your Lord, the Guardian of this world," the priest said. And as he went on talking, Reinhold believed he was listening to the cantor from the Russian forest. "Even if all the Jews and all the Torah rolls burn, the flesh will burn and the bones will burn and the parchment, but the letters, they will fly away from the flames."

"The cantor in the Russian forest said that," exclaimed Reinhold.

"They say it, for it is their truth and it's ours, for ours was born from theirs," said the priest.

And then when Reinhold went home, he promised to come back as soon as possible and as unnoticeably as possible during the night.

Magda and Heinrich were sitting in front of the radio in the kitchen: Major attacks were expected during the night.

"Good that you're here," said Magda.

The march music was drowned out by the sirens. Magda took the bundle with the bare essentials that stood ready in the corner of the vestibule. "Good that you're finally here," she said.

In the streets people were running and yelling. The sirens were howling. In the cellar sat Frau Zopf and Frau Polster, whose husbands had died, and the two women who had moved into Herr Herz's apartment were sitting there.

"The enemy has reached the city limits," said Frau Polster and pressed a sofa pillow on her head. The sirens kept howling. Antiaircraft guns began to roar. A humming, booming, piping began. Magda grabbed Reinhold's hand. Heinrich stood at attention. Everyone was holding his breath. The light on the ceiling flickered — a crashing, bursting, splintering and again and again, one wave after the other.

One strike brought them all to their feet. Everyone was standing, staring at one another. "That was as aerial mine," said Frau Zopf. The lights went out. In the darkness they called one another by name until Magda had lighted a candle.

Heinrich was still standing, long after the sound for the all clear had come. — I'm worried about my father. He stands like a tree that knows it will be felled. But he's standing, he's resisting! So he'll probably also stand when they come and swing the ax of vengeance at him. And I, his son, will take a stand before my father and cry out: "Halt — this man here has seen only the good in the evil!"

More and more attacks came. Reinhold stayed with his parents and the women in the cellar all night long, and wrote in his diary: The air down here is asphyxiating. The stones of the wall are covered with cold sweat. Limbs tremble, hands cramp, and the city above falls into rubble. The prospect of being buried alive is great. Incidentally, you can pretend it was an earthquake, for when all around it crashes, the walls wobble, and the floor slips away, it isn't hard and it makes it easier, for that could come from the hand of God, and that — as it's drummed into our Christian souls — would make sense.

And the Führer? He sits with his henchmen very deep underground and is probably now having a next-to-last unholy last supper. And the Führer's lord and master speaks through him with a fiery tongue, swears his disciples for the six-hundredth-and-sixty-sixth time to that community, and proclaims that he will seal that bond with his sacrificial blood. And that sacrificial blood, so he proclaims, will be transfigured into the new fame of his splendor. And to the empty hulls that sit around their Führer, fed by his stream, whose souls have long since been up and away and wander whimpering in the crowns of German treetops, he will promise that that community, after he has left it to journey home, will come together anew and again and again to bear his emptiness from here out into all the world.

At morning, two hours after the all clear, they climbed from the cellar out into the street. Rubble, conflagrations everywhere. A firestorm had swept through the city. The smoke was asphyxiating, people with damp cloths over their mouths and noses, with sunglasses, diving goggles, homeless people, leftover people, people still in fiery buildings. Window panes shattered, gas lines exploded, rafters flew through the air.

The train station was still standing. The trains were still running. Reinhold fought for a place for his parents in a train that was traveling up to the Vogelsberg, to that place where his mother had been born, where his grandparents' farm was located, on which distant relatives farmed, with whom his parents were welcome.

Magda had begged Reinhold to travel with them and hide in the woods near the farm. Heinrich had remained silent, even when they had walked past his place of work, which was still burning, even when a colleague had spoken to him. Magda took Heinrich's hand, but he pulled it back, and there was no more than a nod of the head from the train window to Reinhold, who stood on the train platform in the crowd and clamor of the many who wanted to get out of the city.

Magda waved, and when Reinhold could no longer see her hand, which went up and down without stopping, a howling rose up in him that he did not suppress, that he let howl out of him, that vanished in the crowding and clamor all around him on the platform.

He walked past the municipal theater, which was still standing, walked past Elsa's building, which was still standing, turned into the godfather's street — nothing more was there. Men with stretchers were running around and taking injured people and corpses away. Others wandered and dug for people and objects.

The godfather was sitting in his easy chair. He had the lion's head in his hand, but the ebony cane had broken off. He was sitting in his study on the third floor. A house wall and two meters of floor remained unscathed. He was sitting still and seemed to be observing what was happening below him.

"I'm coming!" roared Reinhold. "I'll get you down!"

"But young man," said an ambulance man, "the gentleman up there is surely dead! Are you a relative?"

"What do you mean dead!" Reinhold screamed. "He's just quiet and is looking. He has an overview, as always!"

"No, it comes from the blast," said the ambulance man. "The lungs burst, then the dead look as though they are alive."

Reinhold helped rescue and clean up until it was dark. The godfather seemed to watch him doing it. When they finally could put up a long ladder to get him, Reinhold climbed up and said: "Good evening." And then he took the old, fragile man and carried him down to the ground.

"He is my relative," said Reinhold. "I'd like to bury him."

He gave his name and address, the godfather was placed with the other corpses on a truck, a slip of paper with Reinhold's information was tied to his wrist. He was holding the lion's head tightly.

I ran to the church, called out "song of defiance" three times, and knocked three times on the door, and called out and knocked. I was dizzy. It seemed to me that time would stumble here, lean, fall backwards. I called out and knocked until I realized that no one heard me. I tore one of the last white pages from my diary, wrote my name on it, and pushed it under the door.

I ran home, lay down on my bed, and stayed there, too, when the avenging angel plunged from the sky with a howl, when the walls of the old building swayed, when all around the house there was fire.

Now I'm trying to gather my life up by writing: Golda comes on very despondent feet. She merely brushes against me, a stranger. The whole world is strange to me. Not only things left behind, Golda, the forest, and Russia, also the things lost, my home town, the German nation. Hanno, Schade, Gabriel, and you, dear godfather, give me a bit of cover here in my alienation!

The next morning Reinhold found a letter from Mechthild.

Reino, they have assaulted our good, old city. Everything that was beautiful here is now a pile of rubble. But our two old churches are still standing, and their spires rise more proudly than ever and proclaim unbroken German will and the courage to go on living.

I went with awful fear to your parents' house, but it's standing, thank God, entirely and even firmly among all the rubble. And since no one came to the door, I'm writing you this note on the door threshold.

We, too, had good luck at home. Only window glass is shattered. Erika, you know her from the harvest project Vineland, was killed last night. And we found Trudel's parents among the dead in the bunker of horror on Friedrichstraße. Nothing is left for Trudel either. How much must a girl like her endure! But she's courageous and deserves our highest respect. If anyone lives his world-view, then it's Trudel.

The services operation in the city is now as good as crippled. In spite of that, my leave is at an end, I have to return to my post. That inhuman enemy will not bring us down! Mechthild.

I ran through my city, through blocked-off streets, over fields of rubble. I galloped, jubilated. I felt a crazy joy, a spark of giddiness at the destruction. The Café Deibl was still standing. I went inside and sat down at the table at which I had sat first with Gabriel and then with Elsa. There was even a kind of coffee. It was ridiculous, and I drank it with enjoyment. And would like to have remained sitting there as I had remained sitting that time with Elsa.

But then I was driven to go again to the remains of the godfather's study. I walked through the rubble, over the debris, feeling happy doing so. But when I heard a child crying and was struck with the horrible idea that some-one was still buried in the rubble, I started to search and found Mary with her Child Jesus.

"Where is your Joseph," I asked, and had to laugh, for a young woman was sitting there, with a cloth over her head and an infant in her arms. And because the whole image was set under beams that had fallen all over the place, I had to consider it the stall of Bethlehem whether I wanted to or not.

But like every man to whom the Madonna seems familiar, the young woman seemed familiar to me. "Do we know each other?" I asked.

"No, of course not," she said with the voice of a Madonna.

"Do you need help?" I asked stupidly. And was about to burden myself with the young woman and take her home with me for the time being, in the reasonable belief that she had been bombed out, her husband off to war, her parents killed, God knows what, when out of the darkness of the ruins a very small boy stepped over to us and said "Mama" to the image of the Ma-donna. And so then I took the three home.

After I had satisfied their hunger as far as it went with Mother's last pro-visions, they went to sleep. When in the night it again crashed all around, I waked the young woman and said she should go to the cellar for the sake of the children.

"No," said the Madonna, "I can't. I'm Jewish."

At that I was speechless. And it thundered and flashed so terribly around us that I threw myself over her. And then the image came to me: Father with the board out of which he had planned to build me a knight's castle! And then my father struck me from the image, and outside the bombs were falling, and next door the house flew into the air, and my father's blows came blow by blow.

Then came the all clear, and I said: "Rachel Neumann!"

"Reinhold," said the Madonna.

And it was Rachel. Really and truly, it was she. And when I had finally comprehended that, I gave Indian whoops until the children shrieked along piteously.

After the two little ones had cried themselves to sleep, we sat down at the kitchen table. "Tell me about it," I said and couldn't help thinking of Golda.

"From the beginning?" she asked. And the Madonna, who was Rachel Neumann, seemed to me to take on Golda's features.

But then she told me. Her Madonna's mouth became hard, and Golda's childlike face would not fit it anymore: "In January '39 I moved with my parents away from here to Leipzig, where not a single person knew us, and so no one could know that we are Jews."

"But I still remember," I had to interrupt her. "They said that your apartment door had been kicked in. The remainder of your supper had been standing on the table still. Your bed, they said, had been thrown onto the courtyard."

"It was supposed to look like they had dragged us away. No one was supposed to look for us," she said and spoke rapidly so that I wouldn't interrupt anymore: "In July '39 my parents sent me to Berlin. I lived there in the 'House of New Settlers,' a school of the Zionist Movement, studied Hebrew and Jewish history, and I liked it. When transports to Palestine were organized, I wanted to join, but my parents had remained German nationals in spite of everything and didn't want to leave. My father belonged to the National Union of Jewish Front Soldiers and on holidays still wore the Iron Cross that my grandfather had received in the First World War. My father, you know," the young woman exclaimed and tugged at my sleeve, as though I were that father, and she exclaimed: "My father was German to the core, do you understand that? Just imagine, in the spring of '43 that man made a will and made me the sole heir of his estate, with the stipulation that I be within the national borders at the time of his death, and just imagine, please, that otherwise he wanted to make the Association for Germanhood the heir!"

Rachel Neumann! We were sitting at the kitchen table facing one an-other. We had lighted a candle. The children were asleep in the next room in my father's and mother's bed.

But the rupture followed harshly: "Why are you here?" she cried out. "Why not at the front? Are you a Nazi?" And she tugged at my sleeve, and her whole beautiful Madonna face was gone.

"Never mind," I said. "I'll tell you later." But she wouldn't let me. "I de-serted in Russia," I couldn't help saying, "was with Jews in the forest, am engaged to a Jewish girl. Her name is Golda."

The Madonna face then reappeared, and the pale young woman took up her thread again: "After classes I went as a student trainee to Berlin-Weißensee to the Jewish Deaf and Dumb Home for Young Girls. But soon they said: 'Jews are not fit to live!' and the girls were taken away, slapped, kicked, shoved onto trucks, and were mutes, after all, couldn't cry out. But one could whistle — she whistled and whistled."

"Why are you here?" she cried out at me again, "and where is your fian-cée, and how come a deserter is wearing a uniform?"

So I had to tell her, and with that she was calm again, but her face re-fused to be a Madonna's face to me anymore.

"I then worked in the Auerbach Orphanage," she returned to herself, "and got acquainted with Max, who as a half orphan had been there. He had had to take an apprenticeship as a mason and kept living in the Home. He's two years younger than I. I was eighteen, he was sixteen. They made fun of us. But we got married anyway. Max said that only those who were husband and wife could live together in the concentration camp, and he told his mother that he wanted to go to the concentration camp with me, not with her.

"I got pregnant. The orphanage was closed down. But those who could take care of themselves could stay. We stayed. Where else could we have gone? I gave birth in the Jewish Hospital, and the doctors, who had to be understanding, circumcised my son! Max's mother didn't touch him. 'So what! A baby,' she said. Then they picked her up from the factory where she did forced labor. She knew a woman who would have hidden her, but she was pious and peculiar and didn't want to be a burden to anyone."

And as I listened, the young woman went to sleep right in the middle of her story, and then I could observe her in peace and let the image of the child who had stood with serious eyes in the bay window come over me, and the whole horror came over me, which the child at the bay window even with her serious eyes could not have foreseen.

But when I stood up to let her sleep and to go to sleep myself, she awoke in startlement and held tightly to me: "Please, stay and let me tell you!"

"Tell me," I said, and couldn't help thinking of Golda. "When you talk, you can't cry!"

"But I'm not crying," she said, and went on: "The Jewish community had to provide craftsmen who under the supervision of the SS had to build air-raid shelters and repair bomb damage. Max was among them. They said there, 'Work more, work faster, or it's Auschwitz tomorrow!' The craftsmen received slips of paper that were to keep them and their families back for the last transport. But when the Gestapo came to get everybody who was still living in the Auerbach Orphanage, Max was at work and the slip not yet signed. Everyone was taken to a transit camp. Two children's nurses and the cook resisted, saying that through their husbands they had the slip concerned, and I said I had one too, and kept quiet about it not being signed. Then from a list the names were read off of those who could go home. So I went, my baby in my arms and without hurrying, as though my name had been read off. I went back to the orphanage — where else could I have gone! When Max came, we packed the baby carriage full and were up and out of there."

"We went to the woman who wanted to hide Max's mother. The apartment had a lot of rooms. In each one an illegal hid out. But no one who lived there knew who else lived there, so that no one could betray anyone else. But when the woman saw my crying baby, she lost her nerve, gave us sleeping bags, and sent us into the woods. In the middle of the night we heard shots and barking dogs and ran away."

"We traveled until morning, from one end of Berlin to the other. Then we crawled into bombed-out buildings, every night somewhere else — where else could we have gone! We received marks and money from the woman who had the apartment, and so the summer passed, until it got cold, until October."

I had listened speechless. Then suddenly the young woman flew into a rage: "You are a Nazi, after all, and you know that it'll soon be over with. That's why you're hiding here, and you want to use me as an alibi Jew!" She trembled and trembled so much that I picked her up and carried her to her sleeping children. I covered her up and left then.

I couldn't stay in the house. In spite of the daytime and the light, the black-out curtains at Elsa's were still drawn, and again someone was standing on the other side of the street. He looked away when I looked at him, walked back and forth, but did not leave.

In the godfather's neighborhood it was peaceful, not a person far and wide. The sun was shining on the rubble. Torn off pieces were blowing in the spring wind. Torn loose pieces rolled gently over debris and ashes. The first birds were singing.

Suddenly I remembered that I had drunk many a good drink at the godfather's, and so I followed this notion over the ruins, and was in a good mood, exactly as though the dear godfather had been present protecting and leading me. I found the stairs to the cellar, covered with rubble, of course, but still with the requisite opening. Two cellar rooms had not collapsed, and in one of them an excellent wine cellar was laid out. I thanked the dear godfather politely, stuck four bottles of old Bordeaux in my pockets, climbed up to the sunlight, and made my way to the black market. There I traded just like that for butter, plus milk and chocolate.

Proudly laden I went back. The one little rascal was hanging on the white breast of the Madonna, with abandonment the other was tearing one page after the other out of my beloved Karl May books.

There was an opulent meal, but the young woman was not to be stayed, and soon she was continuing: "In October '43 the woman who had the apartment put us up with a madame who for good money accepted guests like us. In December the heavy night attacks by the English began, and in the hellish noise I could finally scream. 'Bomb everything to bits, lay everything flat!' I screamed during those nights. But when an aerial bomb went off, the building collapsed. We were able to get out. 'Go to the National Socialist Women's Organization,' the madame advised. 'Carry your son in your arms, wail, and say that you were bombed out, your papers were lost, that they ought to send you to the country.' I followed her advice, called myself Frieda Gerold, howled and held up my blond son. Then they said: 'This German mother must get into the countryside immediately!' I received a ticket and was sent to Prießenhorst an der Warthe."

"During those days I got news of my mother. To be cautious we had written one another only to general delivery. When she went to pick up a letter from me, she had forgotten to add the necessary Sara to her signature, in accordance with the decree. She was reported and taken away. To Auschwitz. You know what that means."

And when I said No, she was seized again by a fit of rage. Apparently, and no wonder, the young woman had no nerves anymore. But what am I to do, when small fists pound me! I ducked and tried to think about Rachie Neumann, who had been so soft and white, white and holy. "Rachel, what has become of your braids?" I asked under her fists.

And behold, she stopped. "Don't you really know?" she asked.

"Well, what?" I asked back.

"Auschwitz," she said. And then told me about it. And then I had to tell her. And after Auschwitz and the Russian forest we somehow felt even, full of horror.

"Tell me," I said, and wrapped a blanket around her and couldn't help thinking about Golda.

"Yes, I'll tell you," she said. "My mother succeeded in smuggling two letters out of Auschwitz. In the first one she wrote that she was full of confidence, was strong and healthy and would survive the hell. In the second letter, which came much later, she said: 'I can't stand it anymore. I'll not survive. We'll never see one another again.'"

During the night there was a furious ringing of the doorbell. We didn't stir, and the children also remained quiet. When the ringing was gone, she spoke further, softly and quietly, as though no word could cast a cloud over her: "Max returned to the ruins — where else could he have gone! I traveled with my son to Prießenhorst and was put up at a small farm. Cows, pigs, chickens, only a woman and her daughter at home, husband and son on the Eastern front. But then came the attacks by the Americans on Berlin. I was worried about Max and wrote him at general delivery that he should come. He came but couldn't stay long, otherwise the farm women, whom I had told that my husband was on furlough, wouldn't have believed us. And then I got pregnant again."

"Crazy," she anticipates me, "crazy, so what? Why not set our own against the others! Then I didn't see Max for nine months, for weeks at a time received no answer to my letters. Began labor, had to leave my son with the farm women, went into the hospital in Landsberg, gave birth to another son. But I was afraid, and after two days took the baby and ran away. The farm women said that a National Socialist Peoples' Welfare nurse had been there and looked after my son, had looked at my son and noticed that he had been circumcised. I packed my things and ran for the train."

"When I arrived in Berlin with my two sons, I went to the woman who had the apartment. Max was there. The woman gave us some money. We returned to the ruins. The bombs fell day and night, but because of the informers and the search troops we didn't go to the bunkers."

"It got to be winter. We found a basement room in which an electric wire was still working. We found a heating stove. We survived. Then my old nursemaid sent me money by general delivery. I was to go to her with my sons, she would hide us. Max stayed in the ruins, I came here. And when I arrived yesterday, I was standing in front of the nursemaid's bombed-out house."

"But I don't let myself think back on it. I didn't dwell on my mother's death either," she exclaimed and pushed me away and ran to the children and cried herself to sleep.

Now I'm sitting in my room, have hung, like Herr Butz once did, a checkered handkerchief over my lamp and write cautiously so that the scratching of my pen won't wake up the three of them.

"Keeping a diary," Hanno told me, "helps think your thoughts to an end and to evaluate them. Tell things to yourself," Hanno told me, "that way you can write the things out from inside you, understand them, put them in order, change them." And by trying that again, I realize: I have now become the protector of the Madonna and her boys! And at least tonight I can finally believe in the chance for a German to be of use to a Jew.

The next morning Reinhold found two letters in his postbox. *Every night at eleven at the usual place*, it said in the one, which was signed *Song of Defiance*. And in the other, it said: *Reinhold, please, you are putting yourself and me in danger! For God's sake, don't write me again! It's wonderful that you're alive! Go on living! Elsa.*

He went to the Ziegenberg, sat down at the place that he had had with Hanno, looked down at the ruins of the city, drew lines with his finger in the cold dirt, drew rectangles, hexagons, octagons, drew and divided wildly and grimly, and could still not bring any order to the loose March soil.

When he came home, the children were crying. The doorbell had rung persistently. There had been pounding on the door and yelling. It had been men, several of them.

They packed a few things together, went out onto the street, walked through the city of rubble, walked until it struck eleven. Whenever Reinhold saw familiar faces, he hid or embraced the young woman and buried his face in her woolens.

At eleven o'clock he knocked three times on the church door. "Song of defiance," he called out, and the door was opened.

"It's not possible. The cadet colonel," someone said, and Reinhold recognized the girl Gisèle.

He pushed Rachel with the children through the church building, through the door behind the altar, down the stairs into the church basement. There sat the priest with some people whom Reinhold recognized, around the big table. The girl with the red lips and the long curls was sitting there too, but her curls were gone and her lips pale. "Camouflage," she said, grinning.

"Who is the woman with the children?" asked Gisèle.

And Reinhold told the story of Rachel Neumann.

"It won't be very long and the Christian Church will strew its head with ashes and tear its robes," said the priest.

"It won't be very long," Gisèle cried out and hit the table with her fist. "The Soviet troops have reached Königsberg. In Yugoslavia the partisans are storming German positions. The first units of the Red Army are in Austria. In the West the German front is falling apart. The Americans are crossing the Rhine."

Reinhold and Rachel Neumann stayed with the children in the room under the church.

Evenings the friends from the *Song of Defiance* came and brought groceries that they had traded for with wine from the godfather's absolutely inexhaustible cellar. But the priest could not take care of the burial of the godfather, because bombs had fallen on the morgue and the corpses were burned.

Every evening the friends brought more news: Cologne had fallen. Königsberg had capitulated. Berlin was surrounded. American troops were marching into Nuremberg and Munich. The Americans had liberated the prisoners from Dachau and Ravensbrück.

And Reinhold wrote in his diary: When the fliers are over us, I can be sure that my good Rachel raises her fist to the ceiling of the church and screams: "Hit them, hit them!" And when it's striking all around, there's a dance. It seems she's full of good faith that our Christian God is protecting her.

Last night when she did that, it suddenly took the breath out of me, and I would like to have shaken her. But I controlled myself, for she is fragile, and maybe she's already broken to pieces. I ran out of the church, left her alone, for the first time in weeks stood at the church door and could breathe again.

Sirens were howling, people were running, carrying me along. Since many were suffocated and burned in the large bunkers here, many now seek shelter in the two big churches. I let myself be carried along to the Church of St. John, in which the old priest had once read from the Book of Revelations.

Fire bombs were falling, phosphorous bombs, and high-explosive bombs. Through the sky-high stained-glass windows the people saw their city burning.

The lore about ancient sites of mystic power made it possible to erect the St. John structure, which stood firm around me while the walls were falling everywhere. And I looked up into the Gothic splendor, through which the flashes of fire flared up, and realized: Such heights are sometimes required to look at God.

Only, the children screamed so loudly that I, accustomed to being quiet in my hideout, became crazily afraid that those in the air could hear the children and strike. And I saw cracks running through the walls and saw the saint's statue, which was standing beside me holding lilies, split. The lilies tumbled out of his hand, the crack split him vertically, one half fell over and shattered, the other with its hand empty of lilies kept standing helplessly.

But groups had formed around the priest and the preacher to resist fear, and someone was standing near me and roaring against the screaming and the thunder of the bombardment: "...Nights of misery are apportioned to me, doesn't it say that in Job," he roared, "and doesn't it say there, too: His troops ... have encamped around my tent!" And there I recognized Beilharz, one-legged and on crutches, it is true, but with a strong stance on his left leg. And then he, too, didn't believe his eyes, his preacher's voice failed him, and we two were wrapped in one another's arms in the middle of the House of God in the middle of a hail of bombs.

We moved under one of the Gothic cornices, and I found out that my friend's leg had remained in the Crimea. And so we told one another about one thing and another, and when Beilharz wished "the pale criminal" would go to the devil, confident about the coming evening, I invited him to my church when we parted at dawn.

When I came back, pale Rachel had become a little paler but denied that it could have had to do with my long absence and was elated on account of the recent destruction of our home town. So nothing kept me with her, and I withdrew into a church corner.

Miracles do well in churches, and as soon as I write, it's as though every experience were discovering its significance. And that is a miracle, perhaps the greatest. And every time, Hanno looks over my shoulder and admonishes: "Don't get confused about yourself, just go your own way, otherwise the miracle can't happen!"

Golda is so deep in the forest, and there it's so dark that I recognize her here only as an outline, and I keep telling myself: "You must trace her outline thickly with your ink, else she'll fade away entirely!"

The days are now strident with events. Even when I sit within thick church walls, it still goes straight through me, smashes into me, possesses me, and only at night, when I can sleep, does my soul keep watch and is at the same time completely exhausted with aching for Golda.

Until now I've tried in vain to persuade the dear godfather to make his way to me and visit me in my dreams. He smiles and remains where he is.

211

He's also truly very old, and it would be up to my youthfulness to set out on its way. But I still don't know the way. Exactly as with Golda, nothing but external experience blocks the downward and upward climb, as detritus and rock fall. And so I wish with all my heart, and for nothing else — except again and again, Golda and Golda — to gain and experience the solitude that will let me undertake those kinds of travels with words as my wagon.

The world changes faster at some times than at others. My dead ones must add on to their dwelling, and for those of mine who are alive the rooms are getting too big.

At evening his friends came.

"The Führer is demanding the death of the people. The German people should die. He is demanding sacrificial death," Gisèle cried out. "The SS is running through the streets, into buildings and bunkers. They're saying now, 'Do not surrender to the enemy forces, take your own lives. The Russians have no sense and understanding, the Americans have no pride and honor!' From the radio comes, 'Werewolves, make use of the night!'"

"Humiliated, vanquished, destroyed by those to whom the holy Evil One is alien, by inferior average people, that is their end," cried out the priest. "And that end, the Führer says, will be the end of the universe. He challenges the German people to destroy their cities and factories, they're to blow up their dikes and bridges, and all for the legend of the twilight of the Gods!"

"From his bunker the Führer directs armies that no longer exist," cried out the girl with the pale lips and short hair. "Those who still follow him lay hands themselves on the last German walls. He has given the order to flood the Berlin subway, and the order is being followed! Thousands have fled there. Thousand will now die. He wants total destruction, just as he wanted total war — nothing should fall into the hands of the enemy."

"Except for a field of potatoes," cried out the pale Rachel with her boys in her lap.

And then there was silence until the priest said: "The blame is on the just as well as the unjust."

"Show me the just!" Rachel cried out, and the boys began to cry.

"When evil bursts in, it bursts in everywhere, not only into the murderers, but also into those who are murdered, not only into the persecutors, but also into those who are persecuted," said Beilharz in the new stillness.

"Will anyone here take it amiss that I perceive with satisfaction the destruction of Germany as the judgment of God?" Rachel shrieked, and the boys shrieked with her.

Then Gisèle came running through the church, and the nave echoed with her shout: "The Führer is dead! Long live Germany!"

It turned out to be a long night, and out of the godfather's cellar a case of champagne was suddenly there.

"A new Germany is beginning," said the priest, "and the dead will arise and help us to build it."

"*When all the dead arise, then I'll vanish into the void*," sang Beilharz from the *Holländer* and was about to light a candle of mercy for the Führer. But even the priest was opposed to that, and pale Rachel would have lacerated him with her nails, if he had not held her.

"Nothing will be German anymore," she cried out. "What is German will be eradicated! In one or two more seconds, no one in the world will know how to spell that adjective anymore!"

"I've begun secretly to study Hebrew," Beilharz said awkwardly. "Rachel is feminine and red. It seems to me it stands for vengeance there."

"It will be a new beginning, as at the beginning of the world, when the earth was without form and void," said the priest.

The next morning came the news that the Red flag was waving over the Brandenburg Gate.

Reinhold stayed on in the church with Rachel Neumann and the children, waiting for news that his friends brought evenings, waiting until one morning the priest opened up the church doors and tolled the bells and said: "The war is over!"

The sky was blue, the chestnuts were blooming, people wandered around looking for people, American tanks roared through the streets.

Partly on foot and partly by horse-drawn wagon, Reinhold arrived one evening at his parents' place in the Vogelsberg. Heinrich lay in bed and didn't stir. Magda was sitting at the dark window.

The next morning Reinhold persuaded his father to take a walk with him through the woods.

"I know so little anymore what God is that I don't know myself anymore," Heinrich said while walking. "My God has slipped away from me, and I've slipped away from myself."

They walked all day long. At evening Reinhold invited his father to a rural tavern. Heinrich drank like a horse and stood up tall and spoke and could not be stopped: "I am a National Socialist, and I'll remain a National Socialist. And why am I one and why will I remain one? Because National Socialism summoned each one of us out of the confines of his existence, because it put us into a service in which we could grow beyond ourselves. And I say it was a service to mankind. And I say that, even though it is now said that it was a disservice. And why do I say that, and why will I say it? Because I can't re-hang my pictures anymore, even if the wall on which they hang crumbles, even if my pictures fall down from the wall because my wall shatters. Because I can't set candles around anymore, even if they get blown out. And I will not build me a new wall! And I will not light any more candles!"

Heinrich was talking so loudly that the farmers who were sitting at their favorite tables listened, stood up, were so carried away that they joined in with Heinrich's speech like in a liturgy. And so Heinrich for once, for the first and last time, stood tall before the people and was their spokesman. And the people were on his side.

Two days later Reinhold returned to the city and moved back to the apartment with Rachel and the children.

A letter from Mechthild had come.

Reino, a comrade is traveling home and will put this letter in your mailbox, if your building is still standing. Everything's over, Reino, everything's over! The foreigners are stretching their claws over our land, night behind us, darkness ahead of us, no more Germany. Reino, how can I grasp it! Lost, everything lost that we loved! I search for the Führer, search for him in my innermost being, wish, pray that he may receive his justification in history, that he may still receive some satisfaction through it.

Is there no justice in the world anymore, Reino? Will that eternal power in which we believed so deeply be silent? Did we deserve then to plunge into the abyss? Is our guilt then so large?

Reino, I'd like not to miss the end predestined for me. If at the decisive moment I cling cowardly to life, then afterwards I'll bitterly despise myself. But is this the moment?

The capital is now full of foreigners, and I walk around like a criminal. What have I done wrong? Loved my Fatherland, and more than anything else! What is Germany now, Reino, what are we Germans now? An endless army of ghosts, of cripples that chase me through my dreams. And again and again the ghosts press across the threshold of the day and meet me on the destroyed streets.

Why? Why did all this happen? The war lost, so much lost! And everything else suspicious: bright flags and singing people, silent forests, clear stars at night. What remains for us, I wonder? Mechthild.

Rachel came running out of the bedroom, she was screaming, she struck Reinhold: "You were a Nazi, and your father was a Nazi. You don't have to deny it, I found your uniforms, the decorations and papers in the wardrobe!"

That evening there was a gathering in the church. Beilharz came and reported that Gummi had fallen in battle, there was a missing-in-action report about Utz, Hanno's parents and his sister had killed themselves with cyanide, Fräulein Dr. Freitag with gas, and the music teacher had jumped from the city hall tower.

"There the faith of millions now lies bleeding in the rubble of great myths, where the idol has fallen and his place is empty," said the priest, "but still our German people will keep following its urge for self-sacrifice full tilt like a curse. A new sense must now be brought into its emptied existence so that a dark seed does not take root again."

"Yes, Cadet Colonel, how is it," cried the girl with the pale lips and the short hair, "when the little bit of big time that a person has experienced is crossed out, when there's nothing more that calls and demands, nothing that binds, for which life, fighting, dying is worthwhile — what do you plant in such an empty breast?"

"Eberhard Gottschlich," Beilharz cried out in the quiet, "I had forgotten him. He didn't bite into a capsule, he didn't jump from the tower, as one of the first Party members in the city he was denazified yesterday because his wife, according to the newest laws, counts as a kind of resistance fighter, since she sang in the church choir. The House of Comrades is still standing, the shoe store is open again."

And after more quiet, Gisèle said: "Maybe its not flight and compulsion, maybe it's an infection. But healing requires discernment and knowledge. However, the infection is far from being cured. It will smolder and lurk until the graves are closed and the tears dried up, then it will flame up again."

"Because the German defense posture is weakened and, as a matter of fact as it has been for ages, because we don't know the agent, because in distress we try to figure out harum-scarum who the carrier is and in the end always nail the devil to the cross," said the priest.

When Reinhold came home, Rachel had packed her belongings together. "I won't live in a Nazi's apartment and I won't sleep when a Nazi is in the apartment. I just waited until you got here so that I can tell you that and that I remember you: I sensed it, I smelled it!

"Yesterday I was with the Americans and registered myself and my children in their list as survivors. The list wasn't long, and the men couldn't believe that my children are Jewish children. They stared at my children as though they were the remarkable remnant of an extinct species. They will give me an apartment. There I'll wait for Max. If Max doesn't come, then I'll go to Palestine without him, so that I won't any longer have to breathe the same air as those who say here now: I, too, knew a nice Jew."

"What kind of little flag have you pinned on there?" asked Reinhold.

"That's the Jewish flag. Jews who come back from the concentration camps are wearing it, and I'm wearing it so that no one will take me for a German because of my name. I got it from someone who's asleep in your bed in the next room."

Reinhold ran to his room, tore open the door, turned on the light. Herr Herz was startled out of his sleep. And then Reinhold sat for a long time on the edge of the bed with the old man and held his hand.

After Herr Herz had lived with Reinhold for a week because he wanted to wait until the women who had moved into his own apartment had found another, a letter arrived for him. Eberhard Gottschlich complained that Herr Herz had not greeted him on the street. He, who had done much for the Jewish community in the city at the risk of his life, didn't deserve that.

A letter also had come for Reinhold: *I can now give you the answer I owe you. Please visit me in my apartment as soon as you can. Elsa.*

Then Magda and Heinrich arrived in a car from the Red Cross. His father had been instantly dismissed from his office without a claim for a pension or any other kind of support, said Magda. Because of his membership in the SA he had received a summons from the denazification court. He had tried first to be a razor blade salesman, but no one had wanted to buy anything from the desperate man. Then he had gone to work for the woodcutters, and yesterday evening they had brought him home. There hadn't been a doctor far and wide. The Red Cross had come with two medics, and since his father had asked for Reinhold again and again, she had persuaded the medics to drive him home.

All night long Magda and Reinhold kept watch at Heinrich's bed. At noon, when Magda was small and white with exhaustion, Herr Herz took over the watch, and Reinhold went to Elsa.

She was not alone. A man was standing behind her and had laid both his hands on her shoulders. She introduced him as her fiancé.

I congratulated her and started to leave.

"He's a Communist," she said, and asked whether she could explain everything to me over a cup of tea.

I sat in the room. I saw the picture of her father on the bedside table. Then the piano playing began next door. She talked and poured tea into my cup, and poured again, and I wondered what might have become of Golda. But since the piano playing was from an exercise for beginners that was constantly repeated, I constantly repeated my question: What might have become of Golda? and got caught up in the rhythm of the exercise, and I could understand but little of what Elsa said to me.

It was her fiancé who got up to go over and request a pause.

"He's had to put up with that exercise too long," she said. "He was hidden here, in the attic room over the piano room."

The fiancé returned: "The piano teacher will play a little Beethoven now to make up for it."

They joked about the old lady and laughed a little, until I stood up.

She took me to the door. "You were young. That gave me hope," she said.

I walked through the city and arrived at Hanno's house. It was bombed out. Only the lower floor still stood. I went through the iron gate that stood open bent, walked under the old split trees, climbed over debris and ashes, went up the shattered stone steps, pressed the golden doorlatch. The door sprang open. I was standing in the great room. Everything was in rubble and bits. Only the onyx sphinxes were lying in wait unharmed next to the first landing of the stairs. Above me the sky was blue.

I climbed the first steps. The guardians of grave and temple raised their wings, showed their lion's claws, but let me pass. I climbed to the end of the stairs and walked down the long hall to Hanno's room.

Hanno approached me from far away: "Welcome, friend," he called out, "to my sacred four walls!"

And there they all were sitting together, and we greeted one another heartily. Schade and Gabriel were there, the dear godfather had come, Utz and Gummi, Red Charly, my good man ahead, whose name is Willi, and my father had joined them.

"Fathers are mortal," said Hanno. "I told you that."

"You're now the prey of your imagination," Gabriel started out. "This is the wild world of the dead," and his horrible laugh did me good. "You're now the in-spirited poet," and Gabriel bent over with laughter.

Hanno went to his bookcase, took a key from his pants pocket, opened up the doors, whose polished glass flashed in the last evening sunlight, took out a book, leafed through it, found what he was looking for, and read: *Where is the homeland of the poet? In not forgetting, in memory.*

"In resistance," Gabriel cried out.

"In stubbornness," said the dear godfather.

Hanno put the book back into its place, closed the glass door, locked the bookcase, put the key back into his pants pocket.

My father accompanied me as far as the stairs: "Go to the Café Deibl and get two pieces of cake. Now, boy, everything will get better."

When I got home, my mother was sitting beside the bed with my father. My father was dead. Mechthild was there, and my brother had come back.

I went to my room. Now I'm writing it up. It's my last entry. The war is over. There are no more white pages in my book.

Magda had fallen asleep beside the dead Heinrich.

Herr Herz had gone to the kitchen, had laid a handkerchief on his head, and spoken the prayer for the dead for Heinrich.

Mechthild and his brother had come to Reinhold. His brother had told him that he and his comrades of the territorial army militia had taken a stand at a Rhine bridge. Engineering troops had received the order to blow up the bridge, but had run across the bridge to the enemy. Then the militia commander had given the order to the militia, and he and his comrades had run to the bridgehead. But the engineers had destroyed the detonator in their flight, and they hadn't been able to blow up the bridge. Then the militia commander had shot at them. Only a few comrades had survived.

Herr Herz had told them where he had been the whole time, Mechthild had said.

And his brother had said: "Reinhold, how could all this happen?"